LOOKING CLOSER 5

edited by: Michael Bierut, William Drenttel, and Steven Heller

ALLWORTH PRESS
NEW YORK

11 10 09 08 07   5 4 3 2 1

Published by Allworth Press
An imprint of Allworth Communications, Inc.
10 East 23rd Street, New York, NY 10010

Cover and book design by Pentagram, New York
Page composition/typography by Integra Software Services, Pvt., Ltd., Pondicherry, India

Library of Congress Cataloging-in-Publication Data
Looking closer. 5, Critical writings on graphic design / [edited by] Steven Heller, Michael Bierut, William Drenttel.
p. cm.
Includes bibliographical references and index.
ISBN-13: 978-1-58115-471-9 (pbk.)
ISBN-10: 1-58115-471-2 (pbk.)
1. Commercial art.   2. Graphic arts.   I. Heller, Steven.   II. Bierut, Michael.
III. Drenttel, William.   IV. Title: Critical writings on graphic design.
NC997.L6334 2007
741.6—dc22
2006036530

Printed in Canada

CONTENTS

FOREWORD

In 1992, four working designers conceived of an anthology of critical writings about graphic design. Back then—before iPods and Weblogs—there were few books about graphic design that weren't picture-driven annuals or monographs. The numerous trade magazines covering the design professions tended to be equally lacking in critical faculties, and worst of all, there was no anthology of writings for students in design programs across the country. Nevertheless, a generation of new writers was beginning to surface in venues such as the *AIGA Journal, Eye,* and *Emigre*; in catalogs from the American Center of Design and The Cooper Union; and in isolated essays in the mainstream design media, such as *Communication Arts, ID,* and *Print* magazines.

Together, these writers were finding a new critical voice—sometimes shrill, occasionally oblique, often incomplete in its portrayal or analysis of a particular observation about design. But collectively, by 1992 a body of work had emerged that seemed to represent a new kind of awareness about visual thinking, a new voice in graphic design criticism. It wasn't a movement, exactly, since the themes and interests remained (and have remained) deeply divergent, but it was indeed a convergence of talented people writing in new and unusually expressive ways. And they were being published with enough frequency that it soon became impossible not to notice that *something* was going on.

The idea for *Looking Closer* was conceived in that fertile period, with the first volume published in 1994 and this, our fifth volume, published twelve years later. As ever, the goal is to present the most provocative and compelling voices in design criticism. Along the way, it bears saying that we'd been inspired by Massimo Vignelli's credo that there would be no serious design without serious design criticism. This challenge, in many ways, remains unfulfilled; and yet, the quantity and quality of writings anthologized in these five volumes testifies to a kind of extraordinary progress for graphic design literature. It is our hope that this progress—towards sustained scholarship and robust criticism—will continue.

Over five volumes, we have published 254 essays by 165 writers. Volume One compiled its essays from thirteen sources, while this volume includes writings from nearly twice that amount, or twenty-three sources. Our most frequent contributors (with more than three essays each) are Michael Bierut, William Drenttel, Ken Garland, Milton Glaser, Jessica Helfand, Steven Heller, D.K. Holland, Karrie Jacobs, Tibor Kalman, Mr. Keedy, Ellen Lupton, Katherine McCoy, J. Abbott Miller, Rick Poynor, Michael Rock, Veronique Vienne, and Lorraine Wild. (To be fair, many of the promising young writers in the more recent volumes were not publishing their writings yet in 1994.)

In the next few years, there will continue to be new writers as well as new venues, especially as online journals encourage more copious opportunities for self-publishing. The existence of blogs does not, in and of itself, create writers: writers will emerge slowly and infrequently, as individuals take the time to write with the kind of critical perspective that sheds new light on history, theory, and practice. The true promise for these writers lies in curricula provided in our schools and universities, where critical modes of discourse must continue to be encouraged, and from which the next new generation of writers will undoubtedly emerge. Perhaps, too, we will begin to see new opportunities for design writing as it migrates into mainstream media, bringing design criticism to a world of nondesigners.

The challenge for *Looking Closer*, however, has remained the same: to identify new writers with a distinctive and critical voice who can help us better comprehend the work we make. These writers advance our profession through their unparalleled capacity to question everything, adding critical depth to our history through deeply engaged, uniquely perceptive, and thoughtfully inquisitive writing. This, perhaps more than anything else, is what these five volumes of collected essays have given us.

And now, some acknowledgements. Michael Bierut and Steven Heller participated as editors in all five volumes, while William Drenttel participated in four volumes. Together, we wish to warmly acknowledge the input of three other writers who participated as editors of individual volumes: D.K. Holland, Jessica Helfand, and Rick Poynor. On a personal note, the editors would like to acknowledge the continued support, over the life of this series, of our colleague Rick Poynor, who remains for us all the ultimate champion of design criticism.

Among many acknowledgments, a key one goes to our publisher, Tad Crawford, who believed in the spirit of our initiative and who followed through to realize its long-term potential. Even in lean years, Allworth Press continued to keep these books in print at a reasonable price. This series, and its impact on design writing and thinking over a decade, only existed because of Tad's unwavering commitment, and for this we are especially grateful. These volumes also benefited from the input of other talented editors and professionals at Allworth: Theodore Gachot, Michael Madole, Bob Porter, Nicole Potter-Talling, and Cynthia Rivelli. Elinor Pettit was a freelance researcher on the first edition.

We also wish to acknowledge the sponsors who have provided financial support for individual volumes: Adobe Corporation, Aldus Corporation, and Champion International Corporation. Similarly, AIGA should be singled out for its role as a copublisher of three volumes, extending awareness of the Looking Closer series to its broad national membership.

Looking Closer has continued to provide a challenge to its editors, helping each of us grow as writers, thinkers, and practitioners—but most of all, as critics. It is our hope that our readers have derived as much benefit from this wonderful series of writings that collectively celebrate the critical value of design in contemporary culture.

—The Editors

INTRODUCTION

WHERE'S THE CRITICISM?
Steven Heller

Since last we looked closer (August 2002 to be exact), the blogosphere has erupted into new venues for instant commentary on issues and phenomena, individuals and movements. From humble beginnings—"listservs," "newsgroups," and "chat rooms"—to annotated online data compilations, like *Lines and Splines*, to community forums like *Typographica* and *Typophile*, to multiauthored Weblogs, like *Speak Up,* founded in September 2002, and *Design Observer,* in September 2003, to dedicated online design journals and chronicles at AIGA, Core 77, and Unbeige—reams of unedited and edited copy now flow like lava from Vesuvius over Pompeian design fields.

Designers use this new medium (and such programs as Moveable Type and Typepad) to great advantage. Many have launched (and are currently launching) personal blogs replete with all manner of written expression from diaries to essays to papers and speeches. Design students and teachers post ad hoc thoughts as well as tested ideas; critical commentaries about the good, bad, and ugly in design—sometimes unforgiving, often scolding—are not exceptions but the rule. Most blogs are linked to and from other blogs insuring that new audiences are growing exponentially larger than virtually all the traditional print design periodicals—even those featuring Web components. With such fervent activity one might expect more, not less, serious design criticism to have emerged. On a certain level there is more, yet on another there is not.

In fact, this fifth edition of *Looking Closer,* a collection of graphic design and related criticism published since 2000, was not as easy to compile as the first, second, or fourth (and even in the fourth we complained that it was harder than the second, and the third was our historical compendium). The pool of viable texts contained surprisingly fewer than expected—which is not to diminish the valuable selections in this edition, but to suggest an overall lull in the field. The editors assumed that since *Looking Closer 1* premiered in 1994 (at the height of the computer and theory revolutions) graphic design criticism had become *de rigeur* in professional publications and academic journals. We know various voices have been raised at conferences and symposia, therefore we assumed manuscripts suitable for compilation would be much more plentiful than ever before. Instead we were astonished to find a few of the more promising authors from previous editions had nothing to offer this time around—and for whatever reasons they simply stopped writing criticism. Although replaced by a few new articulate voices, we were nonetheless aware that the kind of work we needed for this volume had declined, even as blog posts have zoomed.

Blogs clearly provide stimulating discussions—some quite eloquent and astute—but without the rigorous editorial oversight endemic to magazines and journals the writing is often more raw transcription than polished prose. Where texts are tightly edited, much of this material is pegged to timely moments or events—like how dare those philistines at AT&T scrap Saul Bass' venerable logo, or whether or not Neue Helvetica Round is the next Meta. Since we believe even the most engaging of these discussions might lose relevance by the time *Looking Closer 5* was published, and therefore require detailed editorial contextualization to be made comprehensible, we have backed away from reprinting them. Consistent with *Looking Closer* 1, 2, and 4 we decided not to write prefaces for the selected texts in this edition, believing they should speak for themselves (since *LC3* included historical texts and so brief explanatory précis were necessary).

Actually, only a handful of the pieces in this edition were originally published on the Internet. With the exception of six essays from *Design Observer* (by *LC* editors Michael Bierut, William Drenttel, and former editor Jessica Helfand), seven from *AIGA VOICE* (including one by myself), and one from *Typotheque*, we selected just one, Christine Rosen's "The Image Culture," from a nondesign-dedicated online journal, *TheNewAtlantis.com*. The balance of the content derives from the stalwart journalistic design journals, *Print, Eye, Emigre, Grafik, TypoGraphic,* and *Metropolis*. Yet even some of these seemed to offer less critical analysis on average than were found in the issues published prior to the *LC5* timeframe. Which raises fundamental concerns about the state of criticism since *Looking Closer* premiered.

Has the amount of critical writing increased or decreased? Can graphic design truly sustain an astute body of criticism? Is our field unable to generate enough provocative stimuli for serious graphic design critics to grapple with issues? Addressing these questions, authors in previous editions raised familiar canards: "Criticism is fine until it happens to me"; "The field is too ingrown to allow for honest criticism"; "No one, not even design periodicals, pays a living wage to graphic design critics"; "There are no educational programs devoted to teaching design criticism." These arguments recur because, frankly, graphic design criticism has for too long been a do-it-yourself (D.I.Y.) field. Most graphic design critics are self-taught. They (we) have cobbled together, though brilliantly at times, methods and language from other disciplines. Despite the significant voices on important themes—many of them are represented in this volume—unlike art, architecture, or film there still is no codified critical approach that can be universally adopted or rebelled against. While various theoretical conceits are tapped—like semiotics, connoisseurship, poststructuralism, feminism, even Marxism to a certain extent—they nonetheless seem grafted onto graphic design's critical discourse. In short, after all these years graphic design criticism is still in its infancy.

Nonetheless, as evident from this edition's contents, a kind of informal-formal criticism continues to be practiced in academe and journalism. Writers continue to push for a legitimate discipline, and even without a delineated critical vocabulary (whatever that might be), they continue to build a distinct literature of graphic design. Some writers are even capable of transforming otherwise pedantic discussions of type and its impact on society or tensions between art and commerce into real page-turners. Essays of this caliber included here reveal various analytical, polemical, and cautionary ways of addressing many concerns impacting design practice—such as essays by Alice Twemlow on the new decoration (page 87), Ellen Lupton on new user friendly computer paradigms (page 23), Peter Bilak on typographic experimentation (page 172), and Adrian Shaughnessy on design cults (page 167); as well as design processes that directly impact society—such as essays by Milton Glaser on the designer as citizen (page 144), Phil Patton on the viability of political symbols (page 103), and William Owen on graphically mapping the world (page 13), to name a few. Despite the trepidation expressed above, there is a critical mass of criticism that seems proportional to the apparent interest in the field. (After all, not every designer cares about criticism; some just choose to professionally, or sometimes instinctively, do their work.)

Perhaps the new Web-based venues are the next big thing, but it is still too early to calculate their collective consequence. Popular response to the major design blogs and online journals suggests that interest in reading and writing about design and related issues prevails among some students and practitioners, yet this does not mean universal acceptance. For a few writers the Internet has become the primary outlet; for instance, most of Jessica Helfand's strongest work begins on *Design Observer*. While much online writing has yet to reach a consistent standard, the blogs—or whatever they'll be called in the future—will have to reach a more sophisticated level to be taken seriously. So while print journals remain the dominant venues because their texts are more massaged, gradually blogs are challenging the status quo, which has already begun to change.

After twenty years Rudy VanderLans' *Emigre* ceased publication in late 2005, and with it a valuable outlet, resource, and advocate is gone. And it is with some reluctance the editors of *LC5* must also report this will be the final edition of the series, at least in this book format. Despite our fervent belief in the resonance of print, belief reigns that in the long run the Web may be a more viable archive where access is unlimited and inexpensive. As design writing of all kinds—reportage, analysis, profiles, and criticism—are increasingly available as PDFs and other downloadable documents, various repositories for design authorship are sure to emerge along the information highway. Putting together this edition proved that graphic design criticism has gone directly from infancy to a curious midlife crisis—more mature but in a state of reexamination—and we look forward to where the criticism will come from next.

SECTION I:
GRAPHIC DESIGN AS SYSTEM

THE GRAND UNIFIED THEORY OF NOTHING: DESIGN, THE CULT OF SCIENCE, AND THE LURE OF BIG IDEAS

Randy Nakamura

I n the 1960s and 1970s, George Lois popularized the "big idea" in advertising. With his classic advertisements and covers for *Esquire* he established concept over form. In his book, *What's the Big Idea? How to Win with Outrageous Ideas That Sell,* Lois states:

> I look in vain for the big idea, for that one theme or slogan that says it all, that can be played back by the average consumer after one viewing. If you can't describe the big idea in one sentence or in three or four words, you don't have a big idea. Quick cuts and animation and computer graphics are techniques, and ephemeral techniques, at best. None of these devices is an idea. . . . A great verbal idea can survive even terrible graphics.

Lois' perfect combination of stripped down graphic wit, pop culture references, and clever copy made for memorable ads. Unfortunately, this legacy of concept over form has mutated over the decades into a new and strange form. Instead of merely applying "concept über alles" to actual pieces of design, designers want to engage their entire practice in this manner. This desire to turn design into a total conceptual discipline has its roots in the fact that the cultural and social status of design has always been up for grabs. Being neither fine art nor vernacular art, but sampling, appropriating, and utilizing both domains, design occupies an area Pierre Bourdieu calls the "sphere of the legitimizable," the zone between high and low culture that is constantly being contested, reconfigured, and challenged. This is design as a middlebrow cultural practice. What is fascinating about contemporary design practice is the attempt by its practitioners to raise design above its middlebrow pedigree to a "higher realm" away from the pejorative connotations of merely being "designer" or "stylish." Recently this attempt at upward mobility has often involved the appropriation of ideas

Originally published in *Emigre*, no. 67 (2004).

from the sciences, specifically ecology, and a relatively new branch of knowledge called systems theory (the idea that natural systems are "integrated wholes whose properties cannot be reduced to those of smaller parts"). Terry Irwin, in her essay "A Crisis In Perception," outlines a manifesto for a type of "design ecology." In a fundamental way this is a search for new metaphors. Unfortunately these metaphors are strained and are deeply problematic in how they might be applied to design. At best most of these ideas become comforting platitudes; at worst they are deeply confused and have a dubious value as any sort of corrective or improvement to the way design functions in the world.

NATURE OVER ALL

The ideas and philosophy of Fritjof Capra have deeply influenced Irwin; the title of her essay is a direct lift from the first chapter of Capra's *The Web of Life*. Capra is best known for his book *The Tao of Physics*, a blend of eastern philosophy and quantum mechanics. The *Web of Life* is Capra's attempt to synthesize various elements of deep ecology, evolution, molecular biology, chaos theory, systems theory, and eastern mysticism in order to advocate the interconnectedness of all things. What is most interesting about Capra is the deeply reductionist mindset he uses to juggle all of these disparate disciplines. Extremely controversial concepts like the possibility that evolution is "creative" and "directed" he takes as givens in order to promote his thesis about the "self-organization" of the universe. Everything he assesses and weighs leads back to his singular set of ideas. In a sense this is a perfect reaction to postmodernism (a counter-reformation); culture is entirely subsumed within the idea of nature since "Deep ecology does not separate humans—or anything else—from the natural environment." Problems that exist in culture are explicitly ignored. Direct study of human cultural problems is irrelevant since they occur within larger macroscopic patterns such as evolution, ecology, and self-organized systems.

One gets the sense that Capra's project is deeply modernist in philosophy; his obsession with totalizing systems and the singular directedness of nature would be more disturbing if it wasn't for his relative degree of eloquence and the benign nature he ascribes to the universe. He also has an unfortunate tendency to look like a dwarf standing on the shoulders of giants. Of the 347 pages of *The Web of Life*, the vast majority of space is spent explaining other people's ideas and discoveries. Capra has precious little to add other than repeated catchphrases like "interconnectedness" and "conceptual dimension."

It is hard to see how Capra could be useful for a design practice, seeing how he is philosophically prone to erasing culture rather than investigating it. Since culture really is the basic substance and lifeblood of design, it seems perverse to try to use him as an aid to improve design practice. Nevertheless, Irwin attempts the impossible. The first part of "A Crisis In Perception" establishes Capra's basic principles. In Irwin's view, "nature is a better designer than we are," and she proceeds to paraphrase one of Capra's arguments:

Living systems theory tells us that life's natural tendency is to organize into ever greater levels of complexity—in networks, patterns, and structures that emerge out of seeming chaos without external imposition or direction. Organization wants to happen. Imagine that—the world isn't waiting for designers to impose order upon it. Perhaps many designers weren't laboring under such delusions of grandeur, but I now realize that I was.

The conflation of ideas here is amazing. Apparently "life" is meant to stand for the entirety of human evolution, history, culture, and social development. Although it is tantalizing to mistake metaphor for reality, it is in the end a mistake. The self-organization of living systems takes place on a time scale of *billions of years*. The fact that a human designer has the technological and cultural know-how to design and produce a complex artifact like a book in a matter of a few weeks (or even days) is evidence of an amazing efficiency that no "natural system" has ever equaled. *The world is in fact waiting to be designed*, if only because human beings by necessity have to scale time to their own needs. Maybe nature will sculpt a windbreak for your campsite in a few thousand years, but how much smarter and more efficient to make your own out of a few tree branches and a tarp. There are no delusions of grandeur here, only the necessity of keeping yourself warm.

Irwin also indulges in quite a bit of teleological confusion: either you accept Capra's hypothesis (borrowed from deep ecology) that everything in the world is "nature" and there can be no "external imposition or direction" or you come back to reality, take Ecology 101, and realize that all natural systems have dynamic (and extraordinarily complex) interrelationships with other natural (or human-made) systems, and that most of the vaunted self-organizational capacities of these systems occur because of these external relationships and not from any kind of spooky sounding quality like a "natural tendency." Tautology is no substitute for knowing what the hell you are talking about.

DESIGNING WITHOUT DESIGN

Ultimately in the realm of design, ideas have to be useful. They must have some sort of impact on the process, form, or conception of design. Even George Lois with his legendary disdain of form had to find a photographer sympathetic to his ideas, or the classic *Esquire* covers of Muhammad Ali and Richard Nixon would never have existed except in Lois' head. In the last half of "A Crisis in Perception," Irwin speculates on how Capra's ideas might be implemented within a design practice. Irwin's start is inauspicious. She states:

> *Remember that design is first and foremost a process of analysis and problem solving and isn't always tied to the making of artifacts. Try to better understand how the world works.*

Suddenly design isn't really about design any more, and craft and form are depreci-
ated in the face of "analysis" and "understanding." This appears to be a halfhearted
attempt to recast design as a primarily quantitative and analytical discipline. Yes,
design is about analysis and problem solving, but its fundamental impact on the world
(for better or worse) is *in the artifacts and forms it produces*. This is the only way ideas
survive in design. To denigrate form and artifact making in design is to destroy its
essence and reduce it to a generic role of think tank or consultant. Irwin's continued use of jargon like "waste/energy flows," "interdependencies," and "ecosystem"
only seems to emphasize her tendency towards trying to elevate design using
a quantitative, pseudoscientific language. After depriving design of its distinctive ways
of dealing with the world, Irwin goes one step further into a realm that is almost
messianic:

> I don't think it will be the politicians or the economists or the businessmen
> who will solve the problems of pollution, loss of biodiversity and indigenous
> cultures, poverty or war and violence. The design of a new reality may be
> called for, which doesn't mean creating a "fix" for our current structure. As
> Fritjof Capra said in a lecture at JFK University last fall, "The Stone Age didn't
> end because they suddenly ran out of stones... someone designed something
> better." If a new design is needed, who is better equipped to deliver it than
> a new generation of designers? The first step is to develop a vision that says
> design can make a divergence—perhaps the biggest difference.

Ignoring the weird elision of design and engineering (was the origin of metallurgy
really a moment of design history? Capra's supposed revelation raises more questions
than it could possibly answer), the precedent here is thin, probably nonexistent.
Design has never ended or "solved" war, poverty, or violence. Early twentieth century movements like de Stijl and Russian constructivism attempted to connect design
to larger political, social, and spiritual ideologies. In the case of constructivism,
Alexander Rodchenko and Varvara Stepanova explicitly connected design to "scientific communism." They adopted a rigorous pseudoscientific language and evolved
efficient means of propaganda and self-promotion. In the end they were smashed flat
by the same ideology they attempted to promulgate. Despite its disastrous conclusion, constructivism still generated a meaningful legacy because of the *designed form
and ideas* it left behind.

Deprived of form, Irwin has walked design into a dead end. You cannot be
influential by appropriating the conceptual corpses of someone else's ideas. The design
artifacts you leave behind will be your ultimate legacy.

If design as a discipline of pure ideas is comical, then design as a messiah is
tragic. Irwin diminishes design's real importance while smearing it with a fake veneer
of political and social importance. It is one more design theory destined for the dustbin
of history.

THE CRISIS OF IGNORANCE

If Irwin has a salient point in her essay, it is the observation that there is a crisis in design's relationship with science and technology. Design's increasing immersion in and dependence on digital technology is unquestionable, and the effects of this transformation are far-reaching and unpredictable. Designers accurately reflect society in that they are as ignorant about science as everybody else. The ramifications of this ignorance are vast, affecting our entire society from the educational system (declining enrollments in science and technical disciplines) to government (where politics and big business take precedence over sound scientific research) and even employment (if employers cannot find qualified engineers and scientists domestically then they will inevitably look overseas for the cheaper alternative).

While Rome burns, designers are obsessed with big ideas cribbed from scientific disciplines they can barely understand. The only apparent rationale behind these misguided obsessions is an attempt to drag design from its middlebrow status into a higher arena, or in Pierre Bourdieu's words, the "sphere of the legitimate with universal claims," i.e., the realm of fine arts, poetry, and literature. If it always seems like design will be the bastard child of the art school, then a blind trek through the domain of science is at least an original, if failed, attempt to raise design's status.

Status can never be attained through fake knowledge. If design is in a rut, it can only lift itself out of its rut by its own means, not by dreaming of a *deux ex machina* by systems theory. If design wants to engage with science, it can do so on a multitude of fronts, but it must do so on a plane where science and design can connect as equals, not from a point of veneration and misty-eyed misunderstanding. If the fields of systems theory and self-organized systems are so important, then the challenge for design is to find a way to visualize these exceedingly abstract, relational, macroscopic processes in a form that is understandable to a layperson. This is an extremely tall order that perhaps lacks the glamour of being a guru of "big ideas," but it is absolutely essential to a real design practice that knows one of its most powerful tools is the ability to affect and change perception.

What is, perhaps, the most disappointing part about Irwin's perspective is the total lack of faith in design's ability to offer anything of value to the outside world. Design is an inherently collaborative discipline, yet our intimate knowledge of the collaborative process is taken for granted and even ignored. But from the perspective of "big ideas," most designers are inbred specialists in need of reform by outside collaborators.

But what if the tables were turned? What if design was taken as an object of interest by, say, an anthropologist and design culture was dissected via ethnography? (The immediate model here would be Paul Rabinow's *Making PCR*, which is an ethnography of the scientists who invented PCR, a biochemical copy machine for DNA.) What could the social sciences learn from design? Perhaps that designers have a unique and specific knowledge of making artifacts that embodies a huge array of processes both internal (cognitive, self-critical, creative, and technical) and external (social organizations that are both hierarchical and nonhierarchical, fluid and uniquely self-organized, etc.). And what could designers learn from another discipline reflecting on design culture in a systematic and integrated way?

Now that would be radical, a true "paradigm" buster, a truly "big idea." Design may have much to learn from the sciences, but the hidden truth here might be that science could have much to learn from the culture of design. That would be a true revolution and is one that may yet come to pass.

Bibiliography
Bordieu, Pierre. *Photography: A Middlebrow Art* (Palo Alto: Stanford University Press, 1990).
Capra, Fritjof. *The Web of Life* (New York: Doubleday, 1997).
Irwin, Terry. "A Crisis In Perception," *Communication Arts* (August 2003).
Lois, George. *What's the Big Idea? How to Win with Outrageous Ideas That Sell* (New York: Doubleday, 1991).
Rabinow, Paul. *Making PCR: A Story of Biotechnology* (Chicago: University of Chicago Press, 1996).

TOWARDS CRITICAL AUTONOMY, OR CAN GRAPHIC DESIGN SAVE ITSELF?
Andrew Blauvelt

"Art exists today in a state of pluralism: no style or even mode of art is dominant and no critical position is orthodox. Yet this state is also a position, and this position is an alibi. As a general condition pluralism tends to absorb argument—which is not to say that it does not promote antagonism of all sorts. One can only begin out of a discontent with this status quo: for in a pluralist state art and criticism tend to be dispersed and so rendered impotent. Minor deviation is allowed only in order to resist radical change." —Hal Foster, "The Problem with Pluralism," 1982

It would be an understatement to suggest that the 1990s were an important decade for graphic design. Not only were the technological transformations of the desktop publishing and personal computing revolution of the 1980s fully absorbed, but so too were the lessons of formal experimentation that had developed in the academies and the marketplace.

Originally published in *Emigre*, no. 64 (2003).

Today, we can reflect fondly on those impassioned debates in the nineties about the merits of computer-aided design and the limits of readability and legibility, or the naïveté of whether we needed only ten typefaces and the unbridled enthusiasm of the Internet. These issues and many others formed the basis for much design discourse in the first half of the nineties producing a new generation of voices debating the merits of these changes—many of them in the pages of *Émigré*, myself included.

Slowly the debates subsided. Any tension that may have existed among the factions eased and the marketplace and academy embraced the eclecticism of difference. The globally interconnected and highly disseminated design scene, which really came into the fore in the nineties, could easily transplant even the most provincial tendencies in a matter of months. Graduate programs, whether celebrated or scorned, were once seen as the source of "the problem."

Hal Foster's commentary (cited in the epigraph) about the pluralism of the eighties art scene could be easily applied to contemporary graphic design. Significant aesthetic debates have been superseded by consensus: not a fight over which style but agreement on all styles. The bedrock principle of pluralism asks not in what style we should design, but rather says that we design stylishly. A plethora of these benign styles exists to mix and match according to the logic of the marketplace. Once style was a defining gesture, unapologetically ideological, and a signal that differentiated and codified its subject. Today style has been reduced to a choice, not a matter of conviction but one of convenience. Professional organizations, publications, schools, and even competitions used to be distinct. If they are not now defunct, they are pretty much interchangeable.

This situation of academic and marketplace pluralism as well as a dearth of critical discourse are actually related phenomena, each reflecting the condition of the other. Slowly, but surely, any critical edge—either real or imagined—to design has largely disappeared, dulled by neglect in the go-go nineties or deemed expendable in the subsequent downturn. However, the reason seems not a factor of cyclical economies, but rather the transfiguration of a critical avant-garde into a postcritical *arrière-garde*.

It is no wonder that graphic design today feels like a vast formless body able to absorb any blows delivered to it—lacking coherency and totally dispersed. This absence of a critical mass or resistant body is at the heart of the current malaise. One might argue that graphic design today no longer exists in the form (or body) we once knew it. So scattered and destabilized are its constituent elements that any attempt at definitions becomes meaningless. The expansion of graphic design beyond its roots in print is simply one symptom of this crisis. Even a broad moniker such as "visual communications" loses cohesion in the face of a multitude of providers producing all sorts of "visuals" for divergent media, be it print, television, video, film, or the Internet. Lacking the specificity of a medium, graphic design tends to be identified more through its varied products than any sense of social practice. Thus graphic design is reduced to its commodity form—simply a choice of vehicles for delivering a message: ad, billboard, book, brochure, typeface, Web site, and so on. Implicit in this reductive understanding is the denial of graphic design as a social practice and with it the possibility of disciplinary autonomy.

The late eighties and early nineties produced an assault on the conventions of graphic design through an intense period of formal experimentation. Those inquiries were a desire to rethink prevailing assumptions, principally the legacy of modernism, and succeeded in breaking the link between modernism and the avant-garde. Up to that point, from the late nineteenth century on, an avant-garde in design existed primarily within the rubric of modernism. Indeed those experiments demonstrated that it was possible to produce a design avant-garde independent of modernism. But just like other modernist avant-gardes, these experiments were premised on the notion of inventing new formal languages without historical precedent. Paradoxically, much of the theoretical discourse that formed the basis of these experiments espoused a philosophy that dispensed with such notions as originality altogether. Nevertheless these experiments soon conflated the avant-garde with individual expression (the ultimate "origin" of the designer), as if guarding against the looming anonymity of the designer in the desktop publishing universe. We have become so conditioned to the importance of personal style in design that the subsequent pluralism that it has wrought goes essentially unchallenged.

The results of these experiments moved quickly from polemic to profitability. Both within the marketplace and the academy the consequence was not to invent wholly new languages but rather develop variations of styles. The critical reflexivity that had been the genesis of such experimental work was pushed aside as the promotion of individual expression became paramount. It is no coincidence that the proliferation of design styles corresponded to the increase of the number of brands and the demand for product segmentation in the marketplace. The academy reacted with similar misrecognition by seeing formal experimentation as end in itself; whereby the exercise of individual expression (more commonly called "personal style") is considered experimental. The situation created successive generations of work that had all the look and feel of the experimental without actually being experimental. This should be contrasted with the possibility of experimentation that is itself contextual—tied to the continuity of a historical language of design, for example, or one that is essentially aformal and questions not so much the form of design but the possibilities of its practice. Such an alternative would require both a sense of history and a more contextual understanding of developments within the discipline.

An important way out of the current predicament is for graphic design to reclaim a position of critical autonomy. By autonomy, I do not mean a wholesale withdrawal from the social or the kind of freedoms the fine arts claim. Graphic design, precisely because it is an instrumental form of communication, cannot divorce itself from the world. Rather graphic design must be seen as a discipline capable of generating meaning out of its own intrinsic resources without reliance on commissions, functions, or specific materials or means. Such actions should demonstrate self-awareness and reflexivity; a capacity to manipulate the system of graphic design. A newly engaged form of critical practice is necessary, one that is no longer concerned with originality as defined by personal expression, but rather one dedicated to an inventive contextuality. We also need to imagine a historical language of design that transcends styles and is embedded in the continuity of discourse. The point is not to invent a neomodernist avant-garde and inherit all of its problems. Rather the purpose is to stake a claim for autonomy, which, like an avant-garde, is already a separation from the social demands that limit graphic design to its most marketable features. Autonomy also gives coherency to graphic design in order to resist the dispersal it currently suffers by defining the conditions and terms in which it seeks to operate. Most importantly, a space of autonomy for graphic design affords an opportunity to engage in a more critical examination of its practice, assuming that it does not lapse into a convenient formalism or cannot escape the ideology of expressionism.

METHOD DESIGNING: THE PARADOX OF MODERN DESIGN EDUCATION
Jessica Helfand

Over a century ago, Konstantin Stanislavsky revolutionized the modern theater by introducing a new system of training, in which the actor would draw on his or her own emotions to achieve a true understanding of a character. "We protested against the old manner of acting and against theatricality, against artificial pathos and declamation," Stanislavksy wrote, and, indeed, in an era framed by considerable social and civil unrest, the very notion that characters could be shown to have an interior life was itself remarkably revolutionary. Through the practice of what we have come to know, today, as "method" acting, an actor could explore, identify, and ultimately reveal the degree to which a character could be a hugely complex human being with feelings, emotions, and often conflicting desires.

To this day, method acting remains a highly regarded pedagogical model for training actors. But when did it become an appropriate system for educating designers?

Schools of thought are always hotbeds of ideological controversy: there are always exceptions to the rule, deviations from the principal learning curve. In creative education this a particularly thorny issue: how to teach discipline *and*

Originally published on *www.designobserver.com* (May 2005).

promote invention? Arguably, designers who were trained to understand two-dimensional composition by crafting eight-by-eight inch plaka boards were more conscious of the former than the latter, while today's design students firmly occupy the opposite camp. And while each approach might be said to be imperfect, it is the contemporary condition within which today's design students are expected to "make work" that gives me cause for concern.

In the interest of full disclosure, I should reveal that I was an actress before I became a graphic designer. I struggled with just how difficult it was to understand a role, to be another person—and while the skeptic in me had my doubts about method acting as a kind of religion, I recognized then (and still do) that at its core, it was all about stripped-down emotional honesty. If you could achieve this honesty, your performance would resonate with a kind of pitch-perfect humanity and you had a far better chance of truly engaging your audience as a result.

Engaging the audience, of course, might be said to characterize the designer's goal as well. Perhaps this is why, having spent the better part of the last two weeks participating in year-end reviews at several design schools, I am at once hopeful and discouraged by what I am seeing—in particular, by a kind of self-aware, idiosyncratic abstraction that seems to lie at the core of the theoretical process. And while a good deal of the work I've seen is original, imaginative, and, in more than a few cases, magnificently daring, I find it oddly vexing that somewhere along the line we have allowed our students to appropriate some part of method acting—the part that glorifies feeling and celebrates vanity; the part that amplifies personal memory and replays it as objective truth. It's extremely subjective and it's extremely seductive; and more often than not, it's extremely misplaced as graphic design.

The *good* news is that, in an effort to produce designers who can think for themselves, we ask our students to identify a method which becomes evident through the work that they produce. Such an emphasis on authorship is, by and large, a way to train young designers as thinkers—and not merely as service providers. (So far, so good.) At the same time, we encourage them to seek references beyond the obvious: the richness of their sources testifies to an ability to engage a larger universe, and their work benefits from locating itself along a trajectory they've chosen and defined for themselves.

The *bad* news is that as a consequence of seeking validation elsewhere, there is an unusual bias toward false identity: so the design student, after looking at so much art, believes that s/he is *making* art. The design student, after considering so deeply the intangible forces framing the interpretation of visual form, comes to believe that the very act of interpretation is *itself* the form. This is where the method backfires so paradoxically: in being true to ourselves, we distance ourselves from a more universal truth, the kind that designers, in making messages clear, are so naturally predisposed to understand.

In an age of staged, declarative theater, Stanislavsky's came as a radical response to what was then a stilted performative norm. Yet the reason it has survived since its inception more than a century ago may have more to do with the rigors of form than the emotions of the performer: at the end of the day, there's still a tangible barometer of authenticity—and that's the *script*. (Hamlet can be many things, but in the end, he's still got to deliver his lines.) Perhaps this lies at the core of the problem: where's *our script?* When did we begin to allow, let alone forgive, let alone *encourage* work that is so rhetorical, so impervious to public engagement? The persistent evidence of impenetrable personal work in design schools across America is a serious epidemic, resulting in a kind of method designing that erroneously treats sentiment as substance, and why? It was, after all, Stanislavsky himself who cautioned: "Love the art in yourself, not yourself in the art." Where did we go wrong?

The problem with method designing is not our students' problem. It is *our* problem. Let's teach our students to keep asking difficult questions, to keep solving harder problems, to keep inventing better worlds, and, yes, to be true to themselves. As emissaries of visual communication, our audiences deserve nothing less. To better understand ourselves as authors requires a certain amount of self-reflection, but when did the mirror of autobiography become our canvas, our public lens to the world? If such self-love leads to more honest communication, to more novel form-making, to more meaningful solutions, then so much the better. But for designers, such self-knowledge cannot be a method. It is simply a motive.

PAINTING THE WORLD PINK
William Owen and Fenella Collingridge

By teaching the simple facts of the shape, size, and position of a country relative to all the others, the political map of the world has become intrinsic to our sense of national identity. When we were growing up, in Britain in the mid-1960s, our school maps portrayed the British Isles (we just called it "England") sitting comfortably and naturally at the exact longitudinal center of a flat world, north at the top and south at the bottom, the country subtly and significantly exaggerated in size by the Mercator projection and colored prettily in pink. We learned from the beginning that this was the natural way of things.

A lot of the rest of the world was pink, too: these were the twilight years of the British Empire. The map was probably twenty years old by then and its

Originally published in *Mapping: An Illustrated Guide to Graphic Navigational Systems*, Roger Fawcett-Tang (ed.) and William Owen (contributor), (The United Kingdom: Rotovision, 2005).

representation of demi-global dominion in superabundant pinkness had already been made obsolete by national liberation movements across Africa, the Mediterranean, Arabia, India, East Asia, and the Caribbean. But it wasn't easy for a school geography department to keep up with the winds of change and so we clung to the fiction of empire.

The real use of this map, like most maps, was "to possess and to claim, to legitimate and to name"[1], in this case the assertion by the British state of sovereignty over its people and a large portion of the world, and the expression of the singular point of view that England lay at the center of everything.

In the thirty-five years since, our early schooldays ideas about possession and sovereignty have altered, possibly faster than maps have. The political map of the world has been redrawn, of course, with the creation within the former Soviet and Yugoslav Republics of nineteen new nation states and the destruction of one (the GDR). These are the kinds of absolute changes that conventional maps excel at: the transformation of political boundaries—lines on the ground—or of names, or of regimes. Rights were here being reasserted but, elsewhere, national boundaries were becoming confused. The more interesting and subtle changes—for society and for cartography—have been those arising out of the integration of world trade, communications, politics, culture and population, and the diminishing importance of national political boundaries.

The inexorable progress of globalization is a challenge to mapmakers. How do we define, in cartographic terms, contemporary political relations, or ideas about nearness and remoteness, relative size and wealth, in a world where political alignment is multilayered and distance is measured in air miles and bits per second? Harder still, how do we represent within a figurative geographical construct what is to be British, Japanese, Nigerian, or Turkish and how each nation fits within the world when we each live, either in a literal or metaphorical sense, everywhere?

The inadequacy of the one-dimensional identity and the singular point of view described by a national boundary (and national color, flag, anthem, bird. . .) should be self-evident, although like a school geography department we cling to old truths. Western topographical conventions are fixated on physical space, not just for the needs of navigation but also because they are rooted in asserting property relations and so the accurate description and allocation of private or state ownership is paramount. Space, however, is increasingly distorted by the wealth or continuity of communications or by cultural influence and integration (who needs to be in Seattle when Starbucks is around every corner?). Also, the assertion of absolute rights of ownership has relatively less meaning than *access* to goods and services. The possession of physical space and the representation of "real" physical distance (and even navigation across it) now has relatively less meaning than newer, more complex equations of proximity or privilege.

Take Britain as an example of a vague, ambiguous, and unresolved political state. There is a ghostly fragment of Empire in the Commonwealth and in dominion over Northern Ireland and diminutive offshore redoubts like the Turks and Caicos. There is a degree of internal fragmentation expressed in its one "parliament"—British—and three "assemblies"—Scottish, Welsh, and Northern Irish. Britain's principal legal and economic policies are subject to those of the European Union, of which it is a leading member. However Britain remains outside the common currency Eurozone, and is semidetached from the Schengen Agreement that defines border controls and police cooperation within the EU, dictating the all-important policy of who to let in and who to shut out. Other aspects of national sovereignty are influenced by membership in bodies such as NATO (defense policy) and the World Trade Organization (which defines tight parameters within which the economic and trade policies of its member states can flex).

Now take into account Britain's eclectic ethnic, cultural, or linguistic traditions, or its central position within the global networked subeconomy, in which a substantial minority of its citizens participate in highly mobile supranational industries such as finance, media, software, oil, and professional consulting. In light of these multiple layers (and multiple maps?), what constitutes "Britain" and "Britishness" evidently still matters but has lost its old crispness.

Remapping a world in which global and national space/time coexist requires a radical new approach that allows topographical and topological representations to coexist. Showing the "true" proximity of one place to another in a jet-turbined, video-conferenced, and Internet-enabled world requires a similarly multidimensional understanding of space and time, logical and physical. For example, if we measured distance by the duration, availability, and price of air travel between two locations, rather than miles or kilometers, London would be very much "nearer" to New York than to, say, Athens; or we could measure connectivity not by roads, railways, or shipping lanes—as my mid-sixties atlas did—but by the number of Internet users and ISPs, or the price of voice telephony, the number of mobile users per population, the connection speed and miles of optical fiber, or the number of television stations.

Such a map of proximity and connectivity would reveal a chain of massively connected global cities girdling the earth: in Europe—London, Paris, and Frankfurt; in the Middle East—Dubai; in the Far East—Kuala Lumpur, Singapore, Hong Kong, Shanghai, Tokyo, Sydney; and in the Americas—Sao Paolo, San Francisco, New York. Huge swathes of the world—predominantly but not exclusively in Africa and Asia—would be seen to be almost entirely disconnected from this hyper-concentration of activities and resources.

> The new networked subeconomy of the global city occupies a strategic geography that is partly deterritorialised, cuts across borders, and connects a variety of points on the globe. It occupies only a fraction of its local setting, its boundaries are not those of the city where it is partly located, nor those of the "neighbourhood."[2]

Where are the boundaries located in a world in which the power of a non-governmental organization (say Greenpeace), a media network (CNN), and a global corporation (Shell) are as significant in shaping environmental policy as a national government?

The boundaries lie in multiple dimensions, and not merely along national borders. They cross the routes of cross-border migration and encircle linguistic concentrations; they plot the activities of global corporations and their influence on our food, entertainment, and health; they pinpoint the hotspots of international crime; they lie around trade zones and regions (or philosophies) of political alignment; they follow the contour lines of equal wealth, education, skills, or connectivity; they are intersected and overlaid by specialized human activities (such as finance or media) or key nodal points of physical or digital exchange (Heathrow Airport, Wall Street, Dubai Internet City, the golf course at Palm Springs).

Our sense of place and position, and our understanding of the relations between things, their dimensions and attributes (true or false), is forged and reinforced by their representation on the map. By making these new facts visible, and revealing the coincidence of logical and physical objects or the rapid shifts between global and local points of view, we should have a better map.

Notes
  1. Denis Wood, *The Power of Maps*, The Guildford Press, New York 1992.
  2. *Orbis Terrarum: Ways of Worldmaking*, Cartography and Contemporary Art, ed. Küng and Brayer, Ludion Press, Ghent/Amsterdam 2000.

DEFAULT SYSTEMS DESIGN
A DISCUSSION WITH ROB GIAMPIETRO ABOUT GUILT AND LOSS IN GRAPHIC DESIGN
Rudy VanderLans

When writer/designer Rob Giampietro approached me a few months back with the idea of writing an article about graphic design in the nineties, he brought up an unrelated topic during our conversation that I found intriguing: he mentioned the term "Default Systems Design." He said it was the topic for another article he had been working on for the past few months. It's curious how certain ideas reach critical mass. In Emigre, *no. 64, a number of contributors,*

Originally published in *Emigre*, no. 65 (2003).

independent of each other, noted the emergence of a new kind of graphic design that seems to rely heavily on the use of systems and defaults. Just when you think graphic design has very little new to offer, something's taking root. Reprinted here is how we arrived at the topic, as well as edited segments of the rest of the conversation.

Rudy VanderLans: If the level of graphic design criticism is at all a gauge for the state of design today, then design is as good as dead. We saw a surge of critical writing within design in the early nineties. To some degree this had to do with the times; there was a significant change in technology (the introduction of the Macintosh computer), which coincided with (or caused?) the bankruptcy of the Swiss International Style. But, after many debates, everybody settled down and went about their business. I guess it's difficult to forge a revolution (for lack of a better word) every ten years or so, or maintain a critical opposition indefinitely.

Rob Giampietro: While I understand your frustration, I would say such times of boredom and stagnation are times in which critical opposition is most crucial. It's easy to be righteous when everyone thinks you're right. It's much harder when they've changed their minds.

Rudy: And that's what you think has happened? Designers have become more conservative again, more in line with the status quo? Which is not surprising, of course. In times of economic an uncertainty, when the future looks bleak, there seems to be a tendency to look back, to choose safe solutions. Within graphic design we've seen an upswing in retro themes, nostalgia, and the return of what looks like the Swiss International Style.

Rob: The look of graphic design today is evidence of the pendulum swing back to more conservative and fiscal-minded times. It is a counter-revolution of sorts, and its assumptions are troubling, and real, and on MTV, and in *Emigre* itself.

Rudy: Why are its assumptions troubling?

Rob: Because this kind of work self-consciously positions design as stupid and trivial and says that documents of importance needn't rely on design to shape them. Default Systems are machines for design creation, and they represent design publicly as an "automatic" art form, offering a release from the breathless pace at which design now runs, as clients ask for more, quicker, now. Default Systems are a number of trends present in current graphic design that exploit computer presets in an industry-wide fashion. They are a quasi-simplistic rule set, often cribbing elements from the International Style in a kind of glossy pastiche, a cult of sameness driven by the laziness and comfort of the technology that enabled *Emigre*'s rise, the Macintosh.

Rudy: Do you think this was perhaps an obvious reaction to the hyperpersonal, customized messages of early nineties design?

Rob: Yes, in some part. What's interesting is how much Default Systems owe to early nineties design. The rejection of all systems by these "hyperpersonal" designers was itself systematic. Fussiness for its own sake in the early nineties is the same as reductivism for its own sake in the late nineties and today. Designers from Cranbrook and those mentioned in Steven Heller's "Cult of the Ugly" article in *Eye* magazine (vol. 3, no. 9, 1993) were nothing if not brash and dogmatic. Their ideal of "beauty" was nothing if not relative. Their models, like those of designers using Default Systems, were found in "low" forms, and the ceaseless glorification of these forms was as self-indulgent then as it is now. The stylistic methods of Default Systems design arose from the methods of Ugly design and they are tactically one and the same. Both are based on different kinds of proliferation and limitation. The distinction between the two is largely formal, which is of interest to designers, but their social observations are largely similar, which is of interest to critics.

Rudy: This raises a few questions. First, what do you mean by "Both are based on different kinds of proliferation and limitation"? Secondly, how are the social observations of "Ugly" design and "Default Systems" design similar? What is it that they have in common?

Rob: These two questions are related. The use of terms like "proliferation" and "limitation" is self-conscious on my part. These terms sound as if they come from a Marxist critique rather than a design discussion. I'm not trying to make this discussion overly academic; rather, I am trying to provide design critics with a model for positioning design within a broader social context, which doesn't always happen. The most interesting designs are critiques of the conditions of their own making, and Marxist language is useful for discussing the means of production and consumption because it was developed for that purpose.

Rudy: That doesn't answer my question, though.

Rob: Right. However, if, as I just said, the most interesting designs are critiques of the conditions of their own making, then both Ugly design and Default Systems design qualify as "most interesting." Both exploit certain opportunities presented by the computer as a tool while suppressing other opportunities. Some tactics are allowed to proliferate while others are deliberately limited. For example, the computer is a tool that allows for incredible customization. Typefaces—even individual letterforms—can be altered to a user's tastes. Ugly designers let this kind of customization run self-consciously amok. This was done in the name of a kind of democracy (every user is different), as well as a kind of authenticity (ugliness is pure and therefore true). What's interesting is that although Default Systems design looks so different from Ugly design, its interests are still tied to being authentic and being democratic. Default Systems design claims, "This is how the computer works with minimal intervention." It also claims, "By keeping the designer from intervening, this design language is made available to all." So Default

Systems look new, but they arise from the social concerns of the old. I'd call this "Hegelian," but I wouldn't want to make this discussion any more academic. . .

Rudy: Good, let's not.

Rob: I suspect that Default Systems arose from a kind of shame that plagued designers after accusations that their work had become overly self-indulgent in the face of the limitless possibilities of desktop publishing and a certain version of postmodernity. This notion finds its first theoretical articulation in the summer of 1995, when Dutch critic Carel Kuitenbrouwer wrote in *Eye* of "The New Sobriety" creeping into work of young Dutch designers at that time.

Rudy: Can you describe some of the features and characteristics of this type of Default Systems design?

Rob: Defaults, as we both know, are preordained settings found in common design programs such as Quark, Photoshop, and Illustrator that a user (or designer) must manually override. Thus, in Quark, all text boxes have a one point text inset unless one enters the default settings and changes this. Put simply, defaults automate certain aspects of the design process.

Default typefaces in contemporary design include all Macintosh System Fonts: Arial, Chicago, Courier, Times New Roman, Verdana, Wingdings, etc. Hallmark faces of the International Style that are seen as "uninflected" are also in this category: Helvetica, Akzidenz Grotesk, Grotesque, Univers, etc. Although the latter typefaces are far from meaningless, their original context is as neutral communicators, and this position is simultaneously supported and undermined by Default Systems design.

Defaults also appear in terms of scale. Sameness of size downplays hierarchy and typographic intervention, forcing the reader to form his or her own hierarchical judgments. Default designers argue that this emphasizes reading as opposed to looking, which makes the audience more active, more embodied.

Default placements include centrality as a kind of bluntness and bleeds as a kind of eradication of layout. The center is a default position. One "drops" something in the center; one "places" something off-center. Asymmetrical placement is embodied; central placement is disembodied. To bleed a photograph is to remove the page edge as a frame and emphasize the photograph itself. Placements (or non-placements) such as these allow images and texts to function as such. They are expected. Computer templates and formats that employ modernist grid aesthetics are also included here.

Default colors are black and white, the additive primaries (RGB) and the subtractive primaries (CMY). Default elements include all preexisting borders, blends, icons, filters, etc. Default sizes are 8, 10, 12, 18, 24 point in type, standard sheet sizes for American designers, ISO sizes for Europeans, etc. With standardization, it's argued, comes compatibility. Objects (particularly printed objects) are reproduced 1:1, and images and documents are shown with minimal manipulation.

Rudy: Who stands out for you as Default Systems designers?

Rob: The Experimental Jetset and issue no. 37 of *Emigre* that they designed. To publish their work in *Emigre* served to direct the attention of others to this undercurrent in design, but to mistake their work for anything more than a saccharinely ironic version of the International Style (shaken, not stirred) is to give it a kind of seriousness that their name itself eschews. Set entirely in Helvetica and using only process colors, standard sizes, and arrangements, the art direction of that issue is the epitome of "default." The tone of its essays is jargony and somewhat academic, and the antidesign of the issue provides them with a "serious" backdrop from which to make their points. Included is an archive of data storage formats that have now fallen into disuse, arranged according to their forms. In the center, bracketing the product catalog, Experimental Jetset sets up a bland joke: "Q: How many *Emigre* products does it take to change a light bulb?" After leafing through seventeen pages of products, the reader finds the punch line: "A: Never enough." The joke falls hopelessly flat, humorless. Other variants of the "light bulb" joke are repeated throughout the issue and are presented in ceaseless repetition, like lines of computer code. All are equally disjointed, equally unfunny. Though the joke is a format, the humanity of the joke format has been drained. It, too, is a lost format in need of preservation. Its *unfunniness* here manipulates us into feeling a kind of consumerist guilt over desiring the *Emigre* products within the bounds of its setup and punch line.

Daniel Eatock's "A Feature Article without Content," also comes to mind. The piece mocks a portfolio magazine feature article, demonstrating that expected placement is itself a kind of content.

Another example of Default Systems design is issue number seven of *Re-*, dubbed *Re-View*. It is a self-described "review of a magazine and its formats": cover, contents, review, short story, agenda, fashion, interview, and letters. *Re-View* aims to expose the expected and renders it available to all. The magazine itself has no content: it is an engine for content. "With texts to be written, not to be read, and pictures meant to be taken, not to be seen," it is prescriptive and programmatic while it is descriptive and programmed. Rather than following the traditional route of content leading design, here design leads content because the content is an admission of design's role in generating meaning within the context of a popular magazine. Tactics such as art direction are removed from their everyday associations and presented in a tone that may be mocking, gravely serious, or both. *Re-View*'s Art Director—capital *A*, capital *D*—is eerily similar to a Conceptual Artist—capital *C*, capital *A*—a "brain in a jar," generating visual ideas via programs that are meant to be executed by others. This elevates design while dehumanizing it.

Rudy: You lost me here. How do you both elevate design and dehumanize it?

Rob: The linking of design and Conceptual Art is an attempt to elevate design to the "High Art" level of Conceptual Art. There is a difference between "making" and "generating." By saying the role of the designer is to "make" an object, you are saying one thing; by saying the role of the designer is to "generate" a program by which objects can be made by others, you are saying something else. You've elevated what design produces—ideas, not things—but you've dehumanized it by taking the maker out of the equation and substituting him or her with a program. This is a natural leap for design that's interested in the role the computer plays in the production process, because, at some point, the program is what's making the design. But there is a spectrum, certainly. Design that veers closer to Conceptual Art than Computer Science strikes me as being less dehumanized. I may be oversimplifying, however.

Rudy: While I understand how you have come to use the term "Default Systems Design," I can imagine that designers would have a problem calling their design methods "default." The term has many negative connotations.

Rob: In most contexts, "to default" is to fail. To be "in default" on a loan is not to pay it; to "default" in court is not to appear; to win "by default" is to win because the other team did not play.

The only arena in which the definition of "default" is not entirely negative is in Computer Science, where a default is "a particular setting or variable that is assigned automatically by an operating system and remains in effect unless canceled or overridden by the operator." Defaults, at least in terms of computers, are the *status quo*. Theirs are not the failure to do what's promised but exactly the opposite. Theirs are a promise kept in lieu of an "operator's" (or designer's) intervention. To view a computer through its default settings is to view it as it has been programmed to view itself, even to give it a kind of authority. Naturally, "a default" is produced by systemic thinking—the definition mentions "operating systems" specifically—and "defaults," taken cumulatively, could be defined as the system by which the machine operates when no one is actively operating it. The system makes assumptions that, unchallenged, become truths.

Rudy: The use of Default Systems is not exactly a new phenomenon. It's been a known process for generating work within the world of art and literature. It seems graphic design, again, is coming to the scene late.

Rob: Well, yes and no. Design punishes itself for not being "on trend" too often and to no end. To do so is to be obsessed with style (which is a shallow effort) or to be obsessed with making design the same as art (which is a pointless effort). Anyone would be hard-pressed to identify a governing principle of a new aesthetic movement that wasn't presaged in some form by a prior movement, especially if you include any genre you want. That said, defaults have been used to create art for a long time. In writing, the work of OuLiPo (*Ouvroir Littérature Potentielle*, "Workshop of Potential Literature") comes to mind. Oulipian poetics ascribes a Default System accommodating a series of constraints and then challenges the author to create a product from those constraints. Oulipian poetics are both emulative and emergent. Their constraints arise from mimicking other constraints, but they still manage to be original and meaningful. The texts of OuLiPo are built both by humans and by the systems that humans build.

In the realm of visual art, sixties Conceptualists like Sol LeWitt are helpful in identifying the underpinnings of "default" working procedures because of their twin interests in failure and systems. Many of these artists use strikingly similar working methods, harnessing nonintervention to generate solutions.

Nonintervention is also significant in contemporary film. Gus Van Sant's film *Gerry* and his recent Palme d'Or–winning *Elephant* are based on site-specific improvisation and camerawork. His films are informed by those of Dogme 95 (which arose from the same countries as The New Sobriety), and Dogme 95, in turn, is informed by the French New Wave.

Rudy: In the hands of graphic designers, to what degree are these Default Systems a sort of critique of design?

Rob: In the end, the most potent critiques offered by designers using Default Systems seem to be linked to guilt and loss. Default Systems, and the formats that they include, comment not just on the mechanics of systems but on systemic thinking in general, and on the new life of man in the networked Global Village. The computer has changed design, but it has also changed our process of thinking and making. Formats and systems govern everything from our weaponry systems to our guidelines for citizenship.

Rudy: That's not as much a critique as it is an affirmation of our current situation. Or is it?

Rob: That's the question. In the face of eroding history, vanishing citizenship, bulging landfills, and sprawling consumerism, what is the critique that Default Systems offers? Are they resistant, complicit, or both? Are their strategies effective or clichéd? The answers to these questions will not come from the designers themselves, nor should they. They will come from the critics and from the critical language they derive. To render their forms and tactics available is to open them up for discussion. This discussion is a powerful first step. As design's visual codes become more widely understood, they become more pliable to the designers who employ them. As the assumptions of systemic thinking become popularized, societies may choose more actively to absorb or combat them. Design will play a role in this selection process.

Rudy: Why has so little been written or said about the use of these Default Systems, which we both acknowledge is widespread?

Rob: Because Default Systems are deliberately invisible. To articulate them and the conditions that enable them is an important first step in the critical process. To evaluate their message is an important second step, and this has not been done. The lack of this evaluative mechanism betrays a snag in the fabric of design production with regard to its criticism. The language of criticism must employ its own forms and tactical instruments. Design is still in need of an external critical language, rigorously defined. The development of this language will almost certainly alter the climate and context in which designs are made both now and in the future. The problem is not that Default Systems are bad and haven't been opposed. The problem is that not even designers really understand what they mean. And that problem—along with the irresponsibility that it suggests—is far worse.

THE BIRTH OF THE USER
Ellen Lupton

I n the 1980s and early 1990s, many experimental graphic designers embraced the idea of the readerly text. Inspired by theoretical ideas such as Roland Barthes' "death of the author," they used layers of text and interlocking grids to create works of design that engaged the reader in the making of meaning. In place of the classical model of typography as a crystal goblet for content, this alternative view assumes that content itself changes with each act of representation. Typography becomes a mode of interpretation, and the designer and reader (and the designer-as-reader) competed with the traditional author for control of the text.

Another model surfaced at the end of the 1990s, borrowed not from literary criticism but from human-computer interaction (HCI) studies and the fields of interface and usability design. The dominant subject of our age has become neither reader nor writer but user, a figure conceived as a bundle of needs and impairments—cognitive, physical, emotional. Like a patient or child, the user is a figure to be protected and cared for but also scrutinized and controlled, submitted to research and testing.

How texts are used becomes more important than what they mean. Someone clicked here to get over there. Someone who bought this also bought that. The interactive environment not only provides users with a degree of control and self-direction but also, more quietly and insidiously, it gathers data about its audiences. Text is a game to be played, as the user responds to signals from the system. We may play the text, but it is also playing us.

This essay is revised and excerpted from Ellen Lupton, *Thinking with Type* (New York: Princeton Architectural Press, 2004).

Graphic designers can use theories of user interaction to revisit some of our basic assumptions about visual communication. Why, for example, are readers on the Web less patient than readers of print? It is a common assumption that digital displays are inherently more difficult to read than ink on paper. Yet HCI studies conducted in the late 1980s proved that crisp black text on a white background can be read just as efficiently from a screen as from a printed page.

The impatience of the digital reader arises from cultural habit, not from the essential character of display technologies. Users of Web sites have different expectations than users of print. They expect to feel "productive," not contemplative. They expect to be in search mode, not processing mode. Users also expect to be disappointed, distracted, and delayed by false leads. These screen-based behaviors are driving changes in design for print, while at the same time affirming print's role as a place where extended reading can still occur.

Another common assumption is that icons are a more universal mode of communication than text. Icons are central to the graphical user interfaces (GUIs) that routinely connect users with computers. Yet text can often provide a more specific and understandable cue than a picture. Icons don't actually simplify the translation of content into multiple languages, because they require explanation in multiple languages. The endless icons of the digital desktop, often rendered with gratuitous detail and depth, function more to enforce brand identity than to support usability. In the twentieth century, modern designers hailed pictures as a "universal" language, yet in the age of code, text has become a more common denominator than images—searchable, translatable, and capable of being reformatted and restyled for alternative or future media.

Perhaps the most persistent impulse of twentieth-century art and design was to physically integrate form and content. The Dada and futurist poets, for example, used typography to create texts in which content was inextricable from the concrete layout of specific letterforms on a page. In the twenty-first century, form and content are being pulled back apart. Style sheets, for example, compel designers to think globally and systematically instead of focusing on the fixed construction of a particular surface. This way of thinking allows content to be reformatted for different devices or users, and it also prepares for the afterlife of data as electronic storage media begin their own cycles of decay and obsolescence.

In the twentieth century, modern artists and critics asserted that each medium is specific. They defined film, for instance, as a constructive language distinct from theater, and they described painting as a physical medium that refers to its own processes. Today, however, the medium is not always the message. Design has become a "transmedia" enterprise, as authors and producers create worlds of characters, places, situations, and interactions that can appear across a variety of products. A game might live in different versions on a video screen, a desktop computer, a game console, and a cell phone, as well as on T-shirts, lunch boxes, and plastic toys.

The beauty and wonder of "white space" is another modernist myth that is under revision in the age of the user. Modern designers discovered that open space on a page can have as much physical presence as printed areas. White space is not always a mental kindness, however. Edward Tufte, a fierce advocate of visual density, argues for maximizing the amount of data conveyed on a single page or screen. In order to help readers make connections and comparisons as well as to find information quickly, a single surface packed with well-organized information is sometimes better than multiple pages with a lot of blank space. In typography as in urban life, density invites intimate exchange among people and ideas.

In our much-fabled era of information overload, a person can still process only one message at a time. This brute fact of cognition is the secret behind magic tricks: sleights of hand occur while the attention of the audience is drawn elsewhere. Given the fierce competition for their attention, users have a chance to shape the information economy by choosing what to look at. Designers can help them make satisfying choices.

Typography is an interface to the alphabet. User theory tends to favor normative solutions over innovative ones, pushing design into the background. Readers usually ignore the typographic interface, gliding comfortably along literacy's habitual groove. Sometimes, however, the interface should be allowed to fail. By making itself evident, typography can illuminate the construction and identity of a page, screen, place, or product.

Sources

The writings of Roland Barthes continue to challenge and inspire graphic designers; see *Image/Music/Text*, trans. Stephen Heath (New York: Hill and Wang, 1977). For on screen readability, see John D. Gould, et al., "Reading from CRT Displays Can Be as Fast as Reading from Paper," *Human Factors* 29, no. 5 (1987): pp. 497–517. On the restless user, see Jakob Nielsen, *Designing Web Usability* (Indianapolis: New Riders, 2000). Jef Raskin discusses the failure of interface icons, the scarcity of human attention, and the myth of white space in *The Humane Interface: New Directions for Designing Interactive Systems* (Reading, Mass.: Addison-Wesley, 2000). On density and information design, see Edward Tufte, *Envisioning Information* (Cheshire, Conn.: Graphics Press, 1990) and *The Cognitive Style of PowerPoint* (Cheshire, Conn.: Graphics Press, 2003).

QUANTUM LEAP:
BEYOND LITERAL MATERIALITY
Johanna Drucker

Typefaces, page size, headers, footers, and column width are among the obvious and apparently self-evident graphical features of any textual work. Whether in print, paint, manuscript, or electronic and material formats, such features go largely unnoticed unless they interfere with reading or otherwise call attention to themselves. Works by book artists and designers cleverly exploit these codes to defeat or trick expectations provoked by familiar conventions. Dick Higgins' well-known artist's book *FOEW&OMBWHNW* (New York: Something Else Press, 1969) bears all the conspicuous attributes of a bible or missal—black leather binding, with gold stamping, a red fore edge, and a red-ribbon place holder, and a double-columned layout of sober black type. When we realize the text is a treatise on inter-media intercut with the thinly veiled exploits of Higgins as his alter ego, Thuderbaby, we laugh. The irreverence of the mismatch is obvious and funny. But we quickly move beyond recognition of the book-form clichés and get on with the business of reading the "real" contents of even such a work. Reading the text for what it "says" often means disregarding—even "forgiving"—conspicuous elements of the design. Material presentation is a necessary, even interesting element of a work, but once we get "serious" with a text, we just "read."

Few and far between are the persons whose eyes are trained enough in historical traditions to assess the appropriateness of a type style. Who but a typophile eager to demonstrate expertise cares if a text is set in a face that was invented after that text was written, or three hundred years before it was imagined, or according to a sensibility utterly inimical to that for which it is used? If more blatantly perceived, these fashion errors would be ludicrous—the style equivalent of dressing Pantagruel in a spandex workout suit or costuming the girl-geek character played by Sandra Bullock in *The Net* in a white shirtwaist and black skirt over a corseted frame to indicate her role as a female worker in the bureaucracies of another era's office culture. Most style choices are made to please the eye, make a text legible and presentable, or produce an "aesthetic" design—not as studies in historical understanding. Many uses of a typeface or layout convention can be seen and tolerated as interpretive acts of reinvention, or as innocently ignorant lapses.

Based on a paper given at TEXT (Society for Textual Scholarship), in March 2003 in New York City as "Graphical Aesthetics" and published in *Text* 16 (2006).

But with just a little background into type history, a reader can register striking paradoxes. The descendants of the rational seventeenth-century Roman du Roi, pressed into service for personal ads and various black letter types, take on the endless-seeming task of symbolizing the neo-trans-historical-medievalism that runs rampant in video and online games. This typographic construction of "medievalism" (and its association with "gothic" themes of vampirism, dark magic, and undead forces) would make a wonderful cultural study. A design historian may delight in sighting such peculiarities, but the graphical effects on the commonplace experience usually register only in the case of egregious mismatches of style and form—and even then, as a mere wrinkle, not as a compelling call to historical knowledge or insight. Few of us leave our morning reading of the *New York Times* reflecting on the fate of Stanley Morison's judicious expertise. Nor do we pause to ponder the fall-from-grace effected by changes to once elite Baskerville or Park Avenue in their checkered careers. Few pause to read the IBM logo designed by Paul Rand as the very essence of modern corporate systematicity and global imperialism. The signs are just too familiar to be read. Fewer yet will puzzle through the cultural implications of a genealogical relation between such designers, their training, and the transformation of the communicative sphere. We don't process typefaces on our cereal boxes by their presentation of competing precepts of humanistic and rational-instrumental sensibilities. Every material artifact embodies such aesthetics in its formal properties and history, carrying the legacy of its use and re-use. Too much attention to these graphical properties could get ridiculous—tending towards a dictionary of equivalents in which Neuland + Ezra Pound + wide spacing = fascism through a reductive literalism.

The discussion of the "meaning value" or the "expressivity" of visual means, though unfamiliar in particulars, seems to find more or less ready acceptance as a general idea. With just a little prompting, most readers will admit a begrudging preference for one face or another or admit to the inflecting effect of graphic styles on semantic value. A sample display of posters, type samples, or graphic instances makes clear that such graphical codes affect our reading. Contrasts of early twentieth century journals display marked differences meant to signal appeal to different audiences. Unbroken, measured columns of type composed a page of a serious journal aimed at the masculine sensibility, while broken up chunks of text and graphics aimed at a female reader who clearly suffered from a deficient attention span and was gratified to let her wandering eye fall on ads for domestic labor-saving devices, corsets, and pickling equipment. In an exercise I gave my students a year ago, they transposed the text of the *Wall Street Journal* headlines and those of the *National Enquirer* in a kind of design transvestism—so that the banner headline "Bond Markets See Rates Drop By Slight Margin" took on a screaming impact, while "Two-Headed Boy Gives Birth to Alien Savior with Telepathic Knowledge of Biblical Past-Lives" was modestly set in the grayest and least exclamatory of formats.

Meaning is produced, after all, not exhumed, and such exercises are dramatic demonstrations of this principle. Most literates are fully ready to believe that the message of meaning goes beyond surface effects even if many of these same readers, textual-studies and "lit-crit" persons, will also tend to shrug off these observations as trivial. Most literary types (and common readers) are closet transcendentalists, harboring a not-so-secret belief that after all it is the "sense" that "really matters." (Note here that perverse use of the word "matters"—for what could *matter* more than material, or be more truly "matter" than the manifest text? But more on this in a moment.) We could likely agree without too much dispute that any instance of graphic or typographic form can be read as an index of historical and cultural disposition. Attention to the "character of characters" is laudable, maybe even useful, and similar observations could be made with regard to other elements of layout and design.

Graphical expertise used to be an esoteric art, the province of professionals trained to "spec" type. Desktop publishing changed this and increased general sensitivity to design as a set of familiar variables. The features of graphical expression, when enumerated and described, comprise a set of entities which, not surprisingly, are now present in the menu bar of Word, Quark, InDesign, or other text and page description programs. These graphic elements of a text's "appearance" must be specified or the default settings kick in and provide the "normal" Times, 12 point, single-spaced, unjustified, 5.5" block with standard margins, word space, and letter fit. The desktop user is offered a set of choices for transforming font, format, point size, leading, alignment, tab settings, and so forth. But this approach, like the discussion of historical analysis of style, is premised on a few assumptions that limit the scope of a larger inquiry into graphical aesthetics. Why?

Manipulation of every one of these graphical components assumes that it is an "entity" with an ontologically self-sufficient autonomy and self-evident completeness. This is misleading. Interested as I am in material histories, the crux of my argument is that the very conception of these elements as discrete "entities" is problematic. The menu of options extends an attitude I call "literal materiality"—a sense that a graphical entity is simply "there" and thus available to a rich, descriptive discussion of its self-evident characteristics. Getting nondesigners to pay attention to the material properties of graphical elements is difficult enough. But undoing the assumptions that support the idea of "literal materiality" is even harder. Consider the palette-and-toolbar categories of graphic entities, for instance. These menus reinforce the idea that the appearance of these graphical "entities" are chosen from a list of named, finite, definite, and discrete elements that get put on the page. The problem with this is that graphical elements, like anything else material, are defined circumstantially, in relation to the other elements with which they are juxtaposed or surrounded. Even in the simplest-seeming case—black type on a white background the letters aren't self-identical things that have the same weight, quality, look, and effect of legibility no matter what. They are constitutive elements of a system in which expressivity is acquired relationally. No letter has a "character" in a discrete sense—but rather, it assumes a character according to its use (position, juxtaposition, and context). One senses this vividly when working with a line of hand-set lead, shifting it up and down a galley until its weight can be felt as a combination of factors—placement, juxtaposition, leading, and surrounding space.

The calling into question of the "entity" of any graphical element is most dramatically demonstrated when we try to name and discuss *the ground*—the page, the material support, or the base—essential to a graphic work whether in traditional or electronic format. Each of these terms (page, etc.) suffers from the same sense of "entity" that misleads our sense that graphic elements (type style or size, column-width, or leading) are "things" to be collected from an inventory and then used. In addition, terms like "ground" or "support" reinforce a hierarchy in which the base is subservient to the substantive figures of text and/or graphical elements that are "on" it. I doubt I would have much difficulty convincing readers with the argument I sketched earlier— the value of understanding graphical features in their historical dimensions. But I've set myself a different task here: to dispel the notion of design elements as "graphic entities" and to dislodge the presumptions it carries. That may prove more difficult. I want to rework the conventional approach to the idea of the "page" as an a priori "space" for graphical construction. In its place, I want to propose an understanding of all graphical elements as dynamic entities in what Jerome McGann and I refer to as a "quantum field"—or system.

Not only are graphical codes the very site and substance of historical meaning, rich and redolent with genealogical traces of origin and use, trailing their vestiges of experience in the counters and serifs of their fine faces. Not only are conventions for the organization of text into textual apparatus and para-textual appendices themselves a set of codes that predispose us to read according to the instructions embedded therein. And not only are the physical materials as well as the graphically expressive distribution an arrangement of verbal materials an integral and inherent part of the semantic value of any text—so that any remnant of the old "vehicular" notion can be laid permanently to rest. No, not only do all these elements deserve their particular, specific, descriptively analytic attention for the contribution they make to our processes of interpretation. But also, the very possibility of interpretive acts occurs within this "quantum system," which is not a pregiven physical, metrical "space" in the literal sense, but is a relational, dynamic, dialectically potential "espace" constitutive of, not a precondition for, the graphical presentation of a text.

To reiterate, I'm suggesting that the specific properties of evident and obvious graphical elements, though frequently unnoticed, are an important part of semantic meaning production—the expressivity of these "inflections" is more than superficial, and can and should be understood as integral to textuality. But important as these specifics are, I'm suggesting a radical reconsideration of the process by which these "appearances" are constituted. In this reconsideration, I want to use the example of white space and demonstrate that this space is not inert, not pregiven and neutral, not an a priori fact or entity, but is itself relational and constituted through dynamic relations.

An outstanding example on which to make this clear is the use of white space in William Morris's *Kelmscott Chaucer*. This work offers ample opportunity to reconsider "space" so that it isn't taken as a given, inert and neutral, but as an "espace" or field in which forces among mutually constitutive elements make themselves available to be read. But the points that can be made about the *Chaucer* apply to the garden-variety pages encountered in daily reading. This page, for instance, is divided into text blocks and margins, with linespace, letterspace, space between page number and margin, and so on. Each area of white space has its own quality or character, as if it was a variation in atmospheric pressure in a different part of the graphic microclimate.

Some people may think I am making too much of a simple matter, but, at the very least, I hope to demonstrate that "white" space is visually inflected, given a tonal value through relations rather than according to some intrinsic property.

White spaces can be divided into three basic categories depending on their behavior and character: graphic, pictorial, or textual. I define these as follows: (1) graphic (structural organization, no figural or semantic referent), providing framing and support of the supposed ground; (2) pictorial (as part of an identifiable image or visual meaning in shape or pattern); and (3) textual (organizational convention, keeps characters, lines, and blocks discrete). On any given page, each area takes on a particular graphic value. By this I mean a tone, or color acquired in relation to the density of other graphic elements in proximity, and also a signifying (if not quite semantic) value.

Typographic elements depend upon the use of white space to sustain the careful articulation that gives them their stylistic specificity. Letterforms are as much an effect of the way the spaces breathe through the lines of type as they are of the character of the strokes. The white space plays a primary role as a supporting medium in guaranteeing the typography its stylistic identity. We see evidence of this in the way the space holds open the counters of letters, keeping them to specific degrees of curvature or slant (textual). The incredibly obvious and yet utterly essential space between image and text lines often divides the elements of the graphic universe into word and picture, separating the verbal heavens from the visual earth. This fundamental vocabulary can be subdivided almost indefinitely into the spaces between lines, between the text block and the background, and between other distinct margins within the area of the text, each of which has a place within the visual hierarchy that organizes our reading. Similarly, the space around text blocks creates the measured pace for reading while referencing the specific histories of book design and format features (textual). Lower margins keep the text block from slipping off the page while also giving an indication of textual continuity or termination. All of these distinctions could be refined even further, to a surprisingly high degree of granularity and specificity.

Dwelling on such matters, the minutiae of spaces within letters, and around lines of text, frameworks, and borders, particularly in an elaborately—even excessively—ornate work (as that of Morris), might seem to lavish attention on details that have little or no relevance to "regular" or daily habits of reading. I'd argue the contrary. Another elaborately useful case study would be, of course, Stéphane Mallarmé's 1896 vision of his poem *Un Coup de Dès*. In that work, white space has a spatializing dynamic as well as graphically structuring function. Morris's sense of successive planes and openings, the deep space of representation in relation to the scene of the page, makes a striking contrast with Mallarmé's use of space as relational and active, creating the full three-dimensionality of his work as it is suspended in the full space of a book turned, read, imagined, and conceived.

The conceptual leap required to move beyond a literal, mechanistic under-standing of graphic elements should be easy. We don't think of the atom as a tinker-toy model with balls and sticks, and rings of wire constraining "electrons" in fixed orbits anymore. That notion, so charmingly modular, has the scientific validity of Ptolemaic models of the structure of the solar system—or of Newtonian, rather than quantum, physics. Atoms, molecules—the mechanistic understanding of these "entities" got dispelled in a theoretical frame that replaced entities with forces and introduced the principle of uncertainty into the account of atomic physics in the early twentieth century work of Heisenberg and others. In "quantum physics," a phenomenon is produced by the intersection of a set of possibilities and an act of perceptual intervention. At the level of granularity we are used to experiencing in daily business, matter appears to operate with a certain consistency according to Newton's laws. But at the atomic and subatomic level, these consistencies dissolve into probabilities, not certainties, providing contingent, rather than absolute, identities. We should simply think of letters, words, typefaces, and graphic forms in the same way. Think of the page as a force field, a set of tensions in relation, which assumes a form when intervened through the productive act of reading. Peculiar? Not really, just unfamiliar as a way to think about "things" as experienced. A slight vertigo can be induced by considering a page as a force field, a set of elements in contingent relation, a set of possibilities, instructions for a potential event. But every reading reinvents a text, produces it, as an intervention, and that is a notion we have long felt comfortable invoking. I'm merely shifting our attention from the "pro-duced" nature of signified meaning to the "productive" character of a signifying field.

If I were to put my own methodology into a historiographic perspective, work on typography, printing, and graphic design would form one part of the corpus. Writings on visual representation, printmaking, and literary studies informed by theo-retical investigations of text would form another. Speculative work in the realm of documents, cognitive studies, and systems theory provide yet another element of the intellectual armature on which a concept of emergent properties can be supported. All help mark the significant shift from a *literal* to an *emergent*, codependent conception of materiality. As literary scholars and design critics engage with graphical aesthetics and material properties of text, I suggest we should not limit ourselves to a literalized "read-ing" of materiality, but consider instead a quantum approach to materiality in textual and visual studies.

My debts to Jerome McGann and our ongoing conversations are obvious. I'm also appreciative of Maura Tarnoff's involvement in studying Morris's pages with me.

FROM THE (A) TRIVIAL TO THE (B) DEADLY SERIOUS, LISTS DOMINATE VISUAL CULTURE

Alice Twemlow

I n recent times, the editors of slick style and popular culture magazines have taken it upon themselves to reduce the world and its riches into bite-sized chunks. As a result, lists—and specifically hierarchical ones—have evolved into a new superspecies of the lazy article. The economics of the epidemic are simple. The supply of the "world's most exclusive spas," "badly dressed men," and the "best rock anthems of all time," just waiting to be corralled and enumerated, is endless. And, in a consumer society obsessed as much with the metalanguage of consumerism as it is with actually buying things, the demand is certain. According to *Folio*, a U.S. magazine industry journal, "best of" list issues of magazines are guaranteed bestsellers. It recently ran a how-to article offering some "dos and don'ts" for creating such issues including, under the "dos" heading, such sage advice as: "Be counter-intuitive. Instead of the best hamburger, name the best blue cheese burger." Though they are seductively easy to read and apparently provide a way of getting to the "essence" of a subject, do we lose something by reducing valuable (or even not so valuable) information into a series of bullet points?

The proliferation of lists in magazines results from a collision of conditions: dwindling editorial budgets (when you are paying by the word, conjunctions seem superfluous); the popularity of search engines, such as Google, that allow editors to generate lists in infinite combinations and mean that readers are familiar with viewing information through a listing lens; and the aesthetic appeal of a neat vertical story that provides the illusion of order and completion.

A list—especially one that ranks or categorizes—can be a salve for the anxiety of living in an era of information overload: an authoritative knife with which to slice through the morass of extraneous data. But the relief is short-lived; soon the accumulated lists begin to add to the overload themselves. Listing the options may be

Originally published in *Eye* 12, no. 47 (Spring 2003).

easier than selecting one of them to stand by, but, as lists multiply, all they add to the reader's life is another item on the to-do list: take out newspapers and magazines for recycling.

HARD, UNADORNED FACTS

The ultimate corollary to the publishing industry's current tendency must surely be *List* magazine. First published in June 2000, and with more issues in the pipeline, the magazine compiles image-based and typographic lists that range from the trivial and humorous, such as "Top Ghetto Drinks" and the *Talk* magazine launch party guest list, arranged in a telephone directory format, to the chokingly poignant: in a catalog of last meals requested by death row inmates, John Rock, who died at 2:11 A.M. on September 19, 1986 in Raleigh, North Carolina, asked for "12 hot dogs. (Ate only three)."

    List's conceiver and creative director, the nightclub owner and designer Serge Becker, explains the magazine's impetus: "It seemed very pure. Very much of the moment. We have less time right now. What about a magazine that condenses every-thing down to lists? They're really easy to kind of glance at. You pick it up, you check out one or two, you put it down. It dispenses with the articles concept."

    While *List* does makes an ironic statement, albeit a quiet one, on the reduc-tive nature of our contemporary concerns, more obviously it revels in the richness of the listing device from an art director's perspective. Its creators, Becker and Lisa Ano, were inspired by two of the godfathers of lists: *Colors* magazine and the "Harper's Index"—both highly evolved vehicles for presenting hard, unadorned facts, the former visually and the latter textually. Both examples work so well because of the clarity of their underlying vision and the consistency of their respec-tive voices. *Colors* deals with political and social issues by amassing images in multi-ple that prompt viewers to analyze, compare, differentiate, and decide. *Harper's* exploits the dissonance between carefully paired statistics and thus taps directly into the mainline of the reader's conscience. An example from the December 2002 "Index" reads:

> Hours after Defense Secretary Donald Rumsfeld learned Bin Laden was a
> suspect that he sought reasons to "hit" Iraq: 2.5
> Percentage by which the Pentagon's September order for sun block exceeded
> its last largest such order: 70

THE MAGIC BULLET

Listspeak is not solely a media phenomenon. Far more pernicious in its all-pervasiveness is the kind of bullet-point-list thinking (or lack of thinking) rife in corporate culture that, back in the early 1980s, the inventors of PowerPoint exploited so effectively with software features such as the AutoContent Wizard.

As Ian Parker observed in an article in the *New Yorker*, "PowerPoint also has a private, interior influence. It edits ideas. It is, almost surreptitiously, a business manual as well as a business suit, with an opinion—an oddly pedantic, prescriptive opinion—about the way we should think." PowerPoint templates that insist on a heading followed by bullet points—the InFocus "Presenters University" Web site, for example, pushes the "666 Rule" for visual presentations: "No more than 6 words per bullet, 6 bullets per image and 6 word slides in a row"—lead to a truncated, discontinuous kind of thinking that has seeped out of the corporate boardrooms and into culture at large. Many conference lectures and even church sermons are now delivered in PowerPoint.

While the bullet point's existence certainly predates PowerPoint, its popularity is a curious byproduct of the computer program. Until recently it was merely a typographical mark, a solid dot, used in a particular kind of list, usually in an advertising context, to distinguish items of equal weighting. Typesetters would have created bullets by filling lower case *o*s or by using various dingbats. Now, a plethora of Web sites exists to advise upon its usage: according to one, by adding emphasis to a list with bullets or icons (in PowerPoint you can select animated or sound ones) your list takes on new importance and invites readership. It has become an increasingly noisy sign that requests, with more urgency than a new paragraph can muster, the renewed and exaggerated attention of a reader: "Read This Now!" it seems to demand. Despite the bullet's mysterious past—in typographic histories its origins are either guessed at or omitted completely—and the fact that there is no bullet point button on the computer keyboard (it's Option 8 on Macs and Alt-0149 on Windows); it has somehow finagled its way into popular usage to the extent that it is now the punctuation mark of our era.

Apart from the bullet point, the other visual elements that make a list recognizable include the following: white space; linear arrangement (vertical or horizontal); the use of a colon; a deliberate system of organization (an order indicated by numbers or letters) or non-organization (to expand its free associative potential); and a choice of arrangement on the page (centered, or ranged left, for example.) All these play their part in signaling list-ness.

FROM DAILY CHORES TO ROLLS OF HONOR

The content of a list has an interior logic of its own; a mini universe of principles that make it a purposeful and curated collection of found things or concepts. It can be ordered by rank—as in alphabetical indexes and the "Fortune 500"—by category—as in the case of axes, halbards, and doas in the ethnographic Pitt Rivers Museum—or it can be an unordered assemblage of things. Of the latter category, more often than not the common factor is the personal experience—either real or hypothetical—of the author. Most of us attempt to give our working days some semblance of purpose or control by listing them out—often resulting in laughable abutments of prosaic detail and poetic ambition as in: "call printer, pick up dry-cleaning, quit smoking; get bike fixed, buy deodorant, write memoirs." Our personal notes to self provide a unique space in which both the facts and the possibilities of our lives can coexist.

Other personal lists are compiled to signal inclusion within a particular social group. It is assumed that other cool people such as ourselves know and understand the selection. This is the "the top five Elvis Costello songs" type of list through which Nick Hornby's hero, Rob Fleming, views the world in *High Fidelity*: the type of list in which recognition is its own reward. Most of us relish opportunities such as these to debate nuances in taste and to be "knowing," and the list provides a basis for discussion.

List culture does not only embrace the trivial. Some lists reflect life or death situations: Schindler's list or the anxiously awaited list of Iraq's weapons of mass destruction. Then there are memorials such as Maya Lin's *Vietnam Veterans Memorial* in Washington, D.C., with more than 58,000 names engraved in its marble, or the incantatory recital of the names of the victims at the anniversary memorial service for the attack on the World Trade Center in New York. Nearly every town and village in the United Kingdom lists its dead from two world wars in a cut stone monument. All such quiet memorials and roll calls make a virtue of the respectful, unsentimental quality of an unadorned list.

SHIPS AND WARRIORS

The making and manipulating of lists was one of the earliest forms of literacy. About two-thirds of the tablets excavated from the ancient port of Ugarit in Syria, and dating from 1400 BC, are lists of taxes, rations, supplies, pay, inventories, receipts, census records, and so on. Once information could be stored in a written list, complex forms of analysis, such as categorization and classification—analysis that an oral memory–based culture had precluded—were possible. The list, then, enabled whole new modes of thought.

Listing is an essential literary and linguistic strategy. It can be used as a self-conscious rhetorical device to build the drama of an argument or to create an accumulation of sensation. In the *Iliad*, for example, Homer compiled a catalog of ships and lists of the warriors at Troy to accentuate the drama and the scope of his literary undertaking. And the nineteenth-century transcendentalists Ralph Waldo Emerson and Henry David Thoreau embraced the systematic language of natural history, exemplified by Linnaeus's classification of species, in their list writing.

Later, writers such as Walt Whitman and James Joyce exploited the prosaic/poetic tensions that also characterize the everyday shopping list. For Whitman, the list summoned the subjects into being, calling forth the democratic masses. For Joyce, the list was the definitive modernist device for refuting the descriptive excesses of the Victorian age.

MINUTIAE OF LIFE

Visual practitioners have also made their mark on the evolution of the list. While the kind of lists found in notebooks are frequently mined by critics for the clues they may disclose about the creative process of a maker, lists that may be considered as finished products, as ends in themselves, are discussed much less often.

When the novelist and literary critic William Gass wrote in his beautiful essay, "I've Got a Little List," that "a camera is a list maker, the film nothing but a series of shots in the order of their snapping," he may well have had the photographer Walker Evans in mind. Here is the quintessential visual list maker, documenting the unsung aspects of everyday life through his serial portraits of things, places, and people in "portfolios" such as *Labor Anonymous* and *Beauties of the Common Tool*. In addition to these photographic lists, Evans also made type- and hand-written lists of concepts, objects, and experiences which art critic Sarah Boxer describes as "powerful bits of vertical writing." They tend to make jarring juxtapositions of the ordinary and the emotional details. A two-column list of Evans's 1926–27 European travels, for example, records his physical progress by means of the names and addresses of the places he visits. This humdrum catalog is threaded through with enigmatic hints of the photographer's personal feelings at the various stages of his journey: "Solitude" appears six times (although in one instance it is crossed out).

Among Evans's other lists is one he compiled in 1937 under the heading "Contempt for." In it he itemized: "men who try to fascinate women with their minds, gourmets, liberals, cultivated women, writers, successful artists who use the left to buttress their standing, the sex life of America, limited editions, 'atmosphere,' Bennington College, politics, men of my generation who became photographers during the Depression, journalists, new dealers, readers of the *New Yorker*, the corner of Madison Avenue and 56th St. . . ."

Georges Perec, in 1981, elevated the New Year's resolution list genre to an art form in his log of "Some of the Things I Really Must Do Before I Die," which includes "Take a trip on a bateau mouche" as well as "Arrange my bookshelves once and for all" and "Find the solution to the Rubik cube." More recently, graphic designer Stefan Sagmeister, a self-admitted list-lover, made a similar record of his preoccupations and unfulfilled desires, handwritten and replete with check boxes, that concludes with: "Touch somebody's heart with graphic design."

RELENTLESS DETACHMENT

Many artists have used lists in their work. Some make collections of items, presented, like Gass suggests, as juxtapositions that "exhibit many of the qualities of collage." Ed Ruscha, in a photographic document of every building on Los Angeles' Sunset Strip, for example, observes his environment through a dispassionate listing lens. And Gerhard Richter conveys detachment through relentless amassing in his *48 Portraits*, a visual catalog of philosophers, composers, writers, and scientists depicted in a style reminiscent of encyclopedia illustrations.

A more recent example of this apparently objective cultural portraiture is "Wordsearch," published on four pages of the business section of the October 4 edition of the *New York Times*. Artist Karin Sander collected from 250 New Yorkers, each speaking a different language, a word in their mother tongue, then translated it into the other 249 languages, and compiled the resulting 62,500 words in a work of art analogous to the newspaper's stock market listing. In a similarly taxonomical spirit, French installation artist Christian Boltanski assembled in the South London Gallery 3,000 telephone directories and yellow pages from all the countries of the world. He also inserted in the gallery's newspaper a supplement that listed all registered voters living within ten minutes' walk of the gallery.

At the other end of the spectrum, artists such as Tracey Emin have imported lists based on intensely personal experience ("Everyone I have ever slept with 1963–95") from the private to the public sphere and exploited their incongruence in the new context.

BEAUTY, MYSTERY, AND UTILITY

In a crop of recent design work, too, lists have attained a new prominence. Indexes, directories, checklists—the organizational principles of many graphic design artifacts, especially books, catalogs, and Web sites—are retrieved from ignominious locations in their structures and celebrated. Indexes spill onto book covers, checklists of artists' work become the primary content of promotional posters, and the normally hidden programming language of Web sites is prioritized.

For the catalog of the *Best Book Designs of 1999*, exhibited at the Stedelijk museum, designer Stuart Bailey featured the index of materials, typefaces, designers, and publishers of the winning books on the front and back covers. In such annuals and catalogs, the index is the first place people look, so why not cut to the chase and bring it to the forefront? The Walker Art Center's Andrew Blauvelt and Santiago Piedrafita employed a similarly pragmatic system in their design for the catalog of the American Center for Design's twenty-first annual design competition. Subtitled *The Indexical Archive*, the catalog's cover becomes the checklist of the works in the show, color-coded according to their selection by each juror. The rest of the piece, which Blauvelt describes as "a series of appendices that visualize the competition winners in different ways," continues the listing theme.

When Daniel Eatock and Sam Solhaug of Foundation 33 designed an exhibition about information and architecture at Artists' Space in New York in the Summer of 2002, they created a system in which all the text needed for the exhibition was printed in a continuous list on A1 posters. The same poster was used as a caption for each piece in the show, with the irrelevant information in each case crossed out. And, as a corollary to Bits, his ever-expanding typeface made up of fragments of detritus such as door hinges or bent paperclips, Paul Elliman has compiled a list of materials intended to suggest what he calls "a fluid overlap between language and the built environment." The list, that runs to the hundreds, includes such poetically named metals as "black annealed wire, hot-dipped bright-spangled galv, sheared-edge zintec, friction-welded bright bar," as well as seemingly comprehensive inventories of plastics and processed timbers.

This contemporary fascination with the formal characteristics of lists and indexes echoes, to some extent, the sentiment that surrounded them at their first invention. Walter Ong, in *Orality and Literacy: The Technologizing of the Word* (1982), notes that "Indexes seem to have been valued at times for their beauty and mystery rather than for their utility. In 1286 a Genoese compiler could marvel at the alphabetical catalog he had devised as due not to his own prowess but 'the grace of God working in me.'" While Bailey, Blauvelt, Eatock, and Elliman may not make such divinely inspired claims for their work, their attention to this often-neglected apparatus of order, and their relish in doing so, is undeniable.

And it's not just print designers who are bringing the mechanisms of organization to the fore. Some Web sites, too, reveal their listing backbones, x-ray fashion. *McSweeney's Internet Tendency* uses a centered list that resembles a visual poem like George Herbert's "Easter Wings." Lee Epstein, the site's editor, says of his choice of organizational device, "There is a cleanliness to the list structure, aesthetically, which goes hand-in-hand with the layout of the content of the website." And, another of Elliman's lists, the so-called grrrr.list, provides a live and constantly changing cross section through the various dimensions of anger on the Web. It takes the form of a threaded discussion, one of the mainstays of Web culture, with a message board that collects any postings on the web that use the term "grrrr" (or "grrr" or "grrrrr") as a prefix.

THE UNCHECKED POTENTIAL OF THE ANTI-LIST

With the binary mentality of the A-list—where you can be "on" or "off," "in" or "out," but nothing much in between—and the bullet-point thinking engendered by PowerPoint, a new strain of anti-list arrives like a breath of fresh air. "We need cultural guides that regularly and inevitably explode the notion of their own completeness, consistency, adequacy," challenges critic Mark Sinker. The lists of mundane found data assembled each week on the *McSweeney's* Web site come some way toward answering Sinker's desire to debunk the omnipresent list fever. "It is extremely difficult to know when a list does or does not work," says *McSweeney's* Epstein. "The lists are the hardest pieces to edit, and even harder to explain." Lists such as "T-Shirt Slogans Worn Recently by Contestants on The Price Is Right;" "Names of Squash That Also Make Good Terms of Endearment;" and "Actual Comments Written in the Customer Comments Book in Somerfield's, a Supermarket in Galashiels, in the Scottish Borders" are obsessive to the point of absurdity. But they are also valid and inevitable reactions to our over-reliance on the list construct. Another piece of contemporary satire that deflates its own list format is The Top Ten, a regular feature of David Letterman's

"The Late Show," broadcast weekly on CBS; lists such as "Top Ten Surprises In The 12,000-Page Iraqi Declaration" take the list to its logical and sometimes comic extreme.

Jorge Luis Borges' "certain Chinese encyclopedia" is a literary list that challenges its own boundaries, a mess of conflicting criteria for inclusion in the list that exposes and violates the principles of classification. Borges writes: "animals are divided into (a) those that belong to the emperor; (b) embalmed ones; (c) those that are trained; (d) suckling pigs; (e) mermaids; (f) fabulous ones; (g) stray dogs; (h) those that are included in this classification; (i) those that tremble as if they were mad; (j) innumerable ones; (k) those drawn with a very fine camel's hair brush; (l) et cetera; (m) those that have just broken the flower vase; (n) those that at a distance resemble flies."

Anthropologist Jack Goody's study of the list form in its early history concludes that the list relies on discontinuity rather than continuity. It depends, he says, on physical placement, on location; it has a clear-cut beginning and a precise end, that is, a boundary. Yet on the Web, the list has the potential to become infinite. And, because links allow for multicontextual positioning, the classificatory and hierarchical ordering of elements of the list is inefficient, and perhaps ultimately will become obsolete.

Such concepts don't sit well with graphic design's traditional role as organizer of information and, yet, investigation at the edges of lists, in opposition to lists, and of exploding lists, seems to hold the most promise for the designer interested in building and evolving the genre. Contemporary graphic design's engagement with the list to date is primarily archaeological; the humble list is being retrieved from obscurity, thrust center-stage, and enjoyed as an end in itself. Listing, as a device, fits well with the popular systems-based approach and affords designers distance from their subject matter. But compilers, writers, artists, and designers—or anyone seduced by the simplicity of the list's form—all risk taking a merely passive stance and ignoring the need to make critical choices. In terms of its investigation in design practice, the list still has many possibilities left unchecked.

SECTION II:
GRAPHIC DESIGN AS CULTURE

THE BEAUTY PART
Rick Poynor

In 1993, at the height of the commotion about the "cult of the ugly" in contemporary design, Katherine McCoy sent me a letter at *Eye*, where I was then editor. She explained that, although she found herself looking for something in art and design related to beauty, she would have to use other words to describe it. "Some paradigms work better than others," she concluded. "I prefer integrity and authenticity and quality and appropriateness. But these take a little more work than simple-minded beauty."

As a design educator, everything that McCoy had to say about our problem with beauty rang true. In art, it had long ago become an impossibly difficult word. Picasso's *Les Demoiselles d'Avignon*, in 1907, was a jarring, brutal, deliberately unlovely painting. Marcel Duchamp poured ironic scorn on work that was merely "retinal," and he sought to put art at the service of the mind. In the decades of Pop, Arte Povera, and conceptual art, no artist or critic of any seriousness would have had the temerity to declare beauty as a goal.

Yet, even as McCoy expressed the prevailing wisdom, the first small stirrings of a reevaluation were under way—in Las Vegas, of all places. Art critic Dave Hickey's *The Invisible Dragon: Four Essays on Beauty* threw down the gauntlet with an immensely winning disregard for conventional pieties that made people take notice. "If images don't *do* anything in this culture," he ventured, "if they haven't *done* anything, then why are we sitting here in the twilight of the twentieth century talking about them? . . . this is why I direct your attention to the language of visual affect—to the rhetoric of how things look—to the iconography of desire—in a word, to *beauty!*"

Beauty may have been banished from polite conversation in the academy, but for most people, it hardly needs saying, it never went away. Popular culture is obsessed with it, in the shape of teenage pop singers, supermodels, and movie stars. Glossy magazines and ads relentlessly proclaim an ideal of physical beauty without caring so much as a discarded thong for art's critical discourse. People respond to faces, flowers, gardens, animals, the sky, and the landscape much as they always did. We hunger for

Originally published in *PRINT* (September/October 2000).

these things; we feel their goodness; we are in some way lifted and recharged by them. And then there is design—evidence, for the editors at *Time*, that we are more preoccupied than ever by the appearance of the things we consume. "Function is out. Form is in," trilled a recent cover story. "From radios to cars to toothbrushes, America is bowled over by style."

Little by little, the idea of beauty as an issue for reappraisal is gaining ground. *Uncontrollable Beauty*, a 1998 anthology, gathered essays by Arthur Danto, Thomas McEvilley, and Donald Kuspit, as well as by Hickey. Esthetic rapture is not regressive, argues art critic Peter Schjeldahl. "The self you lose to beauty is not gone. It returns refreshed. It does not make you less intelligent. It gives you something to be intelligent about." Last year, Susan Yelavich of the National Design Museum reported that at a late 1990s "think tank" organized by none other than Kathy and Mike McCoy, beauty was back on the agenda as a hot topic. In London last July, I might add, my daily paper ran a series of weekly articles reassessing beauty's place in contemporary culture.

In graphic design, though, beauty has yet to receive anything like the same kind of attention. If designers don't have much to tell us about beauty, this perhaps stems more from a pervasive sense that the word is unfashionable than from a considered philosophical rejection. From time to time, design competitions are criticized as "beauty pageants"—as if to say they are vain, frivolous, lacking in depth—but leading designers still submit their work and then turn up to collect their prizes, and no one is very surprised that they do.

The reality is that graphic design is a profession wholly in thrall to its own visions of formal beauty. Beauty is the single quality designers most value and crave. In many ways, the debate about ugly design was a red herring. What was actually happening, at that point, was that new forms of expression and a new kind of beauty were emerging, and some people didn't get it. Then, after a while, they did, and this work ceased to be controversial. It was disappointing that there was little attempt, at the time, to talk about what was and wasn't successful—and why. But, looking back, this may have been because, even to its admirers, the work was so new that they hadn't entirely come to grips with it. To enter into a discussion of quality would look like a concession to those who saw no merit in the new.

Most people enter design because they love visual form, respond to it more acutely, perhaps, than to anything else, and want to manipulate it. Anyone motivated solely, or even primarily, by the satisfactions of the eye would have been misguided, in the last three decades, to have chosen art as a career. As Elaine Scarry points out in *On Beauty and Being Just* (a book-length essay of great beauty, by the way), the belief has been that to look is to reify, to do the object of the gaze harm, even in the act of admiring it. Pleasure-filled perception is morally bad. "Aversive" perception—looking at things that offer no pleasure—is morally good. The sensual, celebratory art of, say, Matisse is a no-brainer. Art should be awkward, difficult, aggressive, demanding.

Scarry explains brilliantly why this thinking is mistaken, but for designers it was never necessary to worry too much about it. Frankly, your career was unlikely to depend on it. Naturally, some highly educated designers did deplore thoughtless visuality. They were quick to point out, for instance, how our understanding of real objects' place in history was harmed by colleagues who plundered this imagery for visual effect. They were right, of course, and the determination to think more seriously about design was positive. But somewhere in the struggle to win the argument that design was about a great deal more than form, the profession ceased to make a compelling case for design as a formal activity. It is not that the commitment to form went away—it just went unspoken, like beauty itself. We are surrounded by it, but can't bring ourselves to say what it is.

In design, we have overlooked the degree to which beauty is a vital human need. It is an experience from which people have everything to gain and nothing to lose. For the last year, I have been working on a book about Vaughan Oliver, the British designer. The music graphics he created in the 1980s, with Nigel Grierson, are dark, mysterious, strange—beautiful. I felt this at the time. I still feel it now. Other viewers seem to have felt the same way. There is nothing simple-minded about beauty. It's a shock to the body as much as the head, a radical decentering, as Elaine Scarry puts it, which helps us to find our place in the world. It's enormously hard to discuss, but we have to try. It makes no sense to talk about design and leave beauty out.

THE IMAGE CULTURE
Christine Rosen

When Hurricane Katrina struck the Gulf Coast of Mississippi, Alabama, and Louisiana in late August, images of the immense devastation were immediately available to anyone with a television set or an Internet connection. Although images of both natural and man-made disasters have long been displayed in newspapers and on television, the number and variety of images in the aftermath of Katrina reveals the sophistication, speed, and power of images in contemporary American culture. Satellite photographs from space offered us miniature before and after images of downtown New Orleans and the damaged coast of Biloxi; video footage

---

Originally published in the *New Atlantis*, no. 10 (Fall 2005).

from an array of news outlets tracked rescue operations and recorded the thoughts of survivors; wire photos captured the grief of victims; amateur pictures, taken with camera-enabled cell phones or digital cameras and posted to personal blogs, tracked the disaster's toll on countless individuals. The world was offered, in a negligible space of time, both God's-eye and man's-eye views of a devastated region. Within days, as pictures of the squalor at the Louisiana Superdome and photographs of dead bodies abandoned in downtown streets emerged, we confronted our inability to cope with the immediate chaos, destruction, and desperation the storm had caused. These images brutally drove home the realization of just how unprepared the United States was to cope with such a disaster.

But how did this saturation of images influence our understanding of what happened in New Orleans and elsewhere? How did the speed with which the images were disseminated alter the humanitarian and political response to the disaster? And how, in time, will these images influence our cultural memory of the devastation caused by Hurricane Katrina?

Such questions could be asked of any contemporary disaster—and often have been, especially in the wake of the September 2001 terrorist attacks in New York and Washington, D.C., which forever etched in public memory the image of the burning Twin Towers. But the average person sees tens of thousands of images in the course of a day. One sees images on television, in newspapers and magazines, on Web sites, and on the sides of buses. Images grace soda cans and T-shirts and billboards. "In our world we sleep and eat the image and pray to it and wear it too," novelist Don DeLillo observed. Internet search engines can instantly procure images for practically any word you type. On *flickr.com*, a photo-sharing Web site, you can type in a word such as "love" and find amateur digital photos of couples in steamy embrace or parents hugging their children. Type in "terror" and among the results is a photograph of the World Trade Center towers burning. "Remember when this was a shocking image?" asks the person who posted the picture.

The question is not merely rhetorical. It points to something important about images in our culture: They have, by their sheer number and ease of replication, become less magical and less shocking—a situation unknown until fairly recently in human history. Until the development of mass reproduction, images carried more power and evoked more fear. The second of the Ten Commandments listed in Exodus 20 warns against idolizing, or even making, graven images: "Thou shalt not make unto thee any graven image, or any likeness of any thing that is in heaven above, or that is in the earth beneath, or that is in the water under the earth." During the English Reformation, Henry VIII's advisor Thomas Cromwell led the effort to destroy religious images and icons in the country's churches and monasteries, and was successful enough that few survive to this day. The 2001 decision by the Taliban government in Afghanistan to destroy images throughout the country—including the two towering stone Buddhas carved into the cliffs of Bamiyan—is only the most recent example of this impulse. Political leaders have long feared images and taken extreme measures to control and manipulate them. The anonymous minions of manipulators who sanitized photographs at the behest of Stalin (a man who seemingly never met an enemy he didn't murder and then airbrush from history) are perhaps the best-known example. Control of images has long been a preoccupation of the powerful.

It is understandable why so many have been so jealous of the image's influence. Sight is our most powerful sense, much more dominant in translating experience than taste, touch, or hearing. And images appeal to emotion—often viscerally so. They claim our attention without uttering a word. They can persuade, repel, or charm us. They can be absorbed instantly and easily by anyone who can see. They seem to speak for themselves.

Today, anyone with a digital camera and a personal computer can produce and alter an image. As a result, the power of the image has been diluted in one sense, but strengthened in another. It has been diluted by the ubiquity of images and the many populist technologies (like inexpensive cameras and picture-editing software) that give almost everyone the power to create, distort, and transmit images. But it has been strengthened by the gradual capitulation of the printed word to pictures, particularly moving pictures—the ceding of text to image, which might be likened not to a defeated political candidate ceding to his opponent, but to an articulate person being rendered mute, forced to communicate via gesture and expression rather than language.

Americans love images. We love the democratizing power of technologies— such as digital cameras, video cameras, Photoshop, and PowerPoint—that give us the capability to make and manipulate images. What we are less eager to consider are the broader cultural effects of a society devoted to the image. Historians and anthropologists have explored the story of mankind's movement from an oral-based culture to a written culture, and later to a printed one. But it is only in the past several decades that we have begun to assimilate the effects of the move from a culture based on the printed word to one based largely on images. In making images rather than texts our guide, are we opening up new vistas for understanding and expression, creating a form of communication that is "better than print," as New York University communications professor Mitchell Stephens has argued? Or are we merely making a peculiar and unwelcome return to forms of communication once ascendant in preliterate societies—perhaps creating a world of hieroglyphics and ideograms (albeit technologically sophisticated ones)—and in the process becoming, as the late Daniel Boorstin argued, slavishly devoted to the enchanting and superficial image at the expense of the deeper truths that the written word alone can convey?

Two things in particular are at stake in our contemporary confrontation with an image-based culture: First, technology has considerably undermined our ability to trust what we see, yet we have not adequately grappled with the effects of this on our notions of truth. Second, if we are indeed moving from the era of the printed word to an era dominated by the image, what impact will this have on culture, broadly speaking, and its institutions? What will art, literature, and music look like in the age of the image? And will we, in the age of the image, become too easily accustomed to verisimilar rather than true things, preferring appearance to reality and, in the process, rejecting the demands of discipline and patience that true things often require of us if we are to understand their meaning and describe it with precision? The potential costs of moving from the printed word to the image are immense. We may find ourselves in a world where our ability to communicate is stunted, our understanding and acceptance of what we see questionable, and our desire to transmit culture from one generation to the next seriously compromised.

THE MIRROR WITH A MEMORY

The creator of one of the earliest technologies of the image named his invention, appropriately enough, for himself. Louis-Jacques-Mandé Daguerre, a Frenchman known for his elaborate and whimsical stage design in the Paris theater, began building on the work of Joseph Nicéphore Niepce to try to produce a fixed image. Daguerre called the image he created in 1837 the "daguerreotype" (acquiring a patent from the French government for the process in 1839). He made extravagant claims for his device. It is "not merely an instrument which serves to draw nature," he wrote in 1838, it "gives her the power to reproduce herself."

Despite its technological crudeness and often-spectral images, the daguerreotype was eerily effective at capturing glimmers of personality in its fixed portraits. The extant daguerreotypes of well-known Americans in the nineteenth century include a young and serious Abraham Lincoln, sans beard; an affable Horace Greeley in stovepipe hat; and a dour picture of the suffragist Lucy Stone. A daguerreotype of Edgar Allan Poe, taken in 1848, depicts the writer with a baleful expression and crossed arms, and was taken not long before Poe was found delirious and near death on the streets of Baltimore.

But the daguerreotype did more than capture the posture of a poised citizenry. It also changed artists' perceptions of human nature. Nathaniel Hawthorne's 1851 Gothic romance, *The House of the Seven Gables*, has an ancient moral ("the wrong-doing of one generation lives into the successive ones") but made use of a modern technology, daguerreotyping, to unspool its story about the unmasking of festering, latent evil. In the story, Holgrave, the strange lodger living in the gabled house, is a daguerreotypist (as well as a political radical) who says of his art, "While we give it credit only for depicting the merest surface, it actually brings out the secret character with a truth no painter would ever venture upon, even could he detect it." It is Holgrave's silvery daguerreotypes that eventually reveal the nefarious motives of Judge Pyncheon—and in so doing suggest that the camera could expose human character more acutely than the eye.

Oliver Wendell Holmes called the photo the "mirror with a memory," and in 1859 predicted that the "image would become more important than the object itself and would in fact make the object disposable." But praise for the photograph was not universal. "A revengeful God has given ear to the prayers of this multitude. Daguerre was his Messiah," said the French poet Charles Baudelaire in an essay written in 1859. "Our squalid society rushed, Narcissus to a man, to gaze at its trivial image on a scrap of metal." As a result, Baudelaire worried, "artistic genius" was being impoverished.

Contemporary critiques of photography have at times echoed Baudelaire's fear. In her elegant extended essay, *On Photography*, the late Susan Sontag argues that images—particularly photographs—carry the risk of undermining true things and genuine experiences, as well as the danger of upending our understanding of art. "Knowing a great deal about what is in the world (art, catastrophe, the beauties of nature) through photographic images," Sontag notes, "people are frequently disappointed, surprised, unmoved when they see the real thing." This is not a new problem, of course; it plagued the art world when the printing process allowed the mass reproduction of great works of art, and its effects can still be seen whenever one over-hears a museum-goer express disappointment that the Van Gogh he sees hanging on the wall is nowhere near as vibrant as the one on his coffee mug.

But Sontag's point is broader, and suggests that photography has forced us to consider that exposure to images does not necessarily create understanding of the things themselves. Images do not necessarily lead to meaning; the information they convey does not always lead to knowledge. This is due in part to the fact that photographic images must constantly be refreshed if one's attention is to continue to be drawn to them. "Photographs shock insofar as they show something novel," Sontag argues. "Unfortunately, the ante keeps getting raised—partly through the very proliferation of such images of horror." Images, Sontag concludes, have turned the world "into a department store or museum-without-walls," a place where people "become customers or tourists of reality."

Other contemporary critics, such as Roger Scruton, have also lamented this diversionary danger and worried about our potential dependence on images. "Photographic images, with their capacity for realization of fantasies, have a distract-ing character which requires masterly control if it is not to get out of hand," Scruton writes. "People raised on such images . . . inevitably require a need for them." Marshall McLuhan, the sixties media guru, offered perhaps the most blunt and apt metaphor for photography: he called it "the brothel-without-walls." After all, he noted, the images of celebrities whose behavior we so avidly track "can be bought and hugged and thumbed more easily than public prostitutes"—and all for a greatly reduced price.

Nevertheless, photographs still retain some of the magical allure that the earliest daguerreotypes inspired. As W. J. T. Mitchell observes in *What Do Pictures Want?*, "When students scoff at the idea of a magical relation between a picture and what it represents, ask them to take a photograph of their mother and cut out the eyes." As objects, our photographs have changed; they have become physically flim-sier as they have become more technologically sophisticated. Daguerre produced pictures on copper plates; today many of our photographs never become tangible things, but instead remain filed away on computers and cameras, part of the digital ether that envelops the modern world. At the same time, our patience for the creation of images has also eroded. Children today are used to being tracked from birth by digital cameras and video recorders, and they expect to see the results of their poses and performances instantly. "Let me see," a child says when you take her picture with a digital camera. And she does, immediately. The space between life as it is being lived and life as it is being displayed shrinks to a mere second. Yet, despite these technical developments, photographs remain powerful because they are reminders of the people and things we care about. They are surrogates carried into battle by a soldier or by a traveler on holiday. They exist to remind us of the absent, the beloved, and the dead. But in the new era of the digital image, they also have a greater potential for fostering falsehood and trickery, perpetuating fictions that seem so real we cannot tell the difference.

VANISHING COMMISSARS AND BLOODTHIRSTY PRESIDENTS

Human nature being what it is, little time passed after photography's invention before a means for altering and falsifying photographs was developed. A German photographer in the 1840s discovered a way to retouch negatives, Susan Sontag recounts, and, perversely if not unpredictably, "the news that the camera could lie made getting photographed much more popular."

One of the most successful mass manipulators of the photographic image was Stalin. As David King recounts in his riveting book, *The Commissar Vanishes: The Falsification of Photographs and Art in Stalin's Russia*, image manipulation was the extension of Stalin's paranoiac megalomania. "The physical eradication of Stalin's political opponents at the hands of the secret police was swiftly followed by their obliteration from all forms of pictorial existence," King writes. Airbrush, India ink, and scalpel were all marshaled to remove enemies such as Trotsky from photographs. "There is hardly a publication from the Stalinist period that does not bear the scars of this political vandalism," King concludes.

Even in nonauthoritarian societies, early photo falsification was commonly used to dupe the masses. An exhibit at the Metropolitan Museum of Art in New York, *The Perfect Medium: Photography and the Occult*, displays a range of photographs from the late-nineteenth- and early-twentieth-century United States and Europe that purport to show ghosts, levitating mediums, and a motley array of other emanations that were proffered as evidence of the spirit world by devotees of the spiritualism movement popular at the time. The pictures, which include images of tiny heads shrouded in smoke and hovering over the furrowed brows of mediums, and ghosts in diaphanous robes walking through gardens, are "by turns spooky, beautiful, disturbing, and hilarious," notes the *New York Times*. They create "visual records of decades of fraud, cons, flimflams and gullibility."

Stalin and the spiritualists were not the only people to manipulate images in the service of reconstructing the past—many an angry ex-lover has taken shears to photos of a once-beloved in the hope that excising the images might also excise the bad memories the images prompt. But it was the debut of a computer program called Photoshop in 1990 that allowed the masses, inexpensively and easily, to begin rewriting visual history. Photoshop and the many copycat programs that have followed in its wake allow users to manipulate digital images with great ease—resizing, changing scale, and airbrushing flaws, among other things—and they have been both denounced for facilitating the death of the old-fashioned darkroom and hailed as democratic tools for free expression. "It's the inevitable consequence of the democratization of technology," John Knoll, the inventor of Photoshop, told *Salon.com*. "You give people a tool, but you can't really control what they do with it."

For some people, of course, offering Photoshop as a tool is akin to giving a stick of dynamite to a toddler. Last year, the *Nation* published an advertisement that used Photoshop to superimpose President Bush's head over the image of a brutal and disturbing Richard Serra sculpture (which itself borrows from Goya's painting, *Saturn Devouring One of His Children*) so that Bush appeared to be enthusiastically devouring a naked human torso. In contrast to the sickening image, the accompanying text appears prim: *www.pleasevote.com*. As this and other images suggest, Photoshop has introduced a new fecklessness into our relationship with the image. We tend to lose respect for things we can manipulate. And when we can so readily manipulate images—even images of presidents or loved ones—we contribute to the decline of respect for what the image represents.

Photoshop is popular not only because it allows us visually to settle scores, but also because it appeals to our desire for the incongruous (and the ribald). "Photoshop contests" such as those found on the Web site *Fark.com* offer people the opportunity to create wacky and fantastic images that are then judged by others in cyberspace. This is an impulse that predates software and whose most enthusiastic American purveyor was, perhaps, P. T. Barnum. In the nineteenth century, Barnum barkered an infamous "mermaid woman" that was actually the moldering head of a monkey stitched onto the body of a fish. Photoshop allows us to employ pixels rather than taxidermy to achieve such fantasies, but the motivation for creating them is the same: They are a form of wish fulfillment and, at times, a vehicle for reinforcing our existing prejudices.

Of course, Photoshop meddling is not the only tactic available for producing misleading images. Magazines routinely airbrushed and retouched photographs long before picture-editing software was invented. And of course even "authentic" pictures can be staged, like the 1960s *Life* magazine pictures of Muhammad Ali that showed him training underwater; in fact, Ali couldn't even swim, and he hadn't done any underwater training for his prizefights before stepping into the pool for that photo opportunity. More recently, in July 2005, the *New York Times Magazine* raised eyebrows when it failed to disclose that the Andres Serrano photographs accompanying a cover story about prisoner interrogation were in fact staged images rather than straightforward photojournalism. (Serrano was already infamous for his controversial 1989 photograph, "Piss Christ.") The *Times* public editor chastised the magazine for violating the paper's guidelines that "images in our pages that purport to depict reality must be genuine in every way."

But while Photoshop did not invent image fraud, it has made us all potential practitioners. It enables the average computer user to become a digital prankster whose merrymaking with photographs can create more than silly images—it can spawn political and social controversy. In a well-reported article published in *Salon.com* in 2004, Farhad Manjoo explores in depth one such controversy: an image that purportedly showed an American Marine reservist in Iraq standing next to two young boys. One boy held a cardboard sign that read, "Lcpl Boudreaux killed my Dad then he knocked up my sister!" When the image found its way to the Council on American-Islamic Relations (CAIR), Manjoo reports, it seemed to prove the group's worst fears about the behavior of American soldiers in Iraq. An angry press release soon followed. But then another image surfaced on various Web sites, identical to the first except for the text written on the cardboard sign, which now read, "Lcpl Boudreaux saved my Dad then he rescued my sister!" The authenticity of both photos was never satisfactorily proven, and, as Manjoo notes, the episode serves as a reminder that in today's Photoshop world, "pictures are endlessly pliable." (Interestingly, CAIR found itself at the center of a recent Photoshop scandal, the *Weekly Standard* reported, when it was shown that the organization had Photoshopped a *hijab*, or headscarf, onto several women in a picture taken at a CAIR event and then posted the doctored image on the organization's Web site.)

Just as political campaigns in the past produced vituperative pamphlets and slogans, today Photoshop helps produce misleading images. The Bush-Cheney campaign was pilloried for using a Photoshopped image of a crowd of soldiers in the recent presidential election; the photo duplicated groups of soldiers to make the crowd appear larger than it actually was. The replicated faces of the soldiers recalled an earlier and cruder montaged crowd scene, "Stalin and the Masses," produced in 1930, which purported to show the glowering dictator, in overcoat and cap, standing before a throng of loyal communists. (Other political campaigns—and university publicity departments—have also reportedly resorted to using Photoshop on pictures to make them seem more racially diverse.) Similarly, a seventies-era image of Jane Fonda addressing an antiwar crowd with a young and raptly admiring John Kerry looking on was also created with Photoshop sorcery but circulated widely on the Internet during the last presidential election as evidence of Kerry's extreme views. The doctored image fooled several news outlets before its questionable provenance was revealed. (Another image of Kerry and Fonda, showing them both sitting in the audience in a 1970 antiwar rally, was authentic.)

Photoshop, in effect, democratizes the ability to commit fraud. As a result, a few computer programmers are creating new digital detection techniques to uncover forgeries and manipulations. The Inspector Javert of digital fraud is Dartmouth computer science professor Hany Farid, who developed a software program that analyzes the pattern of pixels in digital images. Since all digital pictures are, in essence, a collection of codes, Farid's program ferrets out "abnormal patterns of information that, while invisible to the eye, are detectable by computer" and that represent possible tampering, according to the *New York Times*. "It used to be that you had a photograph, and that was the end of it—that was truth," Farid said last July. "We're trying to bring some of that back. To put some measure of guarantee back in photography."

But the digital manipulation of images can also be employed for far more enlightened purposes than removing models' blemishes and attacking political opponents. Some artists use Photoshop merely to enhance photographs they take; others have made digital editing a central part of their art. The expansive images of the German photographer Andreas Gursky, whose photos of Montparnasse, the Tokyo Stock Exchange, and a 99-cent store make use of digital alteration, prompt us to look at familiar spaces in unfamiliar ways. The portraits taken and Photoshopped by artist Loretta Lux are "mesmerizing images of children who seem trapped between the nineteenth and twenty-first centuries, who don't exist except in the magical realm of art," according to a *New York Times* critic. Here the manipulation of the image does not intrude. It illuminates. In these pictures, the manipulation of the image at least serves an authentic artistic vision, a vision that relies on genuine aesthetic and critical standards. Ironically, it is these very standards that a culture devoted to the image risks compromising.

THE MTV EFFECT

The still images of daguerreotyping and photography laid the groundwork for the moving image in film and video; as photography did before them, these technologies prompted wonder and sweeping claims about the merits of this new way of seeing. In 1915, after a screening of filmmaker D. W. Griffith's *The Birth of a Nation*, Woodrow Wilson declared that it was "like writing history with lightning" (a judgment Griffith promptly began using in his promotional efforts for the film). Moving images are as powerful as photos, if not more so. Like photographs, they appeal to emotion and can be read in competing ways. Yet moving images change so rapidly and so often that they arrest our attention and task the brain's ability to absorb what we are seeing. They are becoming a ubiquitous presence in public and private life—so much so that Camille Paglia, an astute critic of images, has called our world "a media starscape of explosive but evanescent images."

The moving image, like the photograph, can also be marshaled to prove or disprove competing claims. During the legal and political debate surrounding the case of Terri Schiavo, for example, videotape of her movements and apparent responsiveness to loved ones became central in this family-dispute-turned-national-drama. Those who argued for keeping Schiavo alive used the footage as evidence that she did indeed have feelings and thoughts that rendered attempts to remove her feeding tube barbaric and immoral. Those who believed that she should be left to die (including her husband) thought the tape "grossly deceptive," because it represented a misleading portrait of Schiavo's real condition. Most of the time, her husband and others argued, Terri did not demonstrate awareness; she was "immobile, expressionless." In the Schiavo case, the moving image was both alibi and accuser.

Most Americans consume moving images through the media of television and movies (and, to a lesser degree, through the Internet and video games). In recent years, in what many observers have called "the MTV effect," those moving images have become more nimble and less demanding of our attention. Jumping quickly from image to image in hastily edited segments (in some cases as quickly as one image every one-thirtieth of a second), television and, to a lesser extent, movies offer us a constant stream of visual candy. Former Vice President Al Gore's new for-profit public access television channel, Current TV, is the latest expression of this trend. The network's Web site lists its upcoming programming in tiny time increments: "In 1 min," "In 3 min," "In 10 min," and so on. Reviewing the channel's first few broadcasts, *New York Times* television critic Alessandra Stanley noted the many techniques "designed to hold short attention spans," including a "progress bar" at the bottom of the screen that counts down how much time is left for each of the segments—some of which last as little as fifteen seconds.

According to enthusiasts of television, the speed and sophistication of moving images allows new and improved forms of oral storytelling that can and should replace staler vehicles like the novel. Video game and television apologist Steven Johnson, author of *Everything Bad Is Good for You*, dreams of a world of "DVD cases lining living room shelves like so many triple-decker novels." If television is our new form of narrative, then our storytelling skills have declined, as anyone who has watched the new raft of sitcoms and dramas that premiere (and then quickly disappear) each fall on the major networks can attest. (Shows like *The Sopranos* are perhaps the rare exception.) In fact, television doesn't really "tell stories." It constructs fantasy worlds through a combination of images and words, relying more on our visual and aural senses and leaving less to the imagination than oral storytelling does. Writing some years ago in the journal *Media & Values*, J. Francis Davis noted that although television is in one sense a form of storytelling, the most important messages that emanate from the screen "are those not verbalized—the stories and myths hidden in its constant flow of images."

It is precisely those hidden stories in the moving image that excite critics like NYU professor Mitchell Stephens. In *The Rise of the Image, The Fall of the Word*, Stephens argues that the moving image offers a potential cure for the "crisis of the spirit" that afflicts our society, and he is enthusiastic about the fact that "the image is replacing the word as the predominant means of mental transport." Stephens envisions a future of learning through synecdoche, using vivid and condensed images: "A half second of the Capitol may be enough to indicate the federal government, a quick shot of a white-haired woman may represent age. The part, in other words, will be substituted for the whole so that in a given period of time it will be possible to consider a larger number of wholes." He quotes approvingly the prediction of movie director Ridley Scott, who declares: "Film is twentieth-century theater, and it will become twenty-first-century writing."

Perhaps it will. But Stephens, like other boosters of the image, fails to acknowledge what we will lose as well as gain if this revolution succeeds. He says, for example, "our descendants undoubtedly will still learn to read and write, but they undoubtedly will read and write less often and, therefore, less well." Language, too, will be "less precise, less subtle," and books "will maintain a small, elite audience." This, then, is the future that prompts celebration: a world where, after a century's effort to make literacy as broadly accessible as possible—to make it a tool for the masses—the ability to read and write is once again returned to the elite. Reading and writing either become what they were before widespread education—a mark of privilege—or else antiquarian preoccupations or mere hobbies, like coin collecting.

Stephens also assumes that the people who will be absorbing these images will have a store of knowledge at their disposal with which to interpret them. A quick shot of a white-haired woman might effectively be absorbed as symbolizing "age" to one person, as Stephens says, but it could also reasonably prompt ideas such as "hair dye," "feebleness," or "Social Security" to another. As Camille Paglia observes of her own students, "young people today are flooded with disconnected images but lack a sympathetic instrument to analyze them as well as a historical frame of reference in which to situate them." They lack, in other words, a shared language or lexicon that would allow them to interpret images and then communicate an understanding of what they are seeing.

Such a deficit will pose a unique challenge for cultural transmission from one generation to the next. How, in Stephens's future world of the moving image, will history, literature, and art be passed down to the next generation? He might envision classrooms where children watch The History Channel rather than pore over dull textbooks. But no matter how much one might enjoy the BBC's televised version of *Pride and Prejudice*, it is no substitute for actually reading Austen's prose, nor is watching a documentary about the American Constitutional Convention as effective at distilling the political ideals of the early American republic as reading *The Federalist Papers*. Moving images are a rich aid to learning and understanding, but their victory as the best means of forming rigorous habits of mind is by no means assured.

In addition, Stephens accepts uncritically the claim that the "old days" of written and printed culture are gone (or nearly so) and assumes that video is the language that has emerged, like some species evolving through a process of natural selection, to take its place in the culture. He does not entertain the possibility that the reason the moving image is replacing the written word is not because it is, in fact, a superior form for the communication of ideas, but because the moving image—more so than the written word—crudely but intoxicatingly satisfies our desire for stimulation and immediate gratification.

Like any good techno-enthusiast, Stephens takes the choices that we have made *en masse* as a culture (such as watching television rather than reading), accepts them without challenge, and then declares them inevitable. This is a form of reasoning that techno-enthusiasts often employ when they attempt to engage the concerns of skeptics. Although rhetorically useful in the short term, this strategy avoids the real questions: Did things have to happen this way rather than that way? Does every cultural trend make a culture genuinely better? By neglecting to ask these questions, the enthusiast becomes nearly Panglossian in his hymns to his new world.

There is, of course, a long and thorough literature critical of television and the moving image, most notably the works of Neil Postman, Jerry Mander, and Marie

Winn. And as with photography, from its earliest days there have been those who worried that television might undermine our appreciation for true things. "Television hangs on the questionable theory that whatever happens anywhere should be sensed everywhere," E. B. White wrote in the *New Yorker* in 1948. "If everyone is going to be able to see everything, in the long run all sights may lose whatever rarity value they once possessed, and it may well turn out that people, being able to see and hear practically everything, will be specially interested in almost nothing." Others are even blunter. As Roger Scruton writes, "Observing the products of the video culture you come to see why the Greeks insisted that actors wear masks, and that all violence take place behind the scenes." It is possible, in other words, to see too much, and in the seeing lose our grasp on what is real. Television is the perfect vehicle for this experience, since it bombards us with shocking, stimulating, and pleasant images, all the while keeping us at a safe remove from what we are seeing.

But the power the moving image now exercises over modern American life has grown considerably in recent years. It is as if the Jumbotron television screen that looms over Times Square in New York has replicated and installed itself permanently in public space. Large screens broadcasting any number of images and advertisements can be found in most sports arenas, restaurants, and shopping malls; they even appear in a growing number of larger churches. The dentist's and doctor's office are no longer safe havens from a barrage of images and sounds. A walk through an airport terminal is now a gauntlet of moving images, as televisions bolted into ceilings or walls blare vacuous segments from CNN's dedicated "airport programming"; once on board a plane, we're treated to nonstop displays of movies and TV options like "NBC In Flight." The ubiquity of television sets in public space is often explained as an attempt to entertain and distract, but in fact it seems more successful at annoyance or anesthetization. For people who wish to travel, eat, or pray in silence, there are few options beyond the deliciously subversive "TV-B-Gone" device, a universal remote control the size of a key chain that allows users to turn off televisions in public places. Considering the number of televisions currently in use, however, it would take an army of TV-B-Gone users to restore peace and quiet in public space.

One of the more startling developments in recent years is the moving image's interjection into the classical concert hall. In 2004, the New York Philharmonic experimented with a fifteen-by-twenty-foot screen that projected enormous images of the musicians and conductor to the audience during performances of Wagner and Brahms. The orchestra trustee who encouraged the project was blunt about his motivation: "We want to increase attendance at concerts, change the demographics," he told the *New York Times*. "And the younger generation is more responsive to visual stimuli." A classical music industry consultant echoed the sentiment. "We have to recognize that this is a visual generation," he said. "They are used to seeing things more than they are used to hearing things." Symphonies in Vancouver, San Diego, Omaha, Atlanta, and Philadelphia have all tried using moving images during concerts, and some orchestras are resorting to gimmicks such as projecting works of art during performances of Mussorgsky's *Pictures at an Exhibition*, or broadcasting images of space during Holst's *The Planets*.

Among those less than pleased with the triumph of the moving image in the concert hall are the musicians themselves, who are haplessly being transformed into video stars. "I found it very distracting," a violinist with the New York Philharmonic said. "People might as well stay home with their big-screen TVs," said another resignedly. "It's going the route of MTV, and I'm not sure it's the way to go." What these musicians are expressing is a concern for the eclipse of their music, which often requires discipline and concentration to appreciate, by imagery. The images, flashing across a large screen above their heads, demand far less of their audience's active attention than the complicated notes and chords, rhythms and patterns, coming from their instruments. The capitulation of the concert hall to the moving image suggests that in an image-based culture, art will only be valuable insofar as it can be marketed as entertainment. The moving image redefines all other forms of expression in its image, often leaving us impoverished in the process.

BRAIN CANDY

Concern about the long-term effects of being saturated by moving images is not merely the expression of quasi-Luddite angst or cultural conservatism. It has a basis in what the neurosciences are teaching us about the brain and how it processes images. Images can have a profound physiological impact on those who view them. Dr. Steven Most, a post-doctoral fellow at Yale University, recently found that graphic images can "blind" us by briefly impairing the brain, often for as long as one-fifth of a second. As his fellow researcher explained to *Discovery News*: "Brain mechanisms that help us to attend to things become tied up by the provocative image, unable to orient to other stimuli."

Another study by researchers at the Center for Cognitive Science at Ohio State University found that, for young children, sound was actually more riveting than images—overwhelmingly so, in some cases. The research findings, which were published in *Child Development*, showed that "children seem to be able to process only one type of stimuli at a time" and that "for infants, sounds are preferred almost exclusively," a preference that continues up until at least age four. In their book *Imagination and Play in the Electronic Age*, Dorothy and Jerome Singer argue that "the electronic media of television, film and video games now may contribute to the child's development of an autonomous ongoing consciousness but with particular constraints. Looking and listening alone without other sensory inducements," they write, "can be misleading guides to action."

Research into the function of the primary visual cortex region of the brain suggests that it is not alarmist to assume that constant visual stimulation of the sort broadcast on television might have profound effects on the brains of children, whose neurological function continues to develop throughout childhood and adolescence. One study conducted at the University of Rochester and published in the journal *Nature* in 2004 involved, weirdly enough, tracking the visual processing patterns of ferrets that were forced to watch the movie *The Matrix*. The researchers found some surprising things: The adult ferrets "had neural patterns in their visual cortex that correlated very well with images they viewed," according to a summary of the research, "but that correlation didn't exist at all in very young ferrets, suggesting the very basis of comprehending vision may be a very different task for young brains versus old brains." The younger ferrets were "taking in and processing visual stimuli" just like the adult ferrets, but they were "not processing the stimuli in a way that reflects reality."

These kinds of findings have led to warnings about the long-term negative impact of moving images on young minds. A study published in 2004 in the journal *Pediatrics*, for example, found a clear link between early television viewing and later problems such as attention deficit/hyperactivity disorder, and recent research has suggested troubling, near-term effects on behavior for young players of violent video games. In short: Moving images—ubiquitous in homes and public spaces—pose challenges to healthy development when they become the primary object of children's attention. Inculcating the young into the image culture may be bad for their brains.

THE CLOSING OF THE POWERPOINT MIND

A culture that raises its children on the milk of the moving image should not be surprised when they prove unwilling to wean themselves from it as adults. Nowhere is the evidence of this more apparent than in the business world, which has become enamored of and obedient to a particular image technology: the computer software program PowerPoint.

PowerPoint, a program included in the popular Microsoft Office suite of software, allows users to create visual presentations using slide templates and graphics that can be projected from a computer onto a larger screen for an audience's benefit. The addition of an AutoContent Wizard, which is less a magician than an electronic duenna, helpfully ushers the user through an array of existing templates, suggesting bullet points and summaries and images. Its ease of use has made PowerPoint a reliable and ubiquitous presence at board meetings and conferences worldwide.

In recent years, however, PowerPoint's reach has extended beyond the business office. People have used PowerPoint slides at their wedding receptions to depict their courtship as a series of "priority points" and pictures. Elementary school children are using the software to craft bullet-point-riddled book reports and class presentations. As a 2001 story in the *New York Times* reported, "69 percent of teachers who use Microsoft software use PowerPoint in their classrooms."

Despite its widespread use, PowerPoint has spawned criticism almost from its inception and has been called everything from a disaster to a virus. Some claim the program aids sophistry. As a chief scientist at Sun Microsystems put it, "It gives you a persuasive sheen of authenticity that can cover a complete lack of honesty." Others have argued that it deadens discussion and allows presenters with little to say to cover up their ignorance with constantly flashing images and bullet points. Frustration with

PowerPoint has grown so widespread that in 2003, the *New Yorker* published a cartoon that illustrated a typical job interview in hell. In it, the devil asks his applicant, "I need someone well versed in the art of torture—do you know PowerPoint?"

People endlessly subjected to PowerPoint presentations complain about its oddly chilling effect on thought and discussion and the way the constantly changing slides easily distract attention from the substance of a speaker's presentation. These concerns prompted Scott McNealy, the chairman of Sun Microsystems, to forbid his employees from using PowerPoint in the late 1990s. But it was the exegesis of the PowerPoint mindset published by Yale emeritus professor Edward Tufte in 2003 that remains the most thorough challenge to this image-heavy, analytically weak technology. In a slim pamphlet titled *The Cognitive Style of PowerPoint*, Tufte argued that PowerPoint's dizzying array of templates and slides "weaken verbal and spatial reasoning, and almost always corrupt statistical analysis." Because PowerPoint is "presenter-oriented" rather than content or audience-oriented, Tufte wrote, it fosters a "cognitive style" characterized by "foreshortening of evidence and thought, low spatial reasoning . . . rapid temporal sequencing of thin information . . . conspicuous decoration . . . a preoccupation with format not content, [and] an attitude of commercialism that turns everything into a sales pitch." PowerPoint, Tufte concluded, is "faux-analytical."

Tufte's criticism of PowerPoint made use of a tragic but effective example: the space shuttle *Columbia* disaster. When NASA engineers evaluated the safety of the shuttle, which had reached orbit but faced risks upon reentry due to tiles that had been damaged by loose foam during launch, they used PowerPoint slides to illustrate their reasoning—an unfortunate decision that led to very poor technical communication. The Columbia Accident Investigation Board later cited "the endemic use of PowerPoint briefing slides instead of technical papers as an illustration of the problematic methods of technical communication at NASA." Rather than simply a tool that aids thought, PowerPoint changes the way we think, forcing us to express ourselves in terms of its own functionalities and protocols. As a result, only that which can be said using PowerPoint is worth saying at all.

PSEUDO-EVENTS AND PSEUDO-CULTURE

Although PowerPoint had not yet been created when he published his book, *The Image*, in 1961, historian Daniel Boorstin was nevertheless prescient in his warnings about the dangers of a culture that entrusted its rational decision-making to the image. By elevating image over substance and form over content, Boorstin argued that society was at risk of substituting "pseudo-events" for real life and personal image-making for real virtue. (He described in detail new efforts to create public images for the famous and not-so-famous, a process well illustrated by a Canon Camera commercial of several years ago that featured tennis star Andre Agassi insouciantly stating, "Image is everything.")

"The pseudo-events which flood our consciousness are neither true nor false in the old familiar senses," Boorstin wrote, but they have created a world "where fantasy is more real than reality, where the image has more dignity than its original." The result was a culture of "synthetic heroes, prefabricated tourist attractions, [and] homogenized interchangeable forms of art and literature." Images were wildly popular, Boorstin conceded, but they were, in fact, little different from illusions. "We risk being the first people in history to have been able to make their illusions so vivid, so persuasive, so 'realistic' that they can live in them," he wrote.

Other critics followed Boorstin. In *The Disappearance of Childhood*, Neil Postman wrote about the way the "electronic and graphic revolutions" launched an "uncoordinated but powerful assault on language and literacy, a recasting of the world of ideas into speed-of-light icons and images." Images, Postman worried, "ask us to feel, not to think." French critic Roland Barthes fretted that "the image no longer *illustrates* the words; it is now the words which, structurally, are parasitic on the image." In a more recent iteration of the same idea, technology critic Paul Virilio identified a "great threat to the word" in the "evocative power of the screen." "It is real time that threatens writing," he noted; "once the image is live, there is a conflict between deferred time and real time, and in this there is a serious threat to writing and to the author."

Real events are now compared to those of sitcom characters; real tragedies or accidents are described as being "just like a movie" (a practice Susan Sontag first noticed in the 1970s). Even the imagination is often crippled by our image-based culture. For every creative artist (like Gursky) using Photoshop, there is a plethora of posturing and shallow artists like Damien Hirst, who once proudly told an interviewer that he spent more time "watching TV than ever I did in the galleries."

Is it possible to find a balance between naïve techno-enthusiasm for the image culture and the "spirit of bulldog opacity," as McLuhan described it, which fueled undue skepticism about new technologies in the past? Perhaps devotees of the written word will eventually form a dwindling guild, pensioned off by universities and governments and think tanks, to live out their days in quiet obscurity as the purveyors of the image culture expand their reach. But concern about a culture of the image has a rich history, and neither side can yet claim victory. In the preface to his book *The Essence of Christianity*, published in 1843, Feuerbach complained that his own era "prefers the image to the thing, the copy to the original, the representation to the reality, appearance to being."

Techno-enthusiasts are fond of reminding us, as if relating a quaint tale of reason's triumph over superstition, that new technologies have always stirred controversy. The printing press unnerved the scholastic philosophers and religious scribes whose lives were paced to the tempo of the manuscript; later, the telephone was indicted by a cadre fearful of its threat to conviviality and face-to-face communication, and so on. The laborious copiers of manuscripts did indeed fear the printing press, and some traditionalists did vigorously resist the intrusions of the telephone. But at a time of great social hierarchy, much of this was driven by an elite disdain for the democratizing influence of these technologies and their potential for overturning social conventions (which indeed many of them did). Contemporary criticism of our image-saturated culture is not criticism of the means by which we create images (cameras, television, video). No one would seriously argue for the elimination of such technologies, as those who feared Gutenberg's invention did when they destroyed printing presses. The critique is an expression of concern about the *ends* of an image-based culture, and our unwillingness as yet to consider whether those ends might be what we truly want for our society.

Nor is concern about the image culture merely a fear of losing our grip on what is familiar—that known world with its long history of reliance on the printed word. Those copyists who feared the printing press were not wrong to believe that it would render them obsolete. It did. But contemporary critics who question the proliferation of images in culture and who fear that the sheer number of images will undermine the sensibility that creates readers of the written word (replacing them with clever but shallow interpreters of the image) aren't worried about being usurped by image makers. They are motivated largely by the hope of preserving what is left of their craft. They are more like the conservationist who has made the forest his home only to discover, to his surprise, that the animals with which he shares it are rapidly dwindling in number. What he wants to know, in his perplexed state, is not "How do I retreat deeper into the forest?" but "How might I preserve the few survivors before all record of them is lost?"

So it is with those who resist an image-based culture. As its boosters suggest, it is here to stay and likely to grow more powerful as time goes on, making all of us virtual flâneurs strolling down boulevards filled with digital images and moving pictures. We will, of course, be enormously entertained by these images, and many of them will tell us stories in new and exciting ways. At the same time, however, we will have lost something profound: the ability to marshal words to describe the ambiguities of life and the sources of our ideas; the possibility of conveying to others, with the subtlety, precision, and poetry of the written word, why particular events or people affect us as they do; and the capacity, through language, to distill the deeper meaning of common experience. We will become a society of a million pictures without much memory, a society that looks forward every second to an immediate replication of what it has just done, but one that does not sustain the difficult labor of transmitting culture from one generation to the next.

THINKING INSIDE THE BOX: ASPEN REVISITED
Emily King

*A*spen was the original "Magazine in a Box." Although launched nearly forty years ago, the idea behind it—that of a publication being a gathering of multimedia materials rather than a single block of print—remains as relevant as ever. Contemporary audiences can view *Aspen* at the poetry site UbuWeb. Lovingly rendered by digital archivist Andrew Stafford, the virtual *Aspen* includes images, articles, sound pieces, and film. But, of course, there is no substitute for the real thing. Back issues of *Aspen* are on sale at prohibitive prices, testimony to the magazine's ongoing currency, but there are also complete runs in several art libraries. I found a set in the Special Collections of the library at the Victoria and Albert Museum. To open an issue of *Aspen* is to be immersed in the period of its publication. Indeed, the boxes are often compared to time capsules. That said, the magazine's underlying idea of adopting the form most appropriate for its subject remains highly pertinent. I found it particularly refreshing that *Aspen*'s containers are designed to reflect the nature of their contents. Whereas *Visionaire*, the best known of today's boxed publications, comes in boxes that one way or another scream luxury (be they embossed leather, Louis Vuitton designed, ribbon fastened, or whatever), *Aspen*'s packages are relatively modest. Rather than opulence, they communicate intelligence.

Beyond the obvious function of carrying stuff, boxes have a more intriguing secondary use: that of disguising their contents. Big gift boxes with bows, mysterious boxes of delights, or the box of Pandora's undoing: all are united by their role in raising questions about the nature of their cargo. The container of *Aspen* works in a similar fashion. Where conventional magazines are described by their size and shape, the outline of *Aspen* is merely suggestive. Unlike consumer publications, in which dimensions conform to the expectations of advertisers and in which heft is in proportion to the number of pages those same advertisers are prepared to buy, *Aspen* took whatever form the guest designer might suggest. Sometimes flat like a box containing an expensive shirt and at others a near cube like the package of a pioneering piece of technology, *Aspen* withheld specific information about its insides until the moment of opening.

Initially scheduled to appear six times a year, *Aspen* was in fact published only ten times in the period from 1965 to 1971. Its timetable was consistently irregular.

Originally published in *032c* 6 (Winter 2003/2004).

Four issues were produced between its launch and spring 1967 (vol. 1, no. 1, 1965; vol. 1, no. 2, 1966; vol. 1, no. 3, December 1966; and vol. 1, no. 4, spring 1967). After that a double issue appeared later in 1967 (nos. 5 and 6), which was followed by a long break only interrupted by an unboxed mailing (no. 6A, 1968–9). Two years later, the magazine seemed to have gotten back in its stride. Issue 7 arrived early in 1969 (no. 7, spring/summer 1969), shortly followed by issues 8 and 9 (no. 8, autumn/winter 1969; no. 9, winter/spring 1969–70). Finally, after another break of over a year, the last issue of *Aspen* was published in the middle of 1971 (no. 10, summer 1971).

The magazine was conceived by design and fashion journalist and part-time Aspen resident Phyllis Johnson. Originally acting as editor and publisher, Johnson later handed responsibility for editing Aspen to a series of "guests," but she remained at the helm as publisher throughout its six-year existence. Johnson's consistent presence, and that of her New York–based publishing company the Roaring Fork Press, is belied by the profound changes that took place in the magazine over the course of its ten issues. The first two *Aspens* stay close to the original agenda set out in the editorial letter included in the first issue. Celebrating Aspen, Colorado as "one of the few places in America where you can lead a well-rounded, eclectic life of visual, physical and mental splendor," Johnson committed the magazine to "the civilized pleasures of modern living, based on the Greek idea of the 'whole man.'" Although *Aspen* was published in the city, its early staples were skiing, nature, modern classical music, and lifestyle with an eco-friendly, high-culture twist. Then came *Aspen* no. 3, and everything changed. In the hands of Andy Warhol and New York–based graphic designer David Dalton, the Fab issue included only a single snow-centered lifestyle piece, while the rest of the magazine was devoted to the more urban concerns of pop artists and musicians.

After that the magazine took a series of editorially dramatic twists and turns. Johnson's professional background was robustly consumerist, but her own editorial preferences proved anything but. Unlike the other great female editors of her day, women such as Fleur Cowles who created the landmark fashion magazine *Flair*, Johnson had little time for style. Rather than clothes and cosmetics, her interests centered on the ideas-heavy end of the contemporary art spectrum. The fourth *Aspen* was designed by Quentin Fiore, based on his work with media theorist Marshall McLuhan; double issue 5 and 6 is the product of artist Brian O'Doherty, an extraordinary survey of the conceptual minimalism of the period; and issue 6A is a bunch of cheaply printed documents recording a series of performance art events. *Aspen*'s second burst of energy produced a British issue edited by Mario Amaya, a Fluxus issue edited by Dan Graham, and a psychedelia issue from the hands of Hetty and Angus Maclise. The magazine's swan song was an art-historical issue devoted to Asian art. This last publication may have indicated a new direction for the magazine, one that never came to fruition. Johnson suggested that *Aspen* could be viewed as a "time capsule of a certain period." In fact the magazine moved its focus from place to time, and was just beginning to shift to a broader sense of history when its era came to a close.

★

Aspen, Colorado, the skiing resort from which the magazine took its name, has an exceptional history. Originally a silver-mining town, it grew rapidly in the late nine-teenth century when silver was the commonplace currency of the United States. By the early 1890s the town had a population of 12,000, six newspapers, four schools, two theaters, and an opera house. But its fortunes were changed by a single government act. When the U.S. returned to the gold standard in 1893, commercial silver mining dwin-dled and Aspen was reduced to a rural country seat with ranching as its most valuable resource. By the outbreak of the Second World War, Aspen's population had fallen to around 700 residents. In the 1930s there were a few moves to turn the town into a ski resort, but these did not amount to much. It took the outbreak of war and an influx of mountain-based, skiing soldiers to give the place the impetus it needed. One of these soldiers was Friedl Pfiefer who, in partnership with Chicago industrialist Walter Paepcke, returned to develop the town in the late 1940s.

While Pfiefer's aspirations were centered on sport, Paepcke had an ideal of a different kind. He and his wife Elizabeth were keen participants in Chicago's cultural life: he was a trustee of the University of Chicago and both of them were members of its renowned "Great Books Course." Walter Paepcke always strove to introduce culture to his commercial activities. Among other things, he had commis-sioned a series of modernist artists and designers, many of them European exiles, to create a series of advertisements for his company the Container Corporation of America (CCA). In Aspen, the Paepckes saw an opportunity to expand their commitment to the humanist cause. They wanted to establish "an Athens of the moun-tains," a place in which the important cultural and intellectual issues of the day could be discussed in a beautiful, natural setting.

The first big cultural event in Aspen was the Goethe Bicentennial celebra-tion conference held in 1949. Conducted in a tent designed by Eero Saarinen, speakers included Albert Schweitzer and Jose Ortega y Gasset. On the basis of this event the Paepckes developed the Aspen Institute for Humanistic Studies, a center intended for the introduction of American businessmen to culture, although occa-sionally the businessmen proved somewhat recalcitrant. Alongside activities at the Institute, Aspen hosted other kinds of events including regular music festivals and the annual International Design Conference Aspen (IDCA). During the 1940s and early 50s, Aspen's cultural development outstripped that of its infrastructure and people arriving at the early events had to contend with dirt roads and irregular rail services. In his introduction to a collection of papers from the IDCA, Reyner Banham gives a hilarious account of travelling between Chicago and Aspen in a plane "small enough to be upset by thermal currents caused by cigarette stubs and sunbathers."

An edited selection of papers from the fifteenth IDCA is included in the first issue of *Aspen* magazine and, although not identical, the impulse behind the confer-ence and the publication were closely related. Where the conferences of the early

1950s had been concerned with promoting the value of design to business, later ses-
sions were humanist in a more abstract sense. The papers included in the *Aspen* magazine are from the "Configurations of the New World" conference chaired by
industrial designer George Nelson. The aim of this session was to promote a general-
ized notion of a better way of life and that same sentiment is very much evident in
the first two issues of Johnson's magazine. There is another, possibly specious, link
between the culture created by the Paepckes and the founding of *Aspen* magazine. The
town was developed using funds derived from the sale of paperboard packaging and
its namesake magazine adopted the form of a box. Probably no more than a coincidence, but a neat one.

★

The first *Aspen* magazine is contained in a glossy black box with a large white Bodoni
A on its cover. The box opens at a hinge on its left-hand side and the index is printed
on its matt black lining. Inside are several booklets each containing a single article,
a flexidisk, an advertisements folder and a letter from the editor. Among the trio
of designers who worked on this issue was George Lois, an art director famed for his
witty, typographically taught work at *Esquire* magazine. Johnson described the format
as "rather dignified" and, the innovation of the box notwithstanding, the magazine is
similar to other classy mainstream magazines of its era such as Alexey Brodovitch's
Harper's Bazaar. Possibly Johnson chose to take this elegant-but-conventional design
route to seduce nervous advertisers. In her editorial letter she teases would-be
subscribers by saying "who knows what the next issue will be!"

Issue 2, designed by advertising men Frank Kirk and Tony Angotti, adopts
a different plan. The box is white rather than black and the type on the cover is under-
stated. The inside of the container is divided into four sections, each holding one or
two small black pamphlets. These differences in the form cannot, however, disguise the
similarity in subject of the first two issues. Both have a skiing piece, the first dealing
with off-piste skiing and the second with racing. Both have a music piece with an
accompanying flexidisk, the one about jazz and the other about the radical Russian
composer Alexander Scriabin. Both have an environmental piece, the former about the
Ptarmigan and the latter concerning the destruction of nature through road building.
And both have a lifestyle piece, encompassing a house, a family, and recipes: issue
1 offers Pot au Feu Aspen and issue 2 suggests Boeuf Braise with Spätzle. It is easy to
be dismissive about the agenda of these first two *Aspens*. It is all so bourgeois. But it is
important to look at them through the eyes of the time. Their implied rejection of US
popular culture has become commonplace, but in the mid-1960s these notions still
retained some radical content. To an extent the ideas behind the early *Aspens* have
become victims of their own success; over the last three decades alternative lifestyles
have, paradoxically enough, entered the mainstream.

While issues 1 and 2 steered clear of ordinary American life, issue 3 swept it
up in an exaggerated embrace. Dressed as a packet of a soap powder called Fab, Warhol
and Dalton's magazine eschewed the understatement and elegance of the two previous

issues in favor of a tumble of vernacular graphic styles. They included a series of writings on the effects of LSD in the guise of a book of bus tickets, a "Ten Trip Ticket Book," a flip-book record of a pair of art movies, one by Warhol and the other by Jack Smith, and the only ever issue of *The Plastic Exploding Inevitable*, effectively a one-off Factory newspaper. Warhol and Dalton made good use of the box format as a means of gathering together different kinds of material and, among all the issues of *Aspen*, the Fab issue offers the most variety in look and feel.

In some ways the material included in Warhol/Dalton Aspen runs against the high-cultured humanism that inspired the founding of the Aspen resort and the launch of the magazine. The rhetoric of the Warhol crew often displays an aggression and a desire to shock that did not have a place in the society that was being promoted by the Paepckes. All the same, the defining quality of Aspen life was tolerance, and that includes the recognition of oppositional theories. Looking forward to the demise of *Aspen* five years on, it may have been magazine's willingness to accept ideas of all sorts that led to its eventual exhaustion.

After issue 3 broke the mould, each new *Aspen* adopted a design and editorial policy all of its own. No. 4, the Fiore-designed McLuhan issue, came in a box illustrated with a diagram of an electrical circuit and introduced by a text that begins on the box's cover and ends on its lining. Taken from Fiore and McLuhan's book *The Media Is the Massage*, this paragraph emphasizes the all-pervasiveness of the media. According to the message inside the box "any understanding of social and cultural change is impossible without knowledge of the way media work as environments." Among the nine items included in issue 4 is an indigo press proof of the McLuhan/Fiore book. This piece creates the impression of ideas in progress and flatters the readers' desire to be in on something from the beginning. The advertisements for no. 4 are held in a magenta folder inscribed with McLuhan's theory of effective advertising. The more insidious the better, apparently, but none of the promotions inside appear likely candidates for subliminal success.

Although issues of *Aspen* are very different from one another, there is a degree of continuity between writers and designers. For example Bob Chamberlain contributed pieces to several publications (writing about dancing in no. 3 and motorcycles in no. 4) and David Dalton went from designing the breakaway issue no. 3 to codesigning the double issue, nos. 5 and 6, with Lynn Letterman. The presence of Dalton notwithstanding, the look of *Aspen* 5 and 6 is completely unlike that of the third *Aspen*. So much so that it represents another leap in the life of the magazine. Guest edited by artist Brian O'Doherty (who later wrote the seminal "white cube" essays), it is presented in a square white box constructed from heavy, textured cardboard. This container stands upright and the top rests on the bottom, the one half identical to the other, with no means of closure. It is an object to be displayed rather than toted around. The contents of the box are described schematically: 1 box, 1 book, 4 films, 5 records, 8 boards, 10 printed data. This deadpan index fits with the minimalism of the art inside, including pieces by Sol Lewitt, Dan Graham, and John Cage, and a build-your-own sculpture by Tony Smith.

As well as the innovatory notion of interactivity, *Aspen* 5 and 6 was the first publication to include a reel of Super-8 film. Lasting around fifteen minutes, this movie juxtaposed clips by avant-garde stalwarts Laszlo Moholy-Nagy and Hans Richter with material by younger artists Robert Rauschenberg, Robert Morris, and Stan VanDerBeek. The main texts for 5 and 6 are republished articles by the celebrated authors Roland Barthes, George Kubler, and Susan Sontag. The variety of the contents of O'Doherty's *Aspen* is belied by the uniformity of their presentation. Set in a low-key sans serif, the essays are brought together in a single square leaflet, and all other printed items adopt roughly the same format. The magazine's seductive understatement has contributed to its becoming the most collectible of all ten issues.

The subscription slip enclosed in 5 and 6 asks the question "Is this the *Aspen* Box to end all boxes?" It was the last of the initial six-issue release and it has all the qualities of a grand finale—no. 6A being something of an afterthought. The three-year gap between substantial issues of Aspen raises questions about the efforts that went into producing the second set of the magazine. Certainly the last four issues were published on slightly different terms than those that went before. In particular, there were no advertisements in the magazine after those included in 5 and 6.

Aspen 7, the British Box, was edited by critic and curator Mario Amaya (the man who was shot alongside Andy Warhol). This issue shuns the seriousness of 5 and 6 and professes an "informal theme of fun and games." The box is fronted by a pop-abstract motif designed by Richard Smith and among the items inside are a paper pattern for a pair of "British Knickers" by Ossie Clark and a diary of the future by John Lennon. Written in November 1968, Lennon's diary includes memorable days such as Thursday, 30 January 1969: "got up, went to work, came home, watched telly, went to bed." Although Amaya claims frivolity, his opening essay "The 'London' Decade" is a convincing analysis of London's 1960s ascendancy.

Aspen 8 returns to many of the ideas introduced in 5 and 6. Edited by previous contributor Dan Graham and designed by Fluxus artist George Maciunas, its theme is information and it opens with the statement: "Art information and science information share the same world and languages." The magazine includes a poster-sized image of a parking lot by Ed Ruscha, a description of a sculptural project by Richard Serra, a scheme that involves dropping molten lead from an airplane, and an account of various "Ecologic Projects," artworks that encompass planting and harvesting. But for all they have in common, Graham's Aspen is significantly more various in tone and texture than that of O'Doherty. It creates space for mess and happenstance. By arriving in a light-weight cardboard folder covered in text, it advertises a concern with communication above display.

The penultimate *Aspen* also came in something closer to a folder than a box. The creation of Hetty Maclise, the cover of issue 9 is a composition of bright, abstract swirls. The contents of the magazine are a selection of images and texts largely derived from the North American take on Eastern philosophies and religions. Hetty Maclise coedited the publication with her husband Angus, the drummer and poet who quit the Velvet Underground when the band began to play for money. Angus Maclise's freewheeling musical training took him around the world, from Haiti to the Middle East and on to India and these travels supplied him with a suitcase of alternative ideas, many of which found a home in Aspen. It is possible that the last *Aspen*, no. 10, was a reaction to the Maclise issue. A considered, art-historical survey of Asian art, it provides a welcome corrective to the unfixed hippie sentiments of the previous issue.

★

Coincident with the closure of *Aspen* magazine was a crisis at the Aspen Design Conference. The 1970 event, titled "Environment by Design," had been the scene of unpleasant conflicts between those who believed in systematic, rational action and those who took a more nihilistic view. The latter position was most forcefully argued by a French delegation, whose members ridiculed the Aspen ideal, calling the resort "the Disneyland of environment and design." This contingent proposed that environmentalism was the "opium of the people," a means by which governments distracted their populations from the more urgent issues: in the case of the United States, the ongoing war in Vietnam. Of course they had a point. By the early 1970s the Paepckes' notion of benign capitalism was beginning to look less and less realistic. The antagonism of the 1970 IDCA raged unchecked, thriving in a conference structure that had been established to foster open debate. The liberal-minded humanism that was at the core of the Aspen philosophy was transformed into the mechanism for its own demise.

The events at *Aspen* magazine are not equivalent to those at the conference, but there are some parallels. The magazine was also open to ideas to an almost willful degree, and the extreme contrasts in tone between the last two issues suggest that its editorial path was becoming less certain. It is possible to read *Aspen* 10 as a rebuke to the one before. Perhaps Johnson began to doubt the validity of the hippie, drug-associated view of non-Western culture and was keen to offer an alternative. Could she have felt that the magazine's liberalism had led it to promote values that were not in keeping with its founding ideal?

Whatever the editorial debates at Roaring Fork Press, *Aspen* magazine was finally killed off by a much more prosaic concern: that of postage. On August 20, 1971 the United States Postmaster General rejected Johnson's appeal against the denial of mail privileges for the magazine. Upholding a ruling that *Aspen* was not sufficiently "periodical," the postal service withdrew the lower rates available to more conventional publications. The Postmaster took particular exception to the fact that "each issue of *Aspen* is complete unto itself and bears no relation to the prior or subsequent issues," and that "each issue of *Aspen* could be considered to be an independent work, capable of standing alone." These are, of course, the magazine's great virtues. *Aspen* functioned on the principle of family resemblance rather than that of uniformity: There is enough in common between issues for them to be understood as part of the same body of work, but each issue is very different from all the others. This idea has become very current. Publications such as the aforementioned *Visionaire*, or Jop Van Bennekom's Re-magazine, or indeed this publication, are prone to changes in format, but can still be comprehended as a series. *Aspen* magazine's downfall was the direct result of its openness and flexibility, its ability to absorb a variety of media. It is hugely ironic that, thirty years hence, these same qualities are the source of its ongoing relevance.

WHERE THE GIRLS GO
Maud Lavin

American Girl Place is not for sissies. It's a store that excels in aggressive marketing, specifically in pitching to its customers through layers upon layers of visual and verbal storytelling. The combination adds up to high-volume sales. Opened near Chicago's Magnificent Mile in November 1998, sandwiched between Ralph Lauren and CompUSA, facing the Giorgio Armani store in the Hyatt hotel across the street, the 35,000-square-foot American Girl Place easily leaves its neighbors in the retail dust. In its first year of existence, the AGP store grossed an estimated $25 million. The only outpost of its parent company, Pleasant Co. (now in turn owned by Mattel), AGP serves as an "experience destination" for moms and daughters. It sells and exhibits Pleasant Co.'s historical dolls Felicity, Josefina, Kirsten, Addy, Samantha, Kit, Molly, and the recently introduced Kaya as well as their treasure-chests of accessories; other wares for sale include contemporary dolls in twenty-one different combinations of skin, hair, and eye color, Bitty Baby and Angelina Ballerina dolls, girls' clothes, book series based on each of the historical dolls, historical mysteries, books on contemporary girls' lives (e.g., how to organize a slumber party), and more—much more. The store offers visitors a 150-seat theater and a grandly styled café as well as historical vitrines giving glimpses of what the antique-laden contexts of the historical dolls might have been had they lived and had they been life-sized, instead of eighteen inches high (their actual size). To date, over 4 million people have visited Pleasant Co.'s flagship store.

Pleasant Co. was founded by educator Pleasant Rowland in 1986. Sold to Mattel in 1998, it is still, however, run as a separate entity. Since its inception, Pleasant Co. has sold over 82 million books and 7 million dolls, mainly through its mail-order catalog (paperback versions of the books cost $5.95, the dolls a whopping $84 each). Its target audience is seven- to twelve-year-old girls, and it would be hard to find a girl in that age group in the United States who hasn't read one of Pleasant Co.'s books or played

Originally published in *PRINT* 57, no. 1 (2003).

with one of its products. According to the company's own publicity, over 95 percent of girls ages seven to twelve are familiar with American Girl dolls. I believe it.

Essentially, AGP and the Pleasant Co. products it sells are all about design and marketing. The dolls are relatively generic, but the visual and verbal stories wrapped around them—told through the books, clothes, and accessories—are the phenomenon's lifeblood. Take Molly, a pigtailed "historical" character whose life is set in the year 1944. Molly is the same fairly unremarkable doll as the rest of the historical and contemporary dolls, but she is defined by her own book series, stuff she owns—like her cool camera and scrapbook—and her World War II–era clothes. Every aspect of Molly is designed, from her look to her context. The store and its vitrines are the stage where girls can picture it all coming to life. And they can experience the AGP essence in more intimate ways: The store sells clothes modeled on the dolls' outfits, thus allowing girls to insert themselves, more or less literally, into the dolls' shoes. The store's designer, Nancye Green of Donovan & Green in New York, refers to the store as a "mecca," citing its status as a pilgrimage site for girl consumers. The last time I was there, taking notes for this article, I met a mother in her thirties who was taking her family on a summer vacation, driving cross-country. Their two main destinations were the Grand Canyon and American Girl Place. The store has also become a must-see for designers of all stripes.

Like Rem Koolhaas's $40-million Prada store in New York, the AGP store design was a posh assignment with a high-end budget. AGP, however, is aimed at a sturdier, younger, rollerblading set more inclined to Girls' Clubs and skinned knees than gold-threaded skirts and lace blouses. The AGP store boasts Italian marble floors throughout all three of its levels, patterned velvet couches in signature berry-red offset by cream-colored walls, and leisurely amounts of circulation space where, like the Prada store, products are displayed, lit, and integrated into their surroundings with design as the first priority. Unlike Prada, though, the folks at AGP have figured education and fostering family relationships into their design goals. Says Shane McCall, a designer and the store's visual manager, "We have a lot of seating to encourage parents to sit and enjoy the environment, read books, and spend time with their kids, not rush in and buy something and rush out." Pleasant Co.'s senior art director, Barbara Smith, adds, "All of the graphics at the store were designed to enhance the 'whole world' approach Pleasant Co. takes to branding and showcasing our products. The books and stories introduce entire time periods to girls, and the graphics and products in the store bring these time periods—or 'whole worlds'—to life."

For the last few years, I've been taking design students from The School of the Art Institute of Chicago there. They start out cooler-than-thou—their twenty- or twenty-five-year-old art-student tastes run more to blacks and metals than the cheerful primary colors and dress-like-your-doll esthetic of AGP. But, on the store's belowground historical floor, they end up glued to the vitrines, and then they begin to collect cards from the store's "passport" merchandising system. This clever system provides small complimentary paper slips brightly illustrated with color photographs that show AGP products; these aide-mémoire are ideal for selecting purchases, saving at home, or priming grandma on what her next gift purchase should be. On the top floor of the AGP store, where the "girl-of-today" ersatz living space is set up, the SAIC students get busy pointing out the contemporary doll's collection of goodies: the computer that works, the towel wrap for her dog to use when visiting the day spa, her karaoke machine, her hiking equipment, her picnic spread, her martial arts outfits and many-colored belts, her skis, her cast for when she breaks her leg skiing, her painting outfit, her color wheel, her dog's reindeer antlers for Christmas, her Chanukah outfit for the otherwise inclined, her Chinese New Year's dress. Even Barbie doesn't have this much stuff. Some hate the store (rampant consumerism), most love it (rampant consumerism). All agree, though, that AGP makes Niketown look like a lemonade stand.

My own affair with AGP is also of the romantic comedy variety, the kind where the protagonists start out pitted against each other and then fall in love despite their best efforts. Meanwhile, we in the audience know it was all foreordained from the start.

About a year after the store opened, I was walking around town seeing the sights with my friend Kim, who was visiting from New York. AGP was not high on our list of potential destinations—we tended toward black and metal ourselves—and we were each raising boys, not girls. But we ended up there anyway, cynically expecting froufrou and froth. And I don't know what it was—the marble floors with notches added in each square to make them seem more inviting, the ten-sided display units of finely detailed doll accessories and furniture, the welcoming couches in the library, or the fact that it really is a girl place—that transformed us from scornful to entranced. It dawned on us that whatever was going on at AGP was not at all a bad thing for girls. The dolls themselves are not anorexic Barbies—they look like they could climb a tree or two if they came to life. They come in a variety of skin colors. And Pleasant Co., as I found out later, in creating Addy—an African-American historical doll with a series of accompanying stories set in 1864—not only did a rare thing in depicting the experience of slavery and emancipation for a mass audience (respected novelist Connie Porter was hired to write the books) but also has created an African-American doll equally as popular with white girls as with black girls—a statistical fact almost unheard of in the segregated toy market.

For Kim and me, it was fun to be at a place that girls love, is full of girls, and hosts (almost) only girls and their tow-along moms. Oddly enough, there aren't many public places like that in our culture. And the ones that exist—meeting places for 4-H sewing clubs? for Girl Scouts? for girls-only activities at the Y?—don't tend to have dramatic lighting and spacious, grand bathrooms, every inch beautifully and expensively designed with girls in mind.

Or girls and women, I should say. Like all successful toy stores, AGP is built for adult women, the purchasers, as well as for kids, a design tactic Paco Underhill discusses in his book *Why We Shop*. Most AGP products are displayed at the kids' eye-level (about 31–32 inches high), for example, but some are also laddered up walls for easy adult inspection. (AGP visual manager McCall explains that the girls want to see what the accessories would look like with the dolls—the whole context or story laid out in a vitrine—whereas the parents want to inspect the packages themselves to see what exactly is in the box they're buying.) Neither Kim nor I had grown up with any sisters—she has one brother, I have three—and I think we missed out on some key girl-talk and tea-party time when we were young. We made up for a lot of it that day. We lingered at the door to the café (hardly an impromptu pit-stop: reservations are required) and marveled at the décor—large black and white stripes with red daisies repeated artfully throughout, including black-and-white striped curtains held in place by giant white buttons and light fixtures encrusted with the daisies; we watched the girls sitting at tables accompanied by their dolls, the latter seated in special chairs that clamped to the tables. Then, in a happenstance about as likely as finding a $100 bill on the sidewalk, the maître d' fit us in even though we didn't have a reservation. Settling in for a long tea, Kim and I enjoyed chicken fingers with dipping sauce and other similar delicacies that no doubt prompted designer Jennifer Ehrenberg in the March 1999 *Interiors* to describe the café as McDonald's meets The Drake Hotel. Next, we drifted down the escalators to the ground-floor library and skimmed through some American Girl books. In doing so, we noticed that unlike Nancy Drew mysteries, the female protagonists in these books get to be plucky problem-solvers who resolve their quandaries without calling a dad or a boyfriend to help. The library is situated so that it's the first area store visitors see.

The centrality of the books brings us to the heart of why AGP works. It's a layering of contexts and their accompanying stories: those written by authors commissioned by Pleasant Co., and the stories girls are encouraged to invent themselves. Asked about the role of storytelling in the success of American Girl Place, Pleasant Rowland, herself a legend in both the business and education worlds, granted a rare interview. (Founder Rowland left Pleasant Co. in 2000 to pursue philanthropy. Until then, however, her involvement in the American Girl line, as well as the design of American Girl Place, was hands-on in virtually all details. For the first five years of the company's existence, she even wrote the American Girl catalog copy.) Rowland asserts, "The heart of American Girl is story. The books are what established the brand. Without the stories, the product line wouldn't still be in existence today."

And it's graphic design, words, and product design that deliver the components of the stories to the girls. Each historical doll has a series of six books with titles like *Meet Molly: An American Girl* and *Molly Saves the Day: A Summer Story.* Many of the stories, while referencing crises in the wider world, center on the individual girl's relationships with her friends and family. Each contemporary doll is sold with a Friends Forever book, which tells girls to imagine their doll as their new friend and encourages them to make up personality traits she has and a story about her, and even to design some clothes for her: "Maybe you'll discover that your new best friend . . . is just like you!"

Given my nature, equal parts earnest enthusiasm and suspicious cynicism, I wanted to find out more about how exactly AGP lures its primary target audience. Its marketing pitch was perfect—what message was it relaying exactly? First, it's a message related to gender.

Dan Acuff, in his book *What Kids Buy and Why: The Psychology of Marketing to Kids*, examines play patterns for girls ages eight to twelve. He stresses that girls in this age range are relationship-centered, unlike boys, who are object-oriented. For girls, role-play helps them act out relationships (check—AGP stories), and games that are interactive and social are a draw for them (check—shared AGP stories and products). Girls indulge in imaginative activity, writing stories and plays, and drawing (check—the contemporary dolls' Friends Forever book). On the subject of character identification, Acuff reports that females ages eight to twelve identify with, among others, talented and strong girls of their own age (check—the American Collection books) whereas the boys in the same age group don't seek to emulate their peers. AGP presents contexts and relationships—it's girl all over.

And, for girls, identification is key. Mary Ann McGrath, professor of marketing at Loyola University in Chicago, observes, "The stories from history are about strong girls facing historical crises like slavery and the Depression in a strong way. And the fantasy element is that they're dressed to kill at the same time." Anne Maddox, the general manager of the store when it opened, comments, "Girls really identify with the historic dolls, how their stories interpret into their own lives, learning lessons about loyalty, trust, and bravery. They understand how historical characters lived and apply them to their own lives." In the March 2002 *Journal of Communication*, cultural studies scholars Carolina Acosta-Azuru and Peggy J. Kreshel, writing about girls they interviewed on the subject of Pleasant Co. products, also focus on girls' identification with the dolls' related stories and those suggested by their display: "Girls mirror the catalog's depiction of the American present by stating that American girls love cookouts, slumber parties, and sports" and have "characteristics such as independence, intelligence, and the ability to solve problems."

Encouraging identification was, of course, integral to the product-line concept from the start. As Rowland describes it, "The historical stories allowed girls to imbue the dolls with personality—they came to see the dolls as the characters in the books. The 'girls of today' [doll line] and their stories show the enormous growth in opportunities. Together they give a counterbalance to the historical stories and also a sense of continuum of girls as creative problem solvers. The books provide narratives for play." Rowland sees the way that the historical books encourage girls to act out the stories as key to their educational function, a way of remembering history lessons through creative engagement.

Second, AGP's success is founded on its embodiment of a consumer paradise. It has done this so well as to elicit critical wrath in addition to repeat buyer visits. Dan Acuff observes that both boys and girls enjoy collecting. But AGP's implicit encouragement of kids to acquire complete collections of Pleasant Co. goods raises the usual complaints, and then some. Cultural critic M.G. Lord (who is, it should be noted, a biographer of Barbie), clearly miffed at American Girl's ascendance, complained in the *Washington Post*, "In contrast to Barbie, who has the joyful, uncultivated taste of a lottery winner, the American Girls teach connoisseurship . . . . Take Felicity, an American Girl doll dressed as a New England colonial child, who comes with a Windsor writing chair, a wooden tea caddy and a china tea cup . . . . [O]wners of Felicity may learn some historical trivia, but this doll and her fake antiques, it seems to me, are mostly about teaching your eight-year-old what to bid on at Sotheby's." Rowland has a different take and feels the historical objects in AGP vitrines—echoed by the miniature objects that belong to each historical doll—serve to show girls that "the past wasn't just a story but a time when real girls lived surrounded by material culture."

It's true AGP carries a burden: In being so good at selling to consumers, it has also become scarily representative of larger consumerism issues at play in our culture. Is consumerism our new form of citizenship, more fun and possibly more educational than a public school or museum, its stages more palatable and more inclusive than city hall, more lavish and democratic than an amusement park? Perhaps, but all too easily consumerism can also create exclusions. I've never seen any kids who look homeless or even threadbare at AGP. In this sense, dressing like your doll is not just dressing like the object-for-sale (already a loaded activity) but also, properly, like a consumer. (The dolls themselves are big consumers: They own a lot of stuff and even have their own miniature historical dolls.) On any given day, AGP is crammed with little girls who by all appearances are having a wonderful time, and it's free as only consumer paradises can be—coated with money and with products dangling like sugarplums; the strings are that you don't have to buy anything, but, given the unspoken pressure and "etiquette" of our consumer culture, you feel compelled to look like you could. AGP, then, is a playground for little girls that teaches them to be buyers and how to look like potential buyers. Implicitly, it preaches participation and friendship through buying.

To be ruthlessly honest, though, let's admit that our culture's participatory consumerism (of which AGP is just a small slice) is the largest and, even with its exclusions, still the most populist public arena we have. Fifty million people in the United States will receive a Pleasant Co. mail-order catalog this year. Consider that only about 100.4 million people voted in the last presidential election. Maybe it's time to stop the hand-wringing about how consumerist our culture has become and examine instead what values it can be stretched to carry, what debates it can be pushed to foster, and which, if any, of its exclusions can be erased. This challenge becomes clearer when examined in the context of history. Pioneering publicist Edward Bernays was a nephew of psychoanalyst Sigmund Freud. Pleasant Rowland is the daughter of Edward Thiele, a former president of the Leo Burnett advertising agency. These "family" connections between marketing, psychoanalysis, and education have made pitching to the masses our forte as a culture. Maybe AGP, with its bright colors, mainstreamed feminism, and plucky values, can be seen as one of the more optimistic examples of a consumerist platform that's trying to have something to say in addition to "Buy Here" and is encouraging its junior consumers to do so as well.

GRAPHIC DESIGN IN THE COLLECTION
OF THE MUSEUM OF MODERN ART
Paola Antonelli

Let me please introduce ourselves: we are MoMA's Department of Architecture and Design. I work there as a curator together with several colleagues, under the leadership of our Chief Curator, Terence Riley [ed note: Riley resigned his post in Spring 2006], and a group of passionate members of the Acquisitions Committee. We need to reexamine our collection of graphic design and bring it up to date with the current state of communication design. The portion of the Modern's collection that falls under our jurisdiction comprises about 3,800 design objects, circa 1,000 architectural drawings and models, the mighty Mies van der Rohe archive (20,000 items ca.), the Jan Tschichold collection of ephemera, and short of 5,000 posters. Despite some odd spikes into the eighteenth century, the A&D collection defines "modern" in architecture and design from the second half of the nineteenth century until our days. We are passionate about contemporary design and architecture and destined to revise and update the idea of modern as we go, for in the words of our founding fathers, and especially of director Alfred H. Barr, Jr., the museum's mission is to celebrate the art of our time. However, while our holdings of architecture and objects are *al dente*, the same cannot be said of our collection of graphic design. Even though our posters collection is remarkable, posters do not exhaust graphic design. Especially in recent years, posters have lost their preeminence to other forms of communication design and are in many cases mere vanity projects. Somehow, while our curators have always appreciated architecture and objects in strict design terms, by linking their aesthetic expression to their functional nature, our posters collection has not been able to assert the same autonomy from the fine arts. Rather, they stand as a quieter version of the same. Prompted by our department's history, as well as by our own interests, we need to redirect our focus on graphic *design*.

It is good design form to be able to find opportunity in necessity. This necessary decision to amend the collection indeed presents a unique chance. We will take this as an occasion to discuss not only what graphic design means today and to us, but also the role of design in a museum of art, the nature of our collection, and all design curators' pragmatic need to crystallize for conservation purposes a production that is more and more relying on interactivity and dynamics. Just like we do for objects, we want to be able to analyze goals and means, to follow a design process that is not just

Originally published on *Voice: AIGA Journal of Design* (June 3, 2004).

self-expression, but rather is directed towards other human beings. We want to find beauty beyond all constraints. We want to look at Web sites, interfaces, movie titles, typefaces, TV graphics, printed matter of all kinds, logos, packaging, and magazines. We want to find the right way to acquire them—should an interface exist on its original support? Should it be interactive and should the public be able to experience it? Should it be simulated on a more current machine? Should its use be caught on video? We have a lot of work to do and many favors to call in.

Along the way, we are determined to pick and storm brains and to document the process in many ways. This written account is one, and I begin here by framing the context with a discussion of design in MoMA's collection. Museums exist to preserve selected objects that together build a consistent ensemble, and hopefully support and communicate a strong idea. In so doing, they are meant to educate and stimulate progress. Since design, both of graphics and of objects, has a tremendous impact on everybody's life and a better understanding of it will work to everybody's advantage, a design museum is a meaningful and valuable construct.

At the Modern, all forms of design are introduced in strict relationship with the other forms of visual culture. Among Barr's many innovations was the establishment of six curatorial departments—Painting and Sculpture, Drawings, Prints and Illustrated Books, Film, Photography, and Architecture and Design. Interdisciplinarity facilitates the understanding of design's composite nature. The closeness to such an established discipline as architecture within one department, in particular, highlights the similarity among the design processes and gives depth to the criteria for judging the products by allowing them to go far beyond the consideration of the pure form. It so happens that many design curators at this museum, and I count myself among them, have been and are architects. On the other hand, the magnet of the fine arts has brought us to pay particular attention to aesthetics, by incorporating function in our original brand of sublime. I understand that this declaration might need further explanation.

Philip Johnson curated the Museum's second design exhibition, which also established the collection of design objects, in 1934. *Machine Art*, a unique display of mechanical parts, tools, and objects, revealed to the world a new concept of beauty—defined in 1934 as "Platonic" because of its classical aesthetic derivation and its abstraction—based not only on form, but also on function. In seventy-five years, the department has produced several ideas and exhibitions, and the collection has evolved tremendously. And so has design. In February of 1994, we celebrated the exhibition's sixtieth anniversary with a renewed edition of the catalog, for which Philip Johnson wrote a new preface. I quote from it: "How much has changed! Chaos theory has replaced classic certainties. We prefer Heraclitan flux to Platonic ideas, the principle of uncertainty to the model of perfection, complexity to simplicity." Design's appreciation still has to pass many filters, logic and aesthetics among them, but both logic and aesthetics are definitely not what they used to be. Objects carry baggage of motivations, meanings, and intentions. In order to communicate effectively with the public, today a curator has to explain the process behind every object and the program behind every piece of architecture.

AMERICAN MUTT
David Barringer

I suspect we are bored by the nostrum that art has no social utility; it has meaning and, occasionally, consequence. While it won't mow the lawn, it will allow us to experience the world from the perspective of the teenager mowing it. Graphic design might depict any of this: the mower, the manufacturer, the grass, the fertilizer, the teenager, the digital audio player, the homeowners, the lurking landscapers, the suburb, the gas station, the city planners, the county, the state of nature, the world of apathy. In choosing perspective and defining a worldview, you must make critical judgments. If you choose one perspective, you are rejecting all others. On what basis? On whose behalf? To what end?

You have to put your choices where your cursors are. Choices define you: your priorities, loyalties, hopes. Abstention is impossible. You must make judgments. Where does curiosity hold your eye? Whose perspective do you want your audience to vicariously experience, and why? What story do you want to tell?

Notice I didn't say "what story should be told" or "what story hasn't yet been told." I said, "What story do *YOU WANT* to tell?" The "you" and the "want" are key words here, emphasizing your personality and desire, rather than (a) ethical obligation, (b) a duty to compensate for gaps in the social narrative, or (c) a commitment to the client that trumps all else (that's an excuse for a failure of imagination). We're talking about *desire* desire, not whim, fancy, impulse, or preference—we're talking guts and grit, who you love, why you fight, how you live your life, not what color shirt goes with sullen denial. If you lack passion for your work, if all you have to run in are someone else's floppy clown shoes, then it will show in your sorry performance. Better to stumble on your own than finish an indentured third.

Better to fail in your work than to work for your failure.

PERILOUS FIGHT

Graphic designers are vulnerable to the temptation to overidentify with their clients. Overidentify.

> *WARNING: Overidentification may cause myopia, stiffness, stupidity, intolerance, arrogance, and debilitating codependency.*

Adapted from *Emigre*, no. 68 (2005).

Consider Jesus. Mediating between God and Man stands Jesus, speaking in parables that must be interpreted, telling stories that signify deeper meanings the way chop in the water implies rocks, wind, and current. Graphic designers (and lots of other folks, too) shoulder a dilemma of identification: how to balance the role of emissary with the role of savior, the fact of servitude with the dream of redemption. We designers can always excuse ourselves by appealing to the temporary nature of our assignments, the urgency of paying today's bills, the necessity of commercial relationships, and the possibility of mutual benefit. But what parables can you come up with, and will they have more meat on their bones than the morsel of one interpretation?

What is needed, to paraphrase Nietzsche, is style. Moral style. Outfit your bad self by developing your desires, values, and goals. The lifelong process of challenging convictions to forge new ones revitalizes your imagination. And to hell with a balanced life and a moral compass pointing north to Convention. Work so hard you make yourself sick. Nietzsche did. And Jesus never ate soy burgers, ran on a treadmill, or stayed out of the sun. A balanced life may suffice as a subject for a lifestyle magazine, but if the magazine is laid out well, you can bet the designer is an imbalanced hellcat.

> WARNING: *Overidentification may cause embarrassing gestures in crowded rooms, existential panic at home, and loss of vision.*

To guard against the perils of overidentification, designers must develop a strong sense of self, alarmed with a healthy skepticism triggered by the motives of anyone seeking to buy your brain and grope your person.

THE MARKET FOR TRUTH

Any revaluation of graphic design depends on a review and critique of the market, the water in which the fish of graphic designers swim. When used sloppily as a catch-all category (I indict myself among the guilty), "The Market" is subject to demonization one minute and lionization the next. The market is amoral and tends to reward the concentration of power, resulting in reduced competition and therefore market atrophy, and it is for its innate tendency to self-destruct that it's regulated. A regulated market breeds diversity, by which all of us are able to engage in this argument and expect the opportunity to put our theories into practice. The market deserves criticism for many things, but it can also provide the opportunities for correcting its weaknesses.

We generally employ the term "consumerism" with the precision of a jack-knifing semi, sweeping all traffic conditions ahead of us with this blunt wedge of an implied criticism. Disillusionment with consumerism as a value system is generally the cause of this wrecking hostility, and it is a hostility that begins as self-disgust and is redirected outward toward the external correlative (Big Business) that perpetuates itself by exploiting the self-deluded consumer. As messengers of countervailing value systems, critics, artists, citizens, etc. need to employ their talents in forums somewhat removed from the influences of consumerism. The work of critical thought and artistic achievement is at its best antithetical (and anti-instrumental) to consumerism but in congruence with grander evaluations of human condition and aspiration.

Designers, like many, can do both. They can perform their functions as insiders, as client representatives, and they can marshal their private energies as outsiders, as friends of unwelcome truth and rude art. They can have their jobs—and their work, too.

As independent workers—that is, as those working for one's self or for clients with few to no strings attached—designers may consciously avoid entanglements with consumerism but may still work (risking failure on their own terms) within the broader context of The Market.

HYBRID DESIGNERS

Dr. Frankenstein made a monster way before there was genetic engineering, cloning, or the celebration of free-market incentives. We got it easy. Just come up with some new role, one that combines graphic design with other disciplines (law, writing, anthropology, medicine, engineering), and maybe we'll grow accustomed to these new roles and regard them not as hybrids but as things in themselves. Maybe it won't be so weird to have writer/designers write and design books for clients, anthropologist/designers create and design their own multicultural-training programs for corporations, or statistician/designers crunch the numbers and design their own graphs.

EFFICIENCY OUTSIDE THE DESIGN

Efficiency as an aesthetic value embodied within the design is something you as a designer might be interested in, but efficiency as an instrumental value is what mostly interests your clients. They want your design to do something: move product, raise awareness, save lives.

The client's dream of high efficiency—optimal resource-allocation—is basically that they get the most bang of consumer response for the least buck they can toss to you. If the commercially instrumental value of a design could be measured, would clients want to rely on that as the main index of comparison? When choosing a designer with a lower Adjusted Profitability Index Score, the client, consequently, would have some explaining to do to justify ignoring that low Index Score and going with a second-stringer. It's kind of like college admissions, with a designer's instrumental-value indexes being equivalent to the high school senior's hard numbers of grades and tests. Soft stuff still counts but as a secondary consideration (cronyism and nepotism are always in play).

Designers tend not to evaluate peer work according to instrumental market criteria, possibly for fear of indicting themselves, calling attention to the designer's paradox: context takes all, and this context was made for lying. Market-based indexes measure consumption, not interpretation. Only if you ignore context, authority, intent, and audience, and just focus on aesthetics—the relationships within the given frame—

can you sidestep the paradox by ignoring it. This opens up a way to appreciate the design outside of its function, outside of its instrumental value.

Aesthetic standards will always appeal to the design profession itself, and what ensues in that world is the emergence of predictable aesthetic/instrumental factions likely to paint their clubhouse doors with, say, "Aesthetics Forever!" or "Profit Now!" or "Reasonable Synergists for Inclusion & Liberty!" Great designs are like great artworks: ambiguous, ambivalent, self-critical, subject to deep and divided interpretations. Great designs, therefore, aren't likely to make great money (at least not right away). Aesthetic appreciation endures despite the verdicts of ephemeral commerce. No great designer will lack for the inspiring anecdote of the poor genius. But a great designer lives not on dreams alone. Thus, a designer will be forced, more than ever, to respond to the client's insistence on market-defined instrumentalism (whatever sells) to the exclusion of good design (however defined).

The goal of optimal efficiency in the context of commercial design is, morally speaking, an empty one of ends, not means. The instrumental value—making something happen—trumps not only any aesthetic value but also any moral restraint. In economics, they call it the problem of "moral monstrosity." It refers to the moral vacuity of efficiency calculations, whereby what constitutes the relevant information, known or unknown, is the kind of information that would increase the precision in assessing the instrumental value of a person, an efficiency calculation of that person's contribution to society. The appreciation of a personality is not relevant.

Because we experience life as individuals, we are instinctively repelled by the valuations of our lives that must be made when making decisions on the basis of the most efficient society. We feel undervalued and disposable, and we resist it, denying our very mortality, because no amount of money is likely enough to make us sacrifice our life. But to acknowledge our mortality is not to trade it, to auction off our organs on eBay while we live. Inefficiency has its benefits. Life is itself inefficient.

The irony of this economically idealistic way of weighing the world is that in practice we defer (we in developed countries) to the market to assign value because we don't trust our subjective selves, we who are handicapped by imperfect info and limited perspective. So now it is this imperfect engine of the market we trust, but only insofar as it can be controlled. We regulate it and monitor it, managing the moral monstrosities of illegal markets for slaves, drugs, girls, and kidneys, and keeping a lid on monopolies, price fixing, and insider trading.

So how does efficiency's moral-monstrosity problem apply to design? We defer to the market to assign value to the design because we don't trust our subjective selves, either designers or clients, because we are handicapped by imperfect information and limited perspective (these two limitations reducing the efficacy and import of those instrumental-value indexes; in other words, we can't know everything because we can't see everywhere, so we can't calculate costs/benefits with objective accuracy, and so we estimate as precisely as we can). And now it is this design market that we must control somehow, managing its tendencies to lead to moral monstrosities like:

1. Fungible Designs: When the dollar is the only standard of value, everything is fungible, and fungible designs lead to strange inversions. Clients bargain not for the design itself but for its effects, and if your design falls short in causing the bargained-for effects, you only get paid the proportional amount. Leaving aside measurability issues, imagine your AIDS-awareness poster fails to raise awareness by some number; your magazine print ad fails to increase monthly sales; your *Hamlet* flyers succeed in filling only half the auditorium. Money is money, design is money, money is design, and so your design is only as valuable as the money it makes. Now take it farther: You bid for the project to raise AIDS awareness, and your poster's failure to increase awareness may have cost lives that another bidder's poster might have saved. If lives can be valued in money, then money can be valued in lives, and so your failure to save, say, six lives represents, say, $6 million for which you are responsible. This is absurd, right? Even if you could insure your designs against failures like this, it just doesn't make sense. Does it? Make it about profits instead of lives. Your failure to increase profits costs the company. Maybe you're not responsible for these profits, but maybe you are still responsible for what the company spent for your work. No effect? No pay. The only thing that differentiates you from any other bidding designer is what your design can do. All designs are fungible. And so, to the client, are you.[1]

2. GLAMORALization: In a free unregulated market in which the only value is the instrumentally economic (money), design could promote and glamorize pedophilia, rape, drinking and driving, xenophobia, necrophilia, misogyny, cannibalism, car-bombing, etc., and all with intent to sell related or unrelated products or services (from drugs and guns to slaves and child prostitutes).[2] It would be anything-goes in design, whether the product/service was illegal/immoral or, in more likely scenarios, the illegal/immoral thing was employed to glamorize some legal/moral product/service: serial killers endorsing cologne; rapists, condoms; terrorists, box-cutters; hit men, life insurance; ten-year-old girls, wine coolers. For the most part, consumer horror deters companies from pursuing these controversial tactics, but the point is that companies could target the small demographic that would respond to these kinds of design statements (packaging, posters, direct marketing). All you need to do is use the public-domain list of released child molesters, and you can market whatever you want right to them. Ditto with court records of the incarcerated. Target your demographic by criminal profile. The market is amoral. Money doesn't care how it gets made. Therefore, design doesn't care how it makes money.

3. DissemiNation: The means for disseminating designs are constantly in flux. Fifty years ago, kids may have grown up wanting to be lithographers, but they wouldn't have grown up wanting to be Web designers. Increasingly invasive means of disseminating information, entertainment, advertising, and other media await us in the future, and, in the dystopia we are imagining here, they are all fair game, distinguishable only by profitability. Environmental advertising scans your implanted I.D. chip and displays personalized messages for your eyes only, if not in your eyes only. Push technology shoots wirelessly into your brainchip, hijacking your optic nerve. Design will accept any forms, without misgiving.

4. Design Designs Itself: Designers build the software that renders the profession obsolete. The client enters the design parameters, and the smart-ware craps it out in milliseconds. It doesn't matter whether this is empirically likely; it only matters that you don't matter—in this world.

MORAL CONTENT

Earlier I worked my way toward the necessity of moral content from inside the designer out. Desire could be strongly felt, but that desire could take as its object immoral ends. The desire to work was an internal subjective force that needed moral orientation to enable passionate designers to distinguish promoting a KKK rally from promoting an Eminem concert.

> My object in living is to unite
> My avocation and my vocation
> As my two eyes make one in sight.
>   —Robert Frost, "Two Tramps in Mud Time"

There is an art to harmonizing individual desire and the good, and the opportunity to pursue that art either begins or is denied on the very practical, day-to-day level of economics. Frost recognized that one's avocation cannot survive isolated in a social world but must be linked and even modified by one's vocation, by one's work. But he also suggested that if a person was to fail to unite them, to fail to make one's joy one's work, then the person would end up half-blind.

In talking about efficiency outside the design, I worked my way toward the necessity of moral content from outside the designer in. Efficiency provides a means to evaluate the effectiveness of designs, but, being amoral, efficiency lacks the means to distinguish content. It can't detect immoral intents, goals, or effects. Efficiency provides designers with external incentives, rewarding efficient designs irrespective of whether the designs make money promoting Motrin or Rohypnol.

Because efficiency is amoral doesn't mean it's inevitably immoral. A designer may very well regard efficiency as a value within and without the design, but efficiency is not enough by itself to ensure a good design or even a successful one. While moral content is therefore necessary, I'm not concerned here with directing anyone to a particular store in the great American morality mall, only with noting the necessity of some moral check at key decision-making nodes in the web of creator » creation » dissemination.

Creator: the creator's desire is molded by appeals to The Good, and this requires intelligent self-consciousness (The Good Mind).

Creation: this is where you consider the means of creation (sources of materials and labor, inspiration and limitation) as well as the content of the creation (the kinds of icons, images, ideas, and messages your design contains).

Dissemination: your design has to get out to the public, and this is where you examine how it's getting out there and who controls how it's getting out there.

What is maddening and fascinating about all this is how thoroughly embedded one's personality can become in one's work, whether you like it or not, whether you engage it or not, whether you dig in and resist or sit back and let it ride. Whatever you do, decisions are being made, and you are being made. The more you get used to it, the more it gets used to you, whether "it" is a bad habit or a good life.

Notes

1. And what if you make more than the bargained-for amount? Do you think the client would pay it? If you can contract for it in the way of royalties or performance-based reward, then get it. Do. But more likely you'll just win a little in the way of good will to be leveraged upon the submission of the next bid.

2. We're presuming designs are used sincerely here and not as parody or satire. I can imagine these very designs executed as satire meant to indict the boundless immoralities of greedy companies. Satire only works as corrective when it presumes the reader or viewer to share a sympathetic morality.

SECTION III:
GRAPHIC DESIGN AS FASHION

THE DECRIMINALIZATION OF ORNAMENT
Alice Twemlow

—In which tendrils creep, petals unfurl, and geometric patterns abound

Ornament is the dominant visual currency of the moment. The pages we turn, the screens we summon, and the environments we visit all sprout with decorative detail, dense patterns, mandalas, fleurons, and the exploratory tendrils of lush flora. In a design climate that, for the larger part of a century, has been famously hostile to the generation, application, or even mention of decoration, what has happened to allow for this decriminalization of ornament discernible in today's design? And, beyond the palpable trendiness of these recent kaleidoscopic explosions and fantasy pattern-scapes, what is its significance?

—In which we follow the fluctuations of ornamentation's fortunes, from good to bad and back to good again, possibly

Ornament has had a turbulent past. For a considerable part of the last two centuries, ornament has been the subject of debate in design, at least as it relates to buildings and their interiors. In the mid-nineteenth century, discussion focused on the meaning of decoration, its classification, and its most appropriate uses and sources. The roles of nature, history, and sources from outside Europe were all hotly contested. The development of machine-made decorative detail further complicated the debate. As ornamentation became a more affordable and, thus, widely available feature of household goods such as textiles, wallpapers, books, cups, and saucers, so the discourse that surrounded it began to take on a more moral, social, and even political tone. It became inextricably bound up in discussions of beauty and taste.

Originally published in *Eye* 58, no. 15 (Winter 2005).

The Great Exhibition of 1851—in which the objects on display were, according to architectural historian Brent C. Brolin, "covered with clouds of putti, acres of acanthus, and cornucopiate harvests from the vegetable kingdom"—provided an opportunity for the design reformists to openly and publicly discuss ornament in relation to taste. They saw little to commend among the 100,000 objects on show, and there followed renewed attempts to tame and codify decoration. The most famous and enduring of these was the architect Owen Jones's didactic *Grammar of Ornament*, published in 1856, that laid out thirty-seven propositions relating to the appropriate uses of decoration and pattern and showcased in brilliant color (made possible by the recent introduction of chromolithography) thousands of examples of ornament from around the world. Owens believed that "All ornament should be based on geometrical construction," and he gave very detailed instructions concerning the use and placement of colors and hues. He forbade the use of "flowers or other natural objects" unless they were "conventional representations [. . .] sufficiently suggestive to convey the intended images to the mind, without destroying the unity of the object they are employed to decorate."

Such passionate commitment to the cause of using ornamentation correctly was a central concern for all mid-nineteenth-century design reformists. Henry Cole, the civil servant largely responsible for the Great Exhibition, initiated the *Journal of Design and Manufactures* as a systematic attempt to establish recognized principles of ornament. It was intended for the edification of those who designed, produced, and sold patterns and contained right and wrong examples as well as critical reviews of new patterns. Just as Jones had argued, geometric patterns were considered to be good, and naturalistic design and excessive decorations were considered to be bad, even though naturalistic flower patterns were the most commercially successful in this period. Another example of the evangelizing for correct use of ornament could be found in the Museum of Ornamental Art (now the Victoria and Albert Museum) that was established in 1853 using many of the objects from the Great Exhibition to form the basis of its collections. In it was a gallery titled "Examples of False Principles in Decoration" that showed eighty-seven objects specially selected to represent bad taste for the purpose of illuminating the public. Generally, three-dimensional naturalistic patterns on two-dimensional surfaces received the most criticism. The gallery became known as the Chamber of Horrors and was caricatured in Charles Dickens' weekly magazine *Household Words*.

John Ruskin's writings about architectural ornament, too, helped to cement a connection between appropriate decoration and virtues such as honesty and sincerity. And the moral tone of the critiques was further honed in the early twentieth century by the belief among avant-garde circles that products which disguised their modes of construction with ornament were deceitful and, therefore, fundamentally flawed. The moral resistance to ornamentation found its most vehement spokesperson in Austrian architect Adolf Loos, who in 1908 published a diatribe against decoration titled "Ornament and Crime." In this text Loos used stirring rhetoric to argue that nothing less than cultural evolution and human progress was being hampered by ornament. In his view, ornament was a waste of manpower, health, materials, and capital. "In a highly productive nation," he wrote, "ornament is no longer a natural product of its culture, and therefore represents backwardness or even a degenerative tendency."

In an essay titled "Ornament and Crime: The Decisive Contribution of Adolf Loos," the design critic Reyner Banham traces the passage of Loos's article around Europe through its various reprinting, and speculates as to which architects read it when. Loos himself was quite convinced that ornament's downfall was his own doing. In 1930 he wrote "I have emerged victorious from my thirty years of struggle. I have freed mankind from superfluous ornament." The extent of the impact of Loos's article upon the fate of ornament is still unclear, but the social and economic import of his beliefs certainly fuelled modernism's manifestos, teachings, and practice.

And so ornament began its long fall out of favor in architecture, industrial design, and graphic design, a fall that lasted for the better part of the twentieth century. With postmodernism's revivification of complexity, lent legitimacy by Robert Venturi's writings in the 1960s and 1970s, ornament was granted a reprieve among design thinkers and makers. Even so, ornament has found it hard to shake its second-tier status within the cultural spectrum. It shared this space beyond the pale with the crafts, outsider art, popular or commercial art, and other obsessive or naïve creations such as the kinds of work depicted in Margaret Lambert and Enid Marx's *English Popular and Traditional Arts*, published in 1946, which showcased examples of indigenous crafts such as hand-painted fairground signage, canal boat decoration, intricate lacework, and straw dolls. And, even today, despite its proliferation and the slow emergence of discourse surrounding it, the use of decoration is still regarded by mainstream graphic design as taboo—a testimony, perhaps, to modernism's enduring hegemony. A discussion about decoration on the design blog SpeakUp, for example, saw the terms "candy," "craving," "fluff," "indulge," "eighth deadly sin," "closet," and "guilt"—admittedly taken out of context here—flying around with telling regularity throughout the sixty-two posted comments.

For those willing to embrace decoration's possibilities and explore them through graphic design, there are few historical references or figures to turn to for validation or inspiration. "Ornament has been the subject of debate since classical times in architecture," says designer and educator Denise Gonzales Crisp, "but in graphic design it's as if it was never discussed. It's a stealth ideology." Gonzales Crisp points to the celebrated American type designers W.A. Dwiggins and Frederic W. Goudy as designers who were thinking more deeply than most about decoration, but "that's because ornament was allowed in type," she says. Goudy designed Kennerley in response to what he described as "a real need for types for decorative printing," and Dwiggins used celluloid or acetate stencils in which tiny elements were cut to create typographic ornaments for the surfaces of the books he designed.

—In which we wonder whether today's interest in ornament as it relates to design is anything more than a vagary of fashion?

At first it looks as if ornament's recent reemergence in graphic design can be explained solely by the oscillations of style—the need to find a visual currency as contrary and exotic as possible to the one that preceded it. The early 2000s saw the energies of contemporary practice channeled through what might be broadly characterized as neo-modernism. Among the genre's defining characteristics were systems that generated progeny celebrated for their "default" or "undersigned" qualities and the proliferation of manifestos—those modernist relics—dredged up for ironic reinterpretation. As with all fashionable statements, it is only a matter of time before the pendulum begins its return swing. Thus, only a few short years later we find white spaces furnished with ornamental devices, serifs, borders, and fleurons recalled from the dusty oblivion of archaic type specimens, and, replacing a largely urban and technological image-scape built from the visual language of computer software, and code, we find natural motifs and verdant foliage.

Evident in these expressions of the neobaroque is bizarre nostalgia for a rural past. Bizarre because much of this pattern- and ornament-rich work evokes a time and place that never was—neither part of the designers' personal histories nor their cultural ones. Through the depiction of pastoral scenes, idealized preindustrial landscapes populated with certain wild animals (the stag and the owl in particular), and by seeking recourse to the visual symbolism of heraldry, contemporary and largely urban designers appear to be trying to recreate a past and a rural idyll as an escape from the real urban present.

On closer inspection, however, that pendulum swing might not be such a swing after all. The current fascination with ornament and decoration can be seen not as a reaction against but, rather, as an addition to the work and thinking of the turn-of-the century systems-obsessed designers. Certain tendencies unite the neo-modern and the neobaroque as if they were part of one seamless continuing project. Discernible in both, for example, are similar levels of irony and the use of a set of knowing references directed at fellow designers that help distance the makers from their work and possible engagement with its subject matter. It is as if merely the palettes had been swapped—the one with default type, blurry photographs of forgotten corners of everyday life, and compositions that, with a knowing wink, follow the templates in software programs, replaced by the one with serif and script faces, intensely detailed illustration, and dense patterns that evolve from the step-and-repeat function.

Something else is going on too, however, that may have more lasting implications for design. The other impulse running through this work is a kind of stubborn celebration of uselessness. The modernist-derived philosophy that has dominated twentieth-century design empties ornament of meaning and separates it from function, thus rendering it superfluous in the eyes of the canon. Knowing this, and still continuing to make exuberantly excessive, dense, and sometime exaggeratedly useless work, therefore, can be seen as a provocative thumbing of the nose to the approach to design advocated by many schools and professional organizations in which "problems" are "solved" by following a sequence of codified steps. As Gonzales Crisp puts it, "The super-rational approach to design seems to be all about the client—the idealized client. The decorative speaks to the people using design and not just the clients who commission it."

—In which we delve beneath the surface of things

Amid this dense forest of fashionably ornamental graphic design is work that stands out because, in addition to the irreverence and fun, it delivers complexity, meaningfulness, and a seriousness of intent. Sometimes the decorative elements in a piece of work are not merely sampled from a palette of choices but emanate directly from content and are integrated at a deep level with concept. They do as much work as the word or the image in communicating. What does it take then, to produce this kind of work? It may have to do with the extent to which designers are involved and obsessed, even, with what they do. Many designers, including Canadian designer Marian Bantjes, speak of their obsessive approach to decoration. This obsession can be physical as well as mental—a passion that has as much to do with the act of making as it does with any theoretical intent.

The relationship between craft, decoration, and ornament is a longstanding and a close one. The Arts and Crafts movement helped to reinvest handcraft with social value. William Morris was famously opposed to the mechanization of craft activity but, more recently, the design educator Malcolm McCullough has written about the idea of the computer as a craft tool. He extrapolates "digital craft" as "a blend of skill and intellect accompanied by a blend of work and play, use and beauty, tacit and codified knowledge." The intricacy necessary to make patterns or to construct ornament suggests that real attention is being paid to the craft of making and to detail. Gonzales Crisp also sees the computer as integral to work that uses decoration in a meaningful way. "Amplification, complexity and detail are key to decoration," she says, "and the computer lets you do that. You can noodle the heck out of anything now if you are inclined. It feels like this powerful tool that allows complexity that only crafts-people value. It re-introduces that connection to the making that maybe we lost with the über-designer handing off stuff for production to a typesetter, lithographer, platemaker and so on. It's like it's come full circle."

In product design this connection between the decorative, detail, and craft is already acknowledged and is being probed. In this field there is an emphatic and renewed interest in the humanness and the "tacit knowledge" of making to which McCullough refers. Critic Louise Schouwenberg writes in depth on the subject. "Freed from its negative connotations, craftsmanship can be valued for the psycho-logical effect it exerts on its user: it not only refers to a slower pace, but also implants this deceleration, and the implied attention to detail, into the product," she says. Detail is a contemporary concern of culture more generally, too. In her 1987 book,

Reading in Detail: Aesthetics and the Feminine, historian Naomi Schor posits that the detail, bounded on either side by the ornamental and the prosaic, is something historically gendered as feminine. She emphasizes the ambivalent place that the detail and the feminine have held in traditional Western aesthetics. "For as any historian of ideas knows, the detail until very recently has been viewed in the West with suspicion if not downright hostility," she says. She believes the "rare prominence" it is currently enjoying is thanks largely to poststructuralist thinking.

Product designer Hella Jongerius has created an upholstery fabric for Maharam that has an unusually long repetitive pattern inspired by the jacquard cards (nineteenth century) that tell the loom what to weave, and reconfigures in her ceramics and textiles archetypal patterns like pied-de-poule, stripes, and bird-and-vine, and talks of "the power of decoration, which can transcend the visual to take on a different meaning." She embeds questions in her exaggeratedly ornate Swarovksi chandelier so that decoration is put to work—in this case to ask critical questions. Jongerius was a founding member of Dutch design collective Droog, which, in 1998, held an exhibition called *Inevitable Ornament*. This idea of an inevitable connection between ornament, form, and content is something that graphic design is beginning to deal with right now. Gonzales Crisp has given this notion the label "decorational." By fusing the normally oppositional concepts of decoration and rationality, she attempts "to engage the discourse of ornament with that of rational design," and to suggest that "function is completed by ornament."

The decoration we're seeing today is very particular to the time we live in. In many ways it is dystopian. There's the inclusion of urban, dark, and ironic themes, as evident in Geoff McFetridges's attitude-laden takes on patterning in three designs titled *Red Dawn, Stoner Forest*, and *All Yesterday's Parties*. The last of these designs features camouflage patterns overlaid with a pattern of party detritus (beer cans, bottles, and cigarette butts). Similarly, Daniel van der Velden and Maureen Mooren's identity for the 2005 Holland Festival uses the argyle patterns that the typical middleclass Festival-goer tends to wear as windows onto apocalyptic images, and interweaves street trash with cathedral stained glass to create a tense critique of contemporary Dutch society. British designer Jonathan Barnbrook sums up his feelings on the topic of globalization with the word "globanalization," and expresses this idea visually through a series of works that critique the pervasive reach of multinationals. A series of Tibetan prayer mandalas, for example, are found, on closer inspection, to have been built up from thousands of tiny corporate logos. Even the voluptuous floral wall mural that extended the length of a block in the New York Prada store provides a frame for its own commentary. The installation was created in 1999 by design firm 2 x 4 in collaboration with Rem Koolhaas's Office for Metropolitan Architecture, and was among the first and most prominent of recent reinvestigations of pattern. It uses the silhouettes of full-bodied leaves and flowers as windows for photographic images that reference what designer Karen Hsu describes as "Italianness, consumption, fashion, manufacturing, beauty, and sex."

"The rational aspect of the decorational is its capacity to tell, not only in a story like way, but also in a metonymic way in the same way that icons do," says Gonzales Crisp. If there's a key or operative word to describe what's exciting about the best decorational work, then it's "complexity." She explains: "Much of graphic design's time gets spent on refining and organizing and making things clear. There are all kinds of ways to think about graphic design's service, however. It can also be about establishing empathy or providing escape." This sentiment is shared by Dutch designer van der Velden. "Playfulness and layers, multiple narratives, embedding history, seeking relations, and also political implications are better expressed in a visual vocabulary less dogmatic and more rich than Modernism," he says.

What will give ornament life beyond that of its current popularity, then, is the fact that it provides designers with an alternative to orthodox views of design's role as a problem solver and a simplifier. It is a strategy for thinking and making that has a rich history but that can also be continually reimagined. It can be used as a framing device to direct the viewer's attention or as a carrier for critical or narrative commentary. The most promising aspect of the role of ornament in design's immediate future, therefore, is that it can contain, along with the enchantment of good storytelling, the voice and actual opinions of its designer. Following an era of design in which the responsibility of decision-making was placed in the hands of code, software programs, and systems, and randomness and ironic detachment were valued above conviction, it is indeed refreshing to consider the potential of ornament as a tool that can be used to express personal or political beliefs. Whatever happens, let's not just step and repeat.

STYLE IS NOT A FOUR LETTER WORD
Mr. Keedy

Today, the emphasis on style over content in much of what is alleged to be
graphic design and communication is, at best, puzzling.
—Paul Rand, *Design, Form and Chaos*

The work arises as a methodological consequence—not from streaming
projects through some stylistic posture.
—Bruce Mau, *Life Style*

Looking at other magazines from all fields it seems that "serious"
content-driven publications don't care how they look, whilst "superficial"
content-free ones resort to visual pyrotechnics.
—Editors, *DotDotDot*, issue no. 1

Good design means as little design as possible.
—Dieter Rams, *Omit the Unimportant*

Style = Fart
—Stefan Sagmeister

There has been a long and continuing
feud in design between style and
content, form and function, and even
pleasure and utility, to which Charles
Eames answered, "Who would say that pleasure is not useful?"[1] Maybe we should call
a truce, since it doesn't seem like anyone is winning. Animosity towards style is pretty
much a given in the design rhetoric of the twentieth century. But where did this antag-
onistic relationship between design and style come from? And more importantly, what
has it done for us?

At the end of the stylistic excess and confusion of the Victorian era, the
architect Adolf Loos led the way to a simpler, progressive, and more profitable future.
In 1908 he proclaimed, "I have discovered the following truth and presented it to
the world: cultural evolution is synonymous with the removal of ornament from
articles in daily use."[2] In his polemical and now famous essay "Ornament and
Crime," Adolf Loos established what would be the prevalent attitude towards ornament, pattern, decoration, and style in the twentieth century. He explained, "Shall

Originally published in *Emigre*, no. 67 (2004).

every age have a style of its own and our age alone be denied one? By style they meant decoration. But I said, don't weep! See, what makes our culture grand is its inability to produce a new form of decoration. We have overcome the ornament, we have won through the lack of ornamentation." Far from being a period without style, or new ornament, the end of the nineteenth century was inundated with ornament and style. The Jugendstil, Vienna Secession, Wiener Werkstätte, Art Nouveau, and Arts and Crafts were all in various stages of development. Loos was frustrated because a consensus on style no longer seemed possible, and he believed that "those who measure everything by the past impede the cultural development of nations and of humanity itself." Sounding like an early example of "compassionate conservatism," he explains, "I suffer the ornament of the Kafir, that of the Persian, that of the Slovak farmer's wife, the ornaments of my cobbler, because they all have no other means of expressing their full potential." Loos's condescending conceit became "received wisdom" in modernist design, in which "the lack of ornament is a sign of intellectual power."

In "Ornament and Crime," we see the modernist project as fundamentalist, puritanical, elitism being promoted as progressive enlightenment. Probably very few designers have actually read it, yet they all know that ornament and style are, if not criminal, at least suspect. As Loos points out, "The modern man who tattoos himself is a criminal or a degenerate. There are prisons where eighty percent of the inmates bear tattoos. Those who are tattooed but are not imprisoned are latent criminals or degenerate aristocrats. If a tattooed person dies at liberty, it is only that he died a few years before he committed a murder." And, "The man who daubs the walls with erotic symbols to satisfy an inner urge is a criminal or a degenerate. It is obvious that his urge overcomes such a man: such symptoms of degeneration most forcefully express themselves in public conveniences." The idea that ornament, style, and pleasure are "degenerate" is reinforced today by the fact that pop culture literally wallows in them. The easiest way to differentiate yourself from the all-pervasive "nobrow"[3] monoculture we inhabit is to reject its excesses. Just say "no"—to ornament and style. But for Loos, the fact that ornament was a symptom of "degenerate" sensibilities was not its worst offence. The biggest problem he had with ornament was that it was not economical. As he explained, "Decorated plates are expensive, while white crockery, which is pleasing to the modern individual, is cheap. Whilst one person saves money, the other becomes insolvent," since "the lack of ornament results in reduced working hours and an increased wage. The Chinese carver works sixteen hours, the American laborer works eight hours."[4] For Loos the modern American way, without ornament (or style and history), was not only the most progressive; it was the most cost-effective. Not surprisingly, Loos's style of boxy masses of marble, glass, and wood became the style of corporate America.

Loos was successful at discrediting style and elevating function and economics as the primary goals in design as opposed to older ideas like "truth, beauty, and power."[5] But he did not achieve his main goal of eliminating ornament. As James Trilling points out in his book, *Ornament, A Modern Perspective*, "He did something much more original. He reinvented it, with a completely new character and direction for the twentieth century."[6] He did this by carefully choosing natural substances like marble and wood for their decorative surface effects, which were natural and therefore "authentic." Loos invented "an ornament without images, patterns, motifs, or history. Even this was not enough. Cloaking his achievement in a diatribe against ornament itself, he gave us the only ornament we could pretend was no ornament at all. We went after the decoy and swallowed it whole, a feat of self-deception that shapes our visual culture to this day."[7] We can see evidence of this in the lack of sophistication in the use of pattern and ornamentation in contemporary graphic design. Or as Trilling puts it, "Historically, the abolition of recognizable form in ornament is not just a response to similar developments in painting. It is a final stage in the progressive weakening and dissolution that afflicted ornament throughout the nineteenth century. If we do not recognize the forms of modernist ornament as weak, it is because there are so few forms left to recognize."

That Loos's ideas continue to resonate today is unquestionable. But that an elitist, deceptive, misogynistic, racist, xenophobic, money-grubbing rant would inspire such allegiance is troubling, to say the least. Once ornament was supposedly done away with, or at least "rehabilitated" into modernist dogma, one could have expected that it was only a matter of time before design itself would be recast as a crime against culture. And Hal Foster's diatribe "Design and Crime" does exactly that. Loos condemned ornament for "damaging national economy and therefore its cultural development." Conversely, Foster claims today's design is "a primary agent that folds us back into the near-total system of contemporary consumerism."[8] Foster claims that Art Nouveau designers of the past "resisted the effects of industry" but "there is no such resistance in contemporary design: it delights in postindustrial technologies, and it is happy to sacrifice the semi-autonomy of architecture and art to the manipulations of design." And that "today you don't have to be filthy rich to be projected not only as designer but as designed—whether the product in question is your home or your business, your sagging face (designer surgery), or your lagging personality (designer drugs), your historical memory (designer museums) or your DNA future (designer children). Might this 'designed subject' be the unintended offspring of the 'constructed subject' so vaunted in postmodern culture? One thing seems clear: just when you thought the consumerist loop could get no tighter in its narcissistic logic, it did: design abets a near-perfect circuit of production and consumption, without much 'running room' for anything else."

The paucity of context or specificity in Foster's critique of design is only surpassed by its stunning lack of originality. Once again, design as "scapegoat" is seen as so vacuously amoral and apolitical that capitalism, mass media, and globalization (etc.) have harnessed its mesmerizing emptiness to dupe an unsuspecting, uncritical (inno-cent?) public into duplicitous submission. And design offers no "resistance"! I wish Foster would explain how the art world manages to offer "resistance" and "semi-autonomy" when you do have to be "filthy rich" to be a serious player in it. Talk about no running room! Will designers ever outrun this type of cornball caricature? At the end of the twentieth century, designers find themselves in a world in which ornament, decoration, and style are reduced to meaningless superficial effects; form is only to be derived from function[9]; and design itself is little more than a commercial construct. What a load of crap.

Foster, like most art/culture critics of the twentieth century, seems to be unaware of the fact that culture was developed through design, and that the art culture industry that he is hermetically sealed in is a fairly recent development. Such critics are incapable of imagining that design could have what he calls "political situatedness of both autonomy and its transgression," or "a sense of the historical dialect of disciplinarity and its contestation." If only critics like Foster could allow themselves to see designers as actually possessing some autonomy and self-awareness, instead of reducing us all to commercial hacks, they might realize that design is a cultural practice worthy of their speculative interest. Unfortunately, typical of twentieth-century critics, he is still prattling on about Art, so we'll have to wait for the cultural critics of the twenty-first century for design to be of serious interest. Foster only sees design as a barrier to "resistance" (fight the power, right on!) and a threat to the "distinctions between practices" (art is special!). Design is often erroneously conflated with marketing and consumerism to serve as a whipping boy, to enforce "disciplinarity," and to keep us in our place. He is "attacking the messenger,"[10] because he doesn't like the message. Design is just the messenger. The idea that art doesn't matter is the message.

Foster acknowledges that Loos's "anti-decorative dictate is a modernist mantra if ever there was one, and it is for the puritanical propriety inscribed in such words that postmodernists have condemned modernists like Loos in turn. But maybe times have changed again; maybe we are in a moment when distinctions between practices might be reclaimed or remade—without the ideological baggage of purity and propriety attached." Now that the early modernist dream of "art into life"[11] has succeeded, Foster (like Loos before him) would like to take it back out, and into the protective custody of the art world. Maybe instead of going back to the bad old days of art with a capital *A*, Foster should realize that we are entering an era of design with a capital *D*. Is it actually possible that people are looking at the museum's architecture, and browsing its gift shop instead of the galleries, because the design is not only more fun, but more meaningful to them? Or are they just stupefied by the spectacle of commodification? In "The Age of Aesthetics," isn't it design and style that will matter most? And does that mean that ideas and meaning are out? Not according to Virginia Postrel, who says in her book *The Substance of Style* that you can be "smart and pretty."[12]

Postrel is an economics columnist for the *New York Times*, and a past editor of *Reason* magazine. She has spoken at a number of design venues, including TED 2004. Far from being an "old school" economic critic like Thorstein Veblen, she puts a positive spin on "conspicuous consumption,"[13] and admits, "In a sense my book is a defense of the consumer society."[14] Thus, conservatives tend to be predisposed to listen to her, and liberals of the Adbusters type do not. Her reception by designers has been lukewarm at best. It is ironic that designers were more supportive of Naomi Klein's *No Logo*[15] book, in which the best advice she could muster for them was that they should quit. Postrel has a much better grasp of design in context, and is an advocate for design, if not designers. And as an economist and libertarian, she starts from the assumption that free markets and free choice are, as Martha Stewart would say, "good things." Postrel explains, "Globalization has brought a wide assortment of formerly exotic-seeming styles and products into the mainstream. The challenge is to learn to accept that aesthetic pleasure is an autonomous good, not the highest or the best but one of many plural, sometimes conflicting, and frequently unconnected sources of value."

Postrel breaks up the old bipolar debates between style and substance, or as designers say it, form and function, by recognizing that pleasure is an equally important part of the equation. Artists have been talking about the value of pleasure since day one, but to have an economist say that pleasure is an important value in design—well, it's a lot more than most designers have been willing to say. She takes it even further by warning us against "falling into the puritanical mind-set that denies the value of aesthetic pleasure and seeks always to link it with evil." She believes designers should be asking themselves "How can I provide pleasure and meaning?" Pleasure is not exactly a hot topic among designers. I don't think today's information architects and media directors are ready to admit to such sybaritic impulses. Problem solving, communicating, informing, identifying, or branding: yes. Pleasure? No. But as Postrel points out, "Everyone else is also solving problems and contributing to strategy. The question is what problems can you uniquely solve? Where's your value-added? If you try to sell yourselves as another sort of engineer, the engineers will just scoff at you—and rightly so."[16] It is as if she pointed out that not only does the design "emperor have no clothes," but he is pleasuring himself as well.

Instead of pleasure, perhaps Postrel should have used the more genteel Victorian idea of "repose"[17] as the emotional response one hopes for from design. But Postrel speaks boldly. She even dares to refute the modernist idea of authenticity, described in its various forms as purity, tradition, and the "aura" or "patina" of history. She explains that they are defined "based on rules that have little to do with the desires or purposes of those who create, use, or inhabit the subjects of the critique" and that "'authenticity' becomes little more than a rhetorical club to enforce the critic's taste." Speaking as the voice of the people, she goes on to say, "We can decide for ourselves what is authentic for our purposes, what matches surface with substance, form with identity. We can define authenticity from the inside out. This approach to authenticity challenges the ideal of impersonal authority, replacing it with personal, local knowledge." She believes "what's truly authentic is change and cultural evolution." I applaud her ability to deflate the "gas bags" of authenticity and the puritanical scolds of pleasure and consumerism. But she goes on to say, "Aesthetics have become too important to be left to the aesthetes." I question the faith that she puts in the "we," as in "we the people," with bad taste and no sense of style, to make the best choices. She is careful not to completely discount expertise, as she explains:

"There's a difference between expertise and gatekeeping. Expertise tells you how to achieve what you find aesthetically pleasing. Gatekeeping tells you what you should find aesthetically pleasing. It's the gatekeepers who are upset—people who want to dictate the one true style, whether they're arbiters of fashions in clothing or in architecture."

No doubt that is true, but the idea that it is the expert's job to tell you how to achieve what you have already decided is aesthetically pleasing is even worse. Yes, I could ask Julia Child to help me make a chili cheese dog, or Luciano Pavarotti to sing "Happy Birthday," but that would just be stupid. And it is the expert's job to tell us when we are being stupid. We don't have to agree, or take his or her advice, but we should know what those who have more experience, knowledge, and talent think. Experts should be posted at the "gates" of culture, because the idea that someone has the ability to lock them is absurd. Unfortunately for us, today's "gatekeepers" are not like Ruskin and Morris, or any of the self-proclaimed tastemakers of the past, whose advice was sought, if not always heeded. Today's arbiters of style seem to be people with individually cultivated tastes and opinions, but they are in fact corporate brands like Martha Stuart (Omnimedia), Michael Graves, and Tommy Hilfiger, whose "opinions" are really just products. And today's design academics, critics, and journalists wouldn't presume to be "expert" in anything as potentially contestable, embarrassing, and unimportant as taste. The only real experts and connoisseurs you are likely to run into today are on "make-over" TV shows and eBay. Taste used to be something you developed and learned with the guidance of experts over time; now it's just something you buy. After all, "nobody ever went broke underestimating the taste of the American public."[18]

The idea of taste is problematic and widely contested today. Many people have come to resent high standards of taste as the ability to transform our wardrobes, living rooms, and bodies increasingly becomes an obligation to do so. Where does it all end? How do we keep from being completely consumed by the demands for more style and better taste? Postrel doesn't think that will happen. She believes "most of us won't make that cost/benefit calculation," and in the end people's good sense will prevail. She says, "My own aesthetic preference is to let people do whatever they want." "We live in a momentary—often delightful—chaos that shall inevitably morph into better practices through trial and error. Eventually, aesthetic harmony shall prevail." But why would it? She should know that markets don't always correct themselves by themselves. Sometimes they crash. The "powers that be," the "stakeholders," the ones with the most to lose, are constantly monitoring and regulating the market to keep it going. Yet, in the "age of aesthetics," it is the "gatekeepers" that Postrel would throw out. When pressed for some criteria of judgment, she says, "Quantifying aesthetic value is very difficult. It's not like there is one thing you can measure." Yes Virginia, it is difficult, that's why you ask an expert—you know, someone who actually knows what she is talking about.

Good taste is learned, but no one is teaching it anymore. High culture is supposed to be a reflection of us at our best, while pop culture is a reflection of us at our happiest. The pursuit of happiness and the pursuit of excellence are not the same thing. Style may be coming back in style, but taste is not. What we have now is not so much a "democratization of taste" as a disavowal of any standards. A democratic culture does not mean mob rule. A democratic approach to style would include excellence. But the Darwinian free-market commercial populism Postrel imagines puts too much faith in the market's ability to make the best cost/benefit choices in terms of style. Postrel says, "In the technocratic era of the one best way, correct taste was a matter of rational expertise 'this is good design' not personal pleasure 'I like this.'" However, since she is so keen to point out that style has meaning, I wonder if it has occurred to her that very often the style that says "I like this" has a meaning that says "I'm an idiot." Or is that just the price you pay for pleasure? Not necessarily, because as she points out, "The values of design itself—function, meaning, and pleasure—can exist independently of each other." No doubt this is where all the confusion comes in, and where experience is needed to establish criteria and evaluation. The fact is, as the popularity of TV "design" shows and all those shelter/lifestyle magazines and books prove, people want to be educated about style. But designers are not even debating issues of style and taste among themselves, much less instructing the hoi polloi. They seem to be operating on the assumption that it doesn't matter any more; they are no longer in the business of dictating taste, because there are no rules any more.

In his book on postmodernism in graphic design, Rick Poynor explains that "*No More Rules*'s central argument is that one of the most significant developments in graphic design, during the last two decades, has been designers' overt challenges to the conventions or rules that were once widely regarded as constituting good practice."[19] By using the cliché of "rule breaking," Poynor effectively restricts postmodernism in design to its reactionary emergence and validates the popular misconception that postmodernism ended once its initial shock was absorbed. This reflects the current feeling in design that since there are no more rules, we have arrived at a post-postmodern, post-taste, poststyle, and postdesign free-for-all. In a somewhat nostalgic-sounding tone of resignation, Poynor says, "If fundamental systemic change feels unlikely, then this tends to suggest that the postmodern condition will be our reality for the foreseeable future, imposing operational constraints or 'rules' of its own, whether we like it or not." But the ideas that designers started exploring in the eighties and nineties, like deconstruction, appropriation, technology, authorship, and opposition, which Poynor skillfully outlines in his book, seem more like an attempt to establish new rules, practices, and disciplinarity in place of the "received wisdom" of modernism. Not just rule breaking, or a discarding of rules, but an exploration, expansion, and redefinition of the boundaries of design as a dynamic self-organizing system of possibilities, instead of a top-down hierarchy of rules. It was a project that was "stampeded" by the dot-com "gold rush" and "branding round-up" that seem to have changed the design profession's priorities.

Poynor concludes *No More Rules* by asking, "Given some of the problems of postmodern visual communication discussed in the book, what forms in terms of style might an oppositional graphic design assume at this point?" Setting aside the question of why style has to be "oppositional," my answer is a style that continues to develop and deploy the critical, pluralistic, decentered, postmodern strategies outlined in his book. A style that celebrates the aesthetic pleasure of the unique, idiosyncratic individual through ornamentation, pattern, and decoration, as well as celebrating community and social responsibility through historical continuity. A style that resists easy codification and assimilation with strategic and formal complexity. Okay? But talk is cheap. Designers want to be shown, not told. And that is exactly the problem. Until designers get past their "monkey see, monkey do" approach to designing, they will just be going around in the same old circles, doing the same old "new" work. That is why designers need to think about some different (if not new) ideas about style that come from "outside" the usual discourse. Like Virginia Postrel, who says, "We can enjoy the age of look and feel, using surface to add pleasure and meaning to the substance of our lives." And James Trilling, who says that designers should use "the transformative power of ornament" to "affirm a pervasive, age-old dissatisfaction with structural necessity as the sole determinant of artistic form. The primary function of ornament—and it is a function, make no mistake—is to remedy this dissatisfaction by introducing free choice and variation into even those parts of a work that appear most strictly shaped by structural or functional needs." It's time to "decriminalize" ornament because "communication need not be symbolic, any more than function need be mechanical. Before one even selects a pattern or motif, the decision to use ornament conveys a wealth of meaning, no less real or powerful for being inchoate."[20] The problem is, most designers' ideas about style and ornament have not advanced much since the beginning of the last century.

Unfortunately, the single-minded pursuit of structural meaning and authenticity, decorated only with irony in the aesthetics of the twentieth century, has left style, ornamentation, and beauty in the hands of amateurs. That is where we find an orgy of stylistic expression and exploitation (such as it is). Go to your local shopping mall and you will find Thomas Kinkade, the "painter of light" whose mass-produced contemplations of the sublime represent beauty. And tattoo parlors where "degenerate aristocrats" indulge their "criminal" tastes—one of the few places you are likely to find any interest in ornamentation any more. Or look for a Restoration Hardware or a Design Within Reach, places for "those who measure everything by the past" and who "have no other means of expressing their full potential" except to decorate their homes in a "made for TV" historical style. This is all the proof we need that there is no more "running room" left in the shopping mall of contemporary culture, and we have no one to blame but ourselves. We are our own experts; we know what we like, and we like it like this.

Modernism made the issue of style much easier for designers to deal with, since it gave them a style that they could pretend was not a style. But technology, multiculturalism, globalism, postmodernism, and the "democratization of taste" are demanding a more sophisticated response. Digital technology has made it clear that graphic design is not just about the technical production of objects and information. Now almost anyone with the right software can produce a newsletter, book, Web site, font, or animation. I would argue that a lot of what designers consider specialized knowledge is increasingly becoming part of basic literacy (and software). For example, I just had one of my typography essays reprinted in a very interesting anthology called *Visual Rhetoric in a Digital World: A Critical Sourcebook.*[21] This book is not intended for designers but for writing or composition students who have "begun to engage the visual more seriously as part of the pedagogy." And why wouldn't they? In the information age won't everyone have at least a basic literacy in design? But will everyone have good taste, talent, skill, and a sense of style?

Instead of marginalizing their relationship to style, designers should be capitalizing on their role in developing it. Although they are unlikely to admit it, designers are implicit stylists and tastemakers. If they don't articulate this role explicitly, they won't have much to offer in the age of aesthetics. Culture is expressed and understood through style, which is mostly created and evaluated by designers. In terms of aesthetics, art pretty much had the run of the twentieth century. Now in the twenty-first century, it's design's turn. We don't need a new style or a clearly defined "period style." Nor do we have to proclaim there are "no more rules" or that we should all go off on our own little "autonomous" way. There is no shortage of marginalized artistic geniuses in the world. But if there are going to be design experts in the twenty-first century, what will they be experts in? Graphic designers claim that their expertise is in problem solving, communicating, organizing information, and branding. So to whom should people go for style and taste? Isn't style too important to be left in the hands of amateurs?

Notes

1. Charles Eames, 1972 "Q&A," in *Eames Design,* edited by Charles Miers (Abrams Inc., 1989).
2. Adolf Loos, in *Adolf Loos, 1870–1933 Architect, Cultural Critic, Dandy,* edited by Peter Gossel, English translation by Latido, Bremen (Taschen, 2003).
3. John Seabrook, the blending of highbrow and lowbrow tastes into a new sensibility he calls, "nobrow" from *Nobrow: The Culture of Marketing, the Marketing of Culture* (Vintage Books, 2001).
4. Adolf Loos, "Ornament and Crime," in *Crime and Ornament: The Arts and Popular Culture in the Shadow of Adolf Loos,* edited by Bernie Miller and Melony Ward (Toronto: YYZ Books, 2002).
5. "Truth, Beauty, and Power" was Christopher Dresser's motto that he promoted in his book, *Principles of Decorative Design* (London: Cassell Petter & Galpin, 1873).
6. James Trilling, *Ornament: A Modern Perspective* (University of Washington Press, 2003).
7. Ibid. p.139.
8. Hal Foster, *Design and Crime (and Other Diatribes)* (Verso, 2002).
9. "Functionality was the basis of designing for ages. I was brought up with the slogan 'form follows function,' and later it changed into 'form follows concept.' Droog Design had a major influence there, of course. Until the last years of the twentieth century, there was considerable strictness about what you could and especially what you couldn't do in 'good design.'" *Hella Jongerius* (Phaidon Press, 2003).
10. Addison Whithecomb: "When you resort to attacking the messenger and not the message, you have lost the debate."
11. Vladimir Tatlin is credited with coining the slogan "Art into Life." In 1927 he wrote, "As the founder of the idea 'art into life,' I worked in the woodworking industry on the development of new models for furniture,

and also worked in sewing trusts on the development of a clothing norm." It was a rallying cry for the Russian constructivists to get their art out of the museums and into the world.

12. Virginia Postrel, *The Substance of Style: How the Rise of Aesthetic Value Is Remaking Commerce, Culture and Consciousness* (HarperCollins, 2003).

13. The phrase "conspicuous consumption" was coined by Thorstein Veblen in *The Theory of the Leisure Class: An Economic Study of Institutions* (The Macmillan Company, 1899).

14. Virginia Postrel, from "The Joy of Style," an interview in *Atlantic Unbound*, August 27, 2003.

15. Naomi Klein, *No Logo: Money, Marketing, and the Growing Anti-Corporate Movement* (Canada: Alfred A. Knopf, 1999).

16. Virginia Postrel, from "Pricing Beauty: Reflections on Aesthetics and Value, An Interview," *GAIN*, American Institute of Graphic Arts, March 6, 2003.

17. Christopher Dresser thought that "the attainment of repose is the highest aim of art," from "On the Means by which Repose is Attainable in Decoration," Chapter VI, in *Studies In Design*, by Chr. Dresser, Ph.D.F.L.S. (Gibbs Smith, 1875).

18. H. L. Mencken.

19. Rick Poynor, *No More Rules: Graphic Design and Postmodernism* (Yale, 2003).

20. James Trilling, *Ornament: A Modern Perspective*, p. 75.

21. Carolyn Handa, *Visual Rhetoric in a Digital World: A Critical Sourcebook* (Bedford: St. Martin's, 2004).

NOT YOUR GRANDPARENT'S CLENCHED FIST
Phil Patton

"Let freedom ring—and let it be rung by a stripper," bellows a billboard advertising Howard Stern's new radio show on SIRIUS satellite radio, which started Monday, beneath the silhouetted stencil-like fist that is Howard's new logo. The fist is familiar: it recalls the ones on T-shirts and building walls from the 1960s protest days. But the fist of popular protest, the imagery of the Atelier Populaire in Paris and the grad students at Harvard in 1969, now serves the cause of making the airwaves safe for adolescent jokes about female breasts and human flatulence. It is a long fall from the ideals and ideology of which the fist was previously made the symbol.

As so often, graphic symbols mark a wider change. Yes, we see the little *H* made of the two fingers in the fist, as glib a graphic as the assertion that what Stern is about is powerful political expression. Freedom of speech is Howard Stern's cry. He argues that the new satellite radio offers him freedom from the restrictions of the Federal Communications Commission. That and some, well, serious cash.

The first time as tragedy, the second as farce—Karl Marx long since gave way to Groucho in our expectations of the fate of revolutionary images and routines.

Originally published on *Voice: AIGA Journal of Design*, January 10, 2006.

But along with every other bit of sixties imagery, the graphics of protest seem to be recast with special silliness these days.

The fist of protest has its roots in the deep traditions of revolutionary imagery of 1848 and French Romantic painting. It became a staple of banners and logos of unions and political parties. Raised out of the crowd, the fist clenched in strength, anger, and determination could serve groups of almost any ideological stripe.

Two archives in the United States assemble political graphics: the Center for the Study of Political Graphics in Los Angeles and the All of Us or None (AOUON) Archive of Political Posters in, yes, Berkeley. (The name comes from Brecht.) The Archive's curator Michael Rossman, a writer, scholar, and social historian, and his colleague Lincoln Cushing have surveyed the use of the fist symbol in the archive and report that both the raised fist and the detached fist entered our modern poster vocabulary in posters done by Frank Cieciorka—who also worked as a volunteer for SNCC in the South—in October 1967 for the first genuinely-militant protests against the Vietnam War ("Stop the Draft Week" in Oakland, California).

The fist symbol of the Students for a Democratic Society and the Black Power movement was a simplified and flattened version of the heroic fists of poster art from earlier decades.

The wishful conflation of the student protest with worker protests from Paris in 1968 merged fist and smokestack. (Paris posters were almost immediately torn from the walls and collected in 1968.)

The fist of the Harvard Strike of 1969 was stenciled on walls and T-shirts. Harvard Magazine tracked down the creator of the protest fist image from 1969. He was Harvey Hacker, today an architect and designer.

Today the Socialist Worker's Party still uses a fist, although the Mitterand Socialists in France, which like most Western socialist parties renounced nationalization of industry, turned the fist into a graphic holding a rose. But Slobodan Milosvic liked a red fist of socialist power, which was parodied and challenged by Otpor, a student resistance group, in the 1990s. The Otpor ("Resistance") group used a black fist as their symbol.

In Detroit, the downtown fist sculpture was defaced with spray paint a few months ago, reminding the citizenry of its continuing ambiguities. Robert Graham's sculpture was inspired by the fist of hometown champion boxer Joe Louis. It was paid for by *Sports Illustrated* magazine and unveiled in 1987. The fist and arm suspended from a frame were criticized for not referring explicitly enough to Louis and at the same time for evoking the imagery of Black Power. It was unveiled at a time in the mayoralty of Coleman Young, the city's first African-American mayor, when antipathy between city and suburbs, and black and white, was especially sharp.

The Graham fist is ambiguously horizontal, not vertical. Now the protestors raise fists, but they are a potential battering ram. This evokes the whole history of boxers as symbols of black empowerment and expression. Not as outspoken as either, Louis nonetheless ranks high as a symbol and stands between Jack Johnson and Muhammad Ali. In this regard, he reminds us of the raised fist of the Black Power movement, and specifically the iconic images of the fists of John Carlos and Tommy Smith raised in protest on the medal stand at the 1968 Olympics in Mexico City.

The twenty-four-foot bronze arm was not universally loved. Some citizens wanted a glove on the fist. Some objected to it as a symbol of Black Power. "Making a statue of a fighter would have been a limited image of Joe Louis," Graham said at the time. "People bring their own experiences to the sculpture. I wanted to leave the image open, allowing it to become a symbol rather than make it specific."

That pose is evoked too in the biggest new fist around, and one that has received surprisingly little notice. Looming above crowds and traffic in Times Square, the huge billboard of Sean John with raised fist and inclined head explicitly evokes Carlos and Smith in 1968.

The pair wore black gloves as well as black socks and no shoes. Since the gloves they wore were a pair, each had to wear one on the opposite hand. Smith said he had raised his right fist to represent Black Power in America, while Carlos raised his left fist to represent black unity.

Another commentary on the fate of Black Power was evident in Ron Norsworthy's design for a huge, fist-shaped Reparation Tower included in the show *Harlemworld* at the Studio Museum of Harlem in 2004. The imagined design commented on the gentrification of Harlem by imagining a luxury apartment tower in the shape of a Black Power fist financed by payments made for slavery reparations.

But what is the message of the Sean Jean rendition? Is it—a generous interpretation—an acknowledgement from Puffy that he would not be where he is without Carlos and Smith and their movement? Or is it an assertion that he is continuing their efforts by different means? And how many customers will catch the reference? But let's not romanticize the near past: Tony Judt—whose wonderful new book *Postwar*, a history of Europe since 1945, offers many refreshing new perspectives—points out how stylized the protests of the sixties were and how far from the blood-and-guts demonstrations and revolutions on which they consciously modeled their imagery.

"For all the clenched fists and revolutionary rhetoric," Judt writes, "the student movement of the sixties was mostly about style." He also observes that today the best-selling books about the era are not memoirs or ideological analyses but collections of graffiti and slogans.

THE SHOCK OF THE OLD:
RETHINKING NOSTALGIA
Jessica Helfand

Nostalgia has always been a bad word for designers. Like "retro" and "vintage" it smacks of a sort of been-there-done-that ennui—looking backward instead of forward, nostalgia presents as the very antithesis of the new. Even hard-core historians resist its emotional lure, which can, in an instant, dramatize the truth and distance it from fact. Nostalgia skews by privileging episodic time over chronological time: in this context, "memory" is cast as a curious, dangerous, and rather unreliable lens.

Or is it?

In the late eighteenth and nineteenth centuries, nostalgia was seen as a disease, an ailment to be cured. (One doctor described it as "hypochondria of the heart.") Over time, it came to typify the porous romanticism of bygone eras—Victorianism, for example—conjuring visions both sentimental and ornamental. The streamlined reserve of the International Style obliterated such decorative excess, inaugurating an age of uncompromised neutrality: later, we called it modernism and applauded its appeal to functionality and its celebration of formal rigor.

But the notion of longing never really went away because, at the end of the day, it remains an essential human condition. Equally human is our need to mark time: so we keep calendars and agendas and diaries and albums, all of them gestures of physicality and permanence, tangible, graphic reminders of our own evolution, participation, and engagement with the world around us. (My current research has revealed, among other things, evidence of an astonishing range of visual imagination from civilian diarists proving, rather conclusively I think, that DIY began a long time ago.)

It is easy to classify such efforts as lacking in authority since they are, by their very nature, autobiographical: if they're the micro, then the macro—the big world vision—would seem to require more public forms of expression. As designers, we tend to orient our thinking to the broader demographics, visualizing messages that are read and recorded by multiples. But multiples are made up of singulars: in other words, in order to truly understand how to reach people visually, why wouldn't we start smaller? Why aren't our efforts more centralized, more specific to one person at a time? And in the spirit of such inquiry, why wouldn't we consider, as the grass-roots cultural anthropologists that we really are, what makes people feel and notice and care and think—and remember?

Published on *www.designobserver.com* (October 27, 2005).

The short answer is that, in principle, memory is a fairly unreliable search engine. And while it has received substantial mileage in televised courtroom dramas, where witnesses are asked, under oath, to recall events "to the best of their ability," it is generally thought to be deeply personal and highly flawed. Yet those personal flaws—the ones that our logic tells us should be overlooked—are the ones that sit right up there with nostalgia as qualities we typically resist, loosely on the assumption that our work needs to read to a wider audience rather than resonate with a smaller one.

Nostalgia is fuzzy and utopian, privileging an imagined past over a real one. And indeed, nostalgia can be kitsch—playing on the collective recollections of a generation and teasing the psyche through the occasional retro replay—but why can't it be more than this? Big branding conceits—Old Navy bringing back sixties hip-huggers, for instance—is one way to mobilize nostalgia as a catalyst for sales, but it's a collective memory and, besides, we're all sort of "in" on the irony. Can't the use of personal memory in the public realm be more transcendent, more emotionally raw than this?

A potentially controversial new report released this week claims that sleep, often maligned due to its obvious link to idleness, might be another opportunity for understanding the role of memory: more sleep may actually bring about more clarity— not less. "In different stages of sleep," writes Kate Ravilious in an issue of the *Guardian*, "our brains piece together thoughts and experiences, then file them in a structured way, giving us clearer memories and, ultimately, better judgment." File and structure might not be the first words to come to mind in this discussion, but to the degree that point-of-view remains a key ingredient in so much of what we produce visually, why would we disparage the role of memory in our work? Human memory is more than merely fallible—it's intangible, difficult to pinpoint, virtually impossible to quantify. And yet, bearing witness lies at the core of a very particular kind of history: it is a history that, more often than not, depends on the collective stronghold of a series of highly individualized stories. (Consider the tradition of oral and visual histories—The Shoah Project, for example.)

I've had a growing concern over the past few years that designers in general— and design students in particular—seem predisposed toward a kind of virulent antihistoricism. It's as if a bow to history precludes innovation, that looking back prevents you from looking forward. Such analytical disparity is perhaps deserving of its own post— but for now, I'd like to suggest that the tension between nostalgia (old) and novelty (new) is one of authenticity (personal) versus authority (public). The designer, as maverick, maker, and visual missionary, is perhaps culturally predisposed toward The Next Big Thing. But it's the last little thing—and maybe the thing before that—that really interests me, and which, for that matter, makes me rather nostalgic.

CRIMES AGAINST TYPOGRAPHY:
THE CASE OF AVANT GARDE
Steven Heller

C rimes against typography are committed everyday. But few typefaces have
been victimized more than the late-
sixties/early-seventies gothic, Avant
Garde—and the felonies persist. The reason is a surfeit of angular ligatures that offer too
many cheap tricks. I know, because I am a recovering Avant Garde abuser. Although I
haven't touched the stuff in almost thirty years, when the face was in its prime, I was
hopelessly addicted. Since I had the fonts on my Phototypositor, I got kicks out of making the most flagrantly absurd ligature combinations imaginable. Nobody, not even the
face's creator, Herb Lubalin, could stop me. In fact, having seen so many abominable
applications by addicts like myself, I once heard Lubalin curse the day that Avant Garde
was released to the public. However, the revenue stream made from font sales gives this
a disingenuous ring.

Avant Garde was not originally designed as a commercial typeface. It was the
logo for a magazine that its editor and publisher, Ralph Ginzburg, explains was
"a thoughtful, joyous magazine on art and politics," aimed at people "ahead of their
time." The goal of the magazine, however, was not merely to reflect the cultural zeitgeist but take a lead role in purveying raucous sixties culture. In other words, it was
avant-garde—thus the magazine's title, coined by Ginzburg's wife and collaborator,
Shoshana, was *Avant Garde.*★

Before launching the magazine, Ginzburg was the publisher and editor—with
Herb Lubalin the art director and designer—of the erotic hardcover magazine *EROS*,
which folded after four issues when Ginzburg was arrested and convicted on the charge
of sending prurient materials (e.g. "pandering") through the United States mail. After
the trial, Ginzburg wanted to start a new magazine but was prevented by his lawyers
who feared it might turn out to be a "hellraiser." Ginzburg was out on bail for the
EROS conviction awaiting appeal, but the process took so long—about ten years—that
the magazine ultimately went into production in mid-1967.

To help Lubalin develop the design scheme, Ginzburg sent him a lengthy
editorial outline, and recalls "He came up with two beautiful logos, but they were all
wrong for the publication I had in mind." One was based on the typeface used on the
original Coca-Cola bottles, another on Hebrew letters. "[Lubalin] kept associating the
magazine with the nihilistic avant-garde school of art of the early twentieth century,"

Originally published in *Grafik*, no. 120 (August 2004).

Ginzburg adds, "but this magazine had nothing to do with that." Instead it was for intellectuals who might also possess a sense of humor. "Herb and I had always been on the same creative frequency. The concept of Avant Garde was the lone exception. He just couldn't get it. And though he normally produced designs for me instantaneously, no matter how complex or challenging the job, two weeks elapsed and he still didn't have a clue."

Exasperated, Ginzburg had Shoshana visit Lubalin at his studio to explain the concept of the magazine to him one last time. "I asked him to picture a very modern, clean European airport (or the TWA terminal), with signs in stark black and white," Shoshana recalls, "Then I told him to imagine a jet taking off the runway into the future. I used my hand to describe an upward diagonal of the plane climbing skyward. He had me do that several times. I explained that the logos he had offered us for this project, so far, could have been on any magazine, but that Avant Garde (adventuring into unknown territory), by its very name, was something nobody had seen before. We needed something singular and entirely new." Ginzburg continues, "The next morning, driving to work from his home in Woodmere [New York] he pulled over to the side of the road and phoned me (the first time he ever did that). 'Ralph, I've got it. You'll see.' And the rest is design history."

For his historic solution, Lubalin adapted gothic caps, something between Futura and Helvetica, and angular-ized the *A* and *V* so they fit together like a wedge of pie. He halved the *T* so that one half of it was part of the *N*. The perfectly round *G* carved into the angular *A*, which overlaid the midstroke, and the second *A* in avant was an inclined extension of the *A* in garde, Both words were tightly letter-spaced to be perfectly stacked, and thus could fit as a block anywhere on the cover. According to Shoshana, "The distinctive slant of the *A*, and some other letters, was exactly the line I had made in the air when showing him that ascending jet."

Lubalin turned his rough sketch over to type designer Tom Carnase, his partner at Lubalin Smith Carnase, who rendered the final form. "Herb was a scribbler," recalls Carnase, "but his scribbles were very readable." So it would seem for anyone questioning its provenance that *Avant Garde* was entirely Lubalin's invention. But there were actually more intricate machinations on the way to its becoming a bona fide commercial font.

Lubalin decided that all department headlines should conform to the logo, and Carnase asserts that it was he alone who designed the additional characters and created all the ligatures. After making a handful of these headlines, he further realized there were almost enough characters to complete an entire alphabet, which he eventually drew, and from which a prototype film font was made for the studio's use.

Avant Garde had a modest circulation, but was extremely popular with, among others, New York's advertising and editorial art directors, who were so smitten by the contemporary character of the logo they clamored for freer availability of the face. Carnase recalls that Photolettering Inc. illicitly copied many of the letters and ligatures and sold them without permission. So to counteract this and other unauthorized use, Carnase produced a specimen card pack that offered custom settings to Lubalin Smith

Carnase's clients. Given the high volume of requests, it was clear to Lubalin and his soon-to-be partner, type director Aaron Burns, that Avant Garde should be released as a commercial font. Lubalin Burns was founded (prefiguring Burns' ITC) to produce and sell typefaces.

Before the font could be issued, however, a little matter of the name had to be resolved. "Herb seemed to think I held ownership in the design (I paid him for it, of course), "Ginzburg recalls, "and he asked me for permission to expand the logo into an entire alphabet and to market it under the name Avant Garde. I granted it with alacrity and gratis, with one proviso: That the face's name Avant Garde always be followed by the tiny circled letter *r* connoting that it was a registered trademark, as it was. This was necessary to protect my ownership of (I believe the legal term is to 'police') this valuable mark. Herb blithely ignored this ([and] I can hear him chuckling puckishly over my request) but it infuriated me and caused me legal headaches." Ginzburg later conferred with Burns of the trademark concerns, "and he, too, seemed indifferent to my concerns." The consummate irony, notes Ginzburg, is that Burns invited him to become an investor in ITC, chiefly on the strength of profits it stood to make with the Avant Garde faces. "But the timing of his call couldn't have been worse," says Ginzburg, who says he would have wanted to invest, but was about to start serving his prison term on the *EROS* conviction. Ginzburg's incarceration also put an end to *Avant Garde* magazine, yet the face with its name became ever more successful.

"As I understand it, a number of people got really rich off that typeface, including Herb," notes Ginzburg. But Carnase, who made and retains ownership of all the original drawings for the light, medium, and demi-bold weights (later other designers at ITC designed the additional weights), did not share in any of the profits. "I resented it highly," he says. "This was no way to treat a partner."

Carnase was not, however, as agitated by the way Avant Garde was used as was Lubalin—even though misuse of the ligatures was indeed rampant. Carnase recalls that, among other travesties, many times the lowercase *r* and *n* were so improperly set that the result looked like an *m*. "When you see it you just roll your eyes," he says, "but I didn't want to be a policeman, not then or now."

During every generation at least one typeface represents—often accidentally—the zeitgeist. Through widespread use the font's style then becomes emblematic of aesthetic points of view. Futura was "the typeface of the future." Helvetica was the typeface of corporate modernism. Avant Garde was adopted as symbolic of the raucous sixties and me-generation seventies. While the face had roots in modernism, it was also eclectic enough so as not to be too clean or cold. As a headline face it said "new and improved," and as a text face it added quirkiness to the printed page. It came alive on advertisements, and was appropriate for editorial design too. Eventually, after excessive overuse and rampant abuse, its quirkiness became simply tiresome—something like the paisley of type fonts—no longer fashionable, but not entirely obsolete either. Today,

Avant Garde is having something of a revival, even on the pages of this magazine, sans offending ligatures, and for some is now considered an alternative to the more elegant, contemporary gothics like Meta or Gotham.

I'm happy to say I kicked the habit.

Notes

* The opening page of the first issue of *Avant Garde* bore this dedication set in Avant Garde Gothic: As most of the world's ills are traceable to old imperatives, old superstitions, and old fools, this magazine is exuberantly dedicated to the future.

SECTION IV:
GRAPHIC DESIGN AS POLITICS

A PRESIDENT AND HIS DOG

Karrie Jacobs

Everyone I talk to these days is addicted to political blogs. We are all searching the Web for the latest piece of dirt on Ahmad Chalabi or Abu Ghraib, or the freshest political polling data. We trade URLs the way in decades past we might have traded names of obscure rock bands: Talkingpointsmemo, Buzzflash, Dailykos, Atrios. It's as if somewhere online there is a Rosetta stone that will help us read the swirl of information, misinformation, and disinformation that is all around us.

This is, I figure, about as close as the Web has come to fulfilling its potential. Finally, ten years after the emergence of the Netscape browser, the Web has become indispensable. Not just for getting stuff—books from Amazon, DVDs from Netflix, airline tickets from Orbitz—but for digging up dirt.

Naturally, what works for us—the left-leaning renegades that were destined to turn the Web into a paradise of countercultural thought—works for them, too. The Internet is equally popular with fundamentalist Christians, Muslim extremists, and all manner of conservatives. As it turns out, it has no endemic politics. So while the Howard Dean organization was credited as being the first presidential campaign to build a base of support by using the Internet (and derided for fizzing in dot-com style), the White House of George W. Bush has become one of the Web's most intriguing users.

I've been spending a lot of time exploring the official Web site of the presidency, *www.whitehouse.gov*, looking for insight into the inner lives of the people who live there. I am fascinated by the regularly posted photo essays. I find them very odd—as beguiling as Cindy Sherman photos. Who is this man in the pictures, the one who's always pointing like he's a Soviet-era statue of Stalin, or waving in lieu of speaking, or surrounding himself with multiracial clusters of children that function as photographic human shields?

I find myself watching the streaming video of Bush's tour of the Oval Office again and again, mesmerized as he says, "The rug that Laura designed for the Oval Office captures the sun and helps make this room an open and optimistic place."

Originally published in *Metropolis* (August 2004).

"Do they mean to be ironic?" I ask myself. No, I don't think so.

Then there's the photo of Lynne Cheney presiding over the 2003 Easter egg roll on the White House lawn surrounded by a wacko assortment of storybook characters, including an obscenely overstuffed Easter bunny. "Are these people trying to be bizarre?" I wonder. Again, I'm pretty sure the answer is no.

And then there's the Barney fetish. If you go to *www.barney.gov*, you will be directed to the home page of the president's Scottish terrier. There is now a feature called "Barney's Photo of the Day Archive." You can click on a date, May 6, for example, and discover that on the day President Bush met with King Abdullah II of Jordan and apologized to him for the abuses at Abu Ghraib prison, Barney was hanging out on the South Lawn with his soccer ball. "It's a humanizing feature of the White House and presidency," explains Jimmy Orr, the White House Internet director, who doubles as a White House spokesperson.

A humanizing feature. Somehow the dog, who is almost always depicted alone—looking as isolated as President Johnson during Vietnam's worst days—is the soul of the White House. The president, on the other hand, is routinely shown surrounded by people; he's constantly making physical contact, but somehow their humanity fails to rub off on him. He always looks as if he's on display at Madame Tussaud's.

Although the Bush administration is bedeviled by shocking photographs that it wishes would just go away, the White House Web site depicts a presidency that is seamless and placid, a pageant of protocol and carefully staged public appearances. I don't think I've ever seen a larger or better-organized collection of photo-op moments anywhere.

"Well, it's propaganda," notes Dan Froomkin, keeper of the *Washington Post's* official White House blog. Froomkin directs me to a 1999 Nieman Foundation for Journalism interview with Pete Souza, an official White House photographer who published a book of photos called *Unguarded Moments: Behind the Scenes Photographs of President Reagan*.

Explaining the title of his book, Souza says: "He was such a stage-directed president—'Stand here, do this, stand there, do that'. . . . I hope that I was able to give some sense of what he was like when he was unguarded. I think he got so used to me—there was a staff of photographers so there was always one of us around—that I don't think he really gave a shit if we were around." One of Souza's favorite photos is a shot of Reagan from the back, instantly recognizable from the shape of his hairdo, throwing a paper airplane from the roof of a Los Angeles hotel. It's a completely disarming image—nonpresidential and distinctly human.

Who knows whether the Reagan administration would have put such a photo up on its Web site if there had been such a thing back then, but it's interesting that the official White House photographer was nondogmatic enough to take photos that were not on-message. On *whitehouse.gov*, by contrast, every single photo of President Bush is the visual equivalent of a talking point.

My favorite feature of the site is that you can call up photos by date. You can find out, for example, what the president was doing—or what the president wants to be remembered as doing—in August 2001. On August 6, the day he got the intelligence briefing entitled "Bin Laden Determined to Strike in U.S.," there are no photos. Too bad. On August 8 Bush is depicted on a Waco, Texas Habitat for Humanity worksite wearing a carpenter's apron, his arm around a volunteer—a black woman—who looks distinctly uncomfortable. On August 15 he's opening a Job Opportunity Center in Albuquerque holding a giant pair of scissors. On August 23 he's fielding questions from Crawford, Texas elementary school students. The intended message of these photos is that Bush was hard at work during his month-long vacation. But it's difficult to look at this pageant of forced bonhomie in retrospect and not imagine the menacing Jaws theme welling up in the background.

Then comes September 11, and the Web site's archive spits out images of the president that were chosen to make him look like a decisive, take-charge guy. There's no photo of the president reading to Sarasota school children as his Chief of Staff, Andy Card, whispers in his ear. Such an image might remind us of the long minutes the president continued to read after he learned of the attacks. Instead we see him in a classroom talking on the telephone as his advisors point at a television screen across the room. We see the president on Air Force One talking on the phone to—according to the caption—Dick Cheney; the president on Air Force One jabbing his finger at Card; the president back in the White House waving his arms at his assembled staff. These are the photos the White House wants you to see. This is the official story.

I could look at these pictures forever, trying to tease out the unspoken truths about the White House, trying to find that elusive piece of knowledge that the blogs never quite yield. Trying, but not succeeding.

Of course, the history of presidential Web sites is very short, so it's impossible to say whether the Bush version is typical. However, Froomkin—a student of politics on the Web—notes that the Clinton administration used its official site to give the public access to all sorts of policy documents. "They basically put everything on it, which was fantastic." (The old Clinton Web sites can be found by visiting the National Archives online at *http://searchclinton.archives.gov*.) The archived pages look quite primitive; although there are, of course, propaganda photos, there's nothing as elaborate or insistent as a day-by-day archive.

The Bush administration has figured out exactly what the Internet is for. It's a place to tell the story you choose to tell, free of meddlesome reporters and editors— and free of unwanted drama. Indeed the presidential routine presented on *whitehouse.gov* winds up being as uneventful as the lives cataloged on the myriad of Joe Shmoe blogs out there—you know, the ones in which someone you don't care about records the minutiae of his daily existence. Which is why it's a damned good thing that the president, like so many of his fellow bloggers, has a dog.

THE CITIZEN DESIGNER
Victor Margolin

I

In this age of progress, it is customary to assume that the past has little to teach us and that we need only to look ahead. This ideology of the future drives most businesses and pushes societies in the industrially developed parts of the world into a dizzying vortex of technological innovation that most often eludes the ability of many to either fully understand or assimilate. What is frequently lacking as citizens face this onslaught of new devices, systems, and social practices is a set of core values that can enable them to make judgments about the personal and social worth of these experiences and to then act on those judgments. Too often the public is simply a passive consumer of innovation without being able to grasp clearly whether it is valuable or not. And what is even more serious is that people usually have little room to resist or refuse to participate, particularly where technology is involved.

We lack a *calculus of values* that can enable us to assess the worth of new experiences brought about by social and technological changes and formulate suitable responses to them. The design professions have not been particularly good at fostering such a critical intelligence among their practitioners. Although scholars and critics like Tomás Maldonado, Gui Bonsiepe, Victor Papanek, Ezio Manzini, Clive Dilnot, and Tony Fry have argued for years that designers need to think far more critically about what they are doing and the conditions within which they work, these arguments have yet to reach a place within professional design consciousness where they are central to the way every designer practices.

One of the great values of design history is that it exposes students to voices from the past that might be relevant to the present. These voices have always been powerful when it comes to issues of form. In architecture, the theories of Charles Rennie Mackintosh, Mies van der Rohe, and Robert Venturi, or, to go farther back in history, Palladio, continue to hover over the drawing boards and computer screens of architects, young and old. But the strong social concerns of a John Ruskin, a William Morris, or a Walter Gropius are today mainly drowned out by a cacophony of other voices, many of which return design to an earlier role as a decorative enterprise rather than a fundamental activity that underlies much of human action.

This essay is based on a lecture at the Ontario College of Art and Design, September 19, 2005.

One of the most significant moral voices of the past is that of William Morris, a towering figure among designers of the modern period. Morris was one of the greatest pattern makers of all time and someone whose own activities ranged from weaving tapestries and creating wallpapers to designing typefaces and printing books. He was also a prodigious writer and lecturer who could produce an epic poem as easily as he could give a discourse on the ills of society. Besides his activities as a designer and author, Morris was also active in politics. He joined the Social Democratic Federation in London and was an active Socialist in the latter part of his life. Between 1883 and his death in 1896, he gave almost 580 lectures to many groups, including the Socialist League, the Hampstead Liberal Club, and the Leicester Secular Society.

One of Morris's most powerful indictments of the ruling class of his day is an early lecture, "Art Under Plutocracy," which he delivered at University College, Oxford, on November 14, 1883. John Ruskin, then a professor at Oxford, chaired the event and may well have been the one who invited Morris to speak there. According to A.L. Morton, who wrote a brief introduction to the lecture in a book of Morris's political writings, Morris's talk caused a considerable uproar, primarily because he declared himself to be practicing Socialist and asked the audience to support his cause. Quoting from the *London Times*, Morton speculates that had the authorities at Oxford known what Morris was going to say, they probably would have refused him the use of the hall.

Perhaps we have all learned too well from the most powerful institutions of capitalism how to pacify controversial arguments and relegate them to the periphery of public discourse. This goes for arguments from the past as well as the present. I therefore want to counter that practice by returning to "Art Under Plutocracy" in order to demonstrate the relevance of Morris's strongly stated views to our present situation. In doing so, I also want to perform an intellectual excavation whose purpose is not the literal revival of Morris's arguments but a reinterpretation of those arguments to address a set of contemporary concerns.

At the beginning of his lecture, Morris provides an extremely broad definition of design. He uses the term "art," although he refers to all the applied arts that we call "design" today. He asks his audience "to extend the word art beyond those matters that are consciously works of art to take in not only painting and sculpture, and architecture, but the shapes and colours of all household goods, nay, even the arrangement of the fields for tillage and pasture, the management of towns and of our highways of all kinds; in a word to extend it to the aspect of all the externals of our life."[1] Today we can enlarge Morris's comprehensive division to include the many new technologies that range from computer hardware and software to nanotechnology, design for space travel, and bioengineering. By doing so, we obligate ourselves to take responsibility as designers for the quality of the total environment, including both its material and immaterial forms.

Morris then goes on to state how important the designed environment is to the overall quality of human life. "How does it fare therefore with our external surroundings in these days?" he asks his audience. "What kind of an account shall we be able to give to those who come after us of our dealings with the earth, which our forefathers handed down to us still beautiful, in spite of all the thousands of years of strife and carelessness and selfishness."[2] As we can read in Morris's utopian novel, *News from Nowhere*, he has a poetic vision of how humans should live. He claims that everyone would be happier living in the countryside, eating simple fare, wearing clothes of natural materials, and working as craftsmen in full control of their labor. He juxtaposes this vision of an arcadian life with the ills of Britain's Victorian cities.

Without embracing the specifics of Morris's rustic vision, I would like to interpret *News from Nowhere* as a metaphor for a life in which the qualities that make us most fully and satisfactorily human are at the center of the environment we design. I certainly agree with Morris about the importance of beauty but would extend the understanding of beauty to include the personal sense of well being that comes from living in an environment that satisfies our human needs.

No writer has described the natural environment more poetically than Morris. "To keep the air pure and the rivers clean," he says, "to take some pains to keep the meadows and tillage as pleasant as reasonable use will allow them to be; to allow peaceable citizens freedom to wander where they will, so they do no hurt to garden or cornfield; nay even to leave here and there some piece of waste or mountain sacredly free from fence or tillage as a memory of man's ruder struggles with nature in his earlier days: is it too much to ask civilization to be so far thoughtful of man's pleasure and rest, and to help so far as this her children to whom she has most often set such heavy tasks of grinding labour?"

Following this description of a rural ideal, he delivers a stinging indictment of capitalism. "That loss of the instinct for beauty which has involved us in the loss of popular art is also busy in depriving us of the only compensation possible for that loss, by surely and not slowly destroying the beauty of the very face of the earth. London and other great cities," Morris tells his audience, are "mere masses of sordidness, filth, and squalor, embroidered with patches of pompous and vulgar hideousness, no less revolting to the eye and the mind when one knows what it means; not only have whole counties of England, and the heavens that hang over them, disappeared beneath a crust of unutterable grime, but the disease, which to a visitor coming from the time of art, reason, and order, would seem to be a love of dirt and ugliness for its own sake, spreads all over the country, and every little market-town seizes the opportunity to imitate as far as it can, the majesty of the hell of London and Manchester."[3]

When attempting to apply Morris's concerns to the present, one can easily be put off by his emphasis on the joys of craftsmanship and his claim that many of the world's ills would dissolve if it were possible to return from the factory system's division of labor to an idealized practice of craft production. What is relevant in this juxtaposition, however, is Morris's recognition that many of his countrymen were engaged in "useless toil," rather than "useful work." He says as much when he tells his audience, "[t]o feel that you have to do a thing not to satisfy the whim of a fool or a set of fools, but because it is really good in itself, that is useful, would surely be a good help to getting through the day's work."[4]

Morris is quite clear in diagnosing the root cause of misery in Britain. He sides with Karl Marx in blaming capitalism for a class system that enables the plutocrats at the top to make a profit from the labor of the workers at the bottom. He also indicts the wealthy class that controls the means of production for not understanding how the manufacture of goods can serve human ends well. Under capitalism, he says, "the essential aim of manufacture is making a profit; that it is frivolous to consider whether the wares when made will be of more or less use to the world so long as any one can be found to buy them at a price which, when the workman engaged in making them has received of necessaries and comforts as little as he can be got to take, will leave something over as a reward to the capitalist who has employed him."[5]

And finally, Morris is concerned that the public is unable to see the true face of commerce, especially when it appears to be working well. "Do not be deceived by the outside appearance of order in our plutocratic society," Morris cautions. "It fares with it as it does with the older forms of war, that there is an outside look of quiet wonderful order about it; how neat and comforting the steady march of the regiment; how quiet and respectable the sergeants look; how clean the polished cannon; neat as a new pin are the storehouses of murder; the books of adjutant and sergeant as innocent-looking as may be; nay, the very orders for destruction and plunder are given with a quiet precision which seems the very token of a good conscience; this is the mask that lies before the ruined cornfield and the burning cottage, the mangled bodies, the untimely death of worthy men, the desolated home. All this, the results of the order and sobriety which is the face which civilized soldiering turns towards us stay-at-homes, we have been told often and eloquently enough to consider; often enough we have been shown the wrong side of the glories of war, nor can we be shown it too often or too eloquently. Yet I say even such a mask is worn by competitive commerce, with its respectable prim order, its talk of peace and the blessings of intercommunication of countries and the like; and all the while its whole energy, its whole organized precision is employed in one thing, wrenching the means of living from others; while outside that everything must do as it may, whoever is the worse or the better for it; as in the war of fire and steel, all other aims must be crushed out before that one object."[6] Although the length of Morris's sentences is a Victorian phenomenon, the prescience of his critical insights is as contemporary as that of the trenchant film *The Corporation*, which was made by a group of Canadian filmmakers several years ago.

II

The vehemence with which Morris confronted the prevailing values of British society owes much to his extraordinary powers of oratory, but the clarity of his critique derives a lot from his ability to articulate his own values. Morris did not take naturally to politics nor was he schooled in policy analysis. He was first and foremost a designer who began to engage politically with the world around him as he saw it infringing on his design practice. Although he spoke frequently about the prevalence of shoddy products and the "swinish luxury of the rich," he moved beyond that in his later years to larger issues of labor, economics, and even British foreign policy.

If we in the design community are to propose scenarios for social change, we must address two questions: First, how do we develop a set of core values that can guide us in making judgments about the way we want the world to be; and second, how do we learn to see beneath the deception of order that Morris referred to and understand the true character of the devices, systems, and situations with and within which we and others live?

For all the talk about design ethics and the need for the designer to be ethical, we must remember that designers for the most part function within systems of production, distribution, and consumption whose components are rarely within their control. While I agree that personal ethics is the essential starting point for any designer's strategy of action, I also believe that designers must frequently act within spheres of power whose parameters are frequently determined by others. Thus, the adoption of a professional code of ethics will certainly be part of a designer's core values, but there is also a need for a critical vision that can enable him or her to analyze the economic and political sphere within which he or she is asked to work and to evaluate the multiple material and immaterial artifacts that constitute the social world.

Capitalism at its best is a highly efficient system of delivering goods and services. At its worst it imposes undesirable products, and even environments, on the consumer and citizen. Ultimately, it is the consumer's willingness to purchase a product or service regardless of its quality that determines its presence or absence in the marketplace. Who then should proclaim the true quality of a product or service, and how is this to be done? This is the job of the critic and the citizen. Ideally, the designer will be both. The *calculus of value* can help. It is a conceptual tool that relates a product or service to many different factors: the labor conditions of its production, its materials, its impact on the use of resources and recycling, and its effect on the way human beings communicate in the public sphere.

Unless the designer or the consumer learns to recognize all these factors, and here I must add that such information is frequently difficult to come by, he or she may be unwittingly participating in a situation that has a negative effect on someone or some group involved in the conception, planning, production, distribution, or consumption of the product. Let me offer several examples. The first situation concerns a change in the level of comfort that many hotels, including budget chains, now provide. As a response to consumer demand, hotels are offering exceptionally thick mattresses, piles of new pillows, extra sheets, and heavy duvet covers in a competitive race to provide the closest approximation to Shangri-la for a middle-class guest. Besides upgrading the sleeping accommodations, the chains are also providing a host of new amenities: fancy soaps and shampoos, exotic teas, and specialty coffees.

In order to make these amenities attractive at a competitive price, the hotels have to compensate somewhere for the costs of their customers' added comfort. As has been the case since the factory system was instituted, it is the laborers, in this case, the housekeepers, who must pay the price. As the author of an article in the *Chicago Tribune* for August 23, 2005 notes, housekeepers are being asked to do more work in less time and to lift heavier mattresses, pillows, and duvets besides. The consequence for the housekeepers is not only added stress but also an increase in back and shoulder injuries. Even though the union that represents them pushed through a law in Cook County that mandated two fifteen-minute breaks to compensate for the added labor, it was temporarily overturned by a judge with the full support of hotel officials who want to eliminate it altogether.

How is design implicated in this scenario? This is not an easy question to answer. Should one blame the designers and manufacturers of pillows and duvets, or the ten-layer Heavenly Bed mattress that was introduced in the late 1990s? Based on the success of these mattresses in hotels, the manufacturer has sold several thousand more for home use, where they don't have to be lifted every day under stressful conditions. And should we consider this to be a design problem at all? I think we should. I would not put the blame on the objects themselves, although I might question the excessive use of materials. However, I would strongly criticize the plan that added stress and a greater possibility of injury to the housekeeper's job.

This situation is a perfect example of a set of human actions that doesn't become codified as a problem unless there is some public response. In this case, a journalist for the *Chicago Tribune* brought the situation to public attention and characterized it as a problem because its consequences corresponded to what we already know to be problems: human stress and bodily injury.[7] By writing the article, the journalist demonstrated how designed objects can be incorporated into a situation that has undesirable consequences for human beings.

Knowing that such uses are possible, a designer of house wares might have second thoughts about designing a new luxury mattress. As a citizen, the designer could write a letter to the hotel chain or organize a letter-writing campaign against the chain's labor practices. One design solution would be to create several levels of comfort and charge more for the higher levels. If a hotel chain were to act fairly, it might use the additional revenue to improve the housekeepers' working conditions. It might also set a limit on mattress weight, adding to the *calculus of value* the physical effect on the housekeeper of lifting heavy mattresses all day. Were the problem to gain greater public awareness, it might even lead to legislation that would limit mattress weight for hotel use or establish more favorable work rules for the housekeepers. I am sure that there is comparable legislation in industry to limit the weight of materials that workers are asked to carry. Finally, a public exposure of hotel working conditions can ultimately lead to consumer boycotts. This was certainly the case after the exposure of the Asian sweatshops where Western clothing and sporting goods are produced. Articles and books by journalists such as Naomi Klein's *No Logo* had a strong effect on consumer boycotts of such goods and resulted in the ultimate improvement in at least some of the manufacturing facilities.

For the most part, consumers and consumer advocates rather than designers have led the charge against companies that engage in unfair labor practices or manufacture products that are unsafe or not inaccessible to all users. The installation of air bags in automobiles, for example, was strongly influenced by consumer advocate Ralph Nader's book *Unsafe at Any Speed*. Consumers or users, rather than designers, were also the strongest advocates for legislation related to design for the disabled, notably the requirement that buildings and public transportation systems be wheel-chair accessible, whether with ramps, elevators, or special lifts. These and other design changes were mandated in the United States by the Americans With Disabilities Act, which took effect in 1992.

As a second example, I will make reference to the computer industry. Despite all that has been done for people with disabilities, there is still a long way to go. It is finally widely recognized that poorly designed office furniture can lead to back pain and other ailments, but it is not yet accepted that poorly designed computer keyboards are frequently the cause of carpal tunnel syndrome and other physical and neurological ills. Yet we have no legislation to mandate such keyboards. It is less expensive for major computer manufacturers to push the health issue aside and continue to provide a cheap standard keyboard with all their computers. Despite the fact that carpal tunnel syndrome is rampant among typists, why is there not more research on ergonomic keyboards and why are such keyboards not mandatory com-ponents of every computer system? Here again, we return to the *calculus of value*, recognizing that improved keyboards would increase the price of a computer even though medical costs and personal discomfort far outweigh the cost of such an increase. In fact, the computer industry fobs off the problem on the health care industry, which further taxes public and private health plans as well as personal finances. Since young consumers are far less likely than older people to consider the long-term costs of poorly designed keyboards and computer furniture, the computer companies can ignore potential health problems without seriously offending the strongest segment of their market. Similarly, mobile phone manufacturers play down the possibility of radiation from holding a cell-phone receiver to one's ear. Were William Morris alive today, he might easily be overwhelmed by the multitude of health and safety hazards, actual and potential, known and unknown, that consumers must deal with in selecting products for use.

III

In 1883, when Morris urged his listeners at Oxford not to be deceived by the "outside appearance of order" in a society ruled by wealthy plutocrats, the destructive consequences of plutocracy could be easily observed. One had only to consider the "sordidness, filth, and squalor" of London and Britain's other great commercial cities. While people living in most cities today can easily detect patches and even large sectors of urban despair, it far more difficult to identify the contours of the large electronic systems that increasingly determine our behavior and influence our lives. Whereas in ancient times, the pyramids or the Great Sphinx of Giza stood out as the foremost design objects of their day, at present, we are hard pressed to imagine a material object that exceeds the immaterial complexity of Google, Amazon, or eBay. These systems at their best are the building blocks of a new global community based on shared interests, and in recent years they have grown far beyond the wildest visions of their founders.

At the same time, such systems have become part of an electronic environment that is gradually usurping numerous social functions that were once carried out between human beings face to face. These systems, which range from online banking and bill-payment to remedial courses for traffic offenders, have become central to our lives and now mediate many of our daily activities. If participation in electronic systems was always a matter of choice, there might be less cause for concern. But to the degree that people are forced to conduct parts of their daily life online when they might prefer to relate to another human being instead of to a machine, such systems radically affect the way we live.

The gradual shift of social transactions to the electronic sphere has the potential to change the conduct of human society as much as the factory system transformed the handicraft traditions that William Morris so adamantly defended. In fact, rather than the nineteenth-century worker being oppressed by the factory system, it is now the twenty-first-century consumer who is tyrannized by impersonal systems through which he or she must access necessary services.

The shift from human actors to automatic systems began with replacing telephone operators and now continues with the replacement of a multitude of service providers, from airline ticket agents to insurance counselors. Whereas Morris railed against the cheap and nasty products of the Victorian era, today we are confronted with cheap and nasty systems that cause far more human misery than a poorly designed Victorian chair. How often have any of any of us been lost in the funhouse of an electronic service system, trying to speak to a live body when none are around?

Consumers are the victims of these systems created by large corporations in order to save money. By automating the jobs of live operators or agents, the extra work involved in completing a transaction is passed on to the end users. It is we who have to work harder to find a document, get to the right node or automated process, and then bare our souls to a fake floozy who politely tells us that we have confused her the moment we get off message. For the most part, we have no choice except to pay for services that we once received without cost. To purchase an airline ticket from an agent, the consumer must now pay an additional fee. Whereas customers were previously able to profit from the specialized knowledge of the ticket agent, now they must spend their own valuable time, if they choose not to make the extra payment, to do research on fares and routes themselves.

As these shifts from human service to electronic systems continue, they introduce social practices that will be difficult to change, given the large costs of designing and implementing such systems. And yet these systems are put into place with virtually no public debate. Decisions are made in corporate boardrooms and implemented on the wager that customers will not protest. Virtually invisible, such systems are designed, tested, and implemented without the consumer's awareness. Suddenly they are launched and a social process is transformed. Although there may be a lot of grumbling, there is never any protest and rarely any criticism of them. Few people are aware that these systems are even designed. The "true face of commerce" is even less visible than it was when Morris attacked British plutocracy in 1883.

At their best, Web sites such as eBay and Amazon are electronic global bazaars that offer the consumer a far larger choice of merchandise than could ever be provided in a physical space. Among the achievements of such sites is the creation of secondary and even tertiary markets for used goods that might not otherwise find a home. Given the commercial opportunities that such Web sites provide, not to mention the sites for small enterprises that can sell a single product globally, it is impossible to come to a singular conclusion about the human value of electronic systems. On the one hand, their potential is enormous; on the other, their effect can be devastating. This brings us back to the very difficult question: How do we live humanely in an age of rapid technological change?

To be honest, I find the answer elusive, particularly as someone who grew up and matured well before the electronic age. But I have a nagging feeling that there is something inhuman about the onslaught of technological innovation and some of the social changes that it is inducing. Lewis Mumford, the late historian of technology and urbanism, explained in his seminal book of 1934, *Technics and Civilization*, the difficulty we have in evaluating technology:

> Because the process of social evaluation was largely absent among the people who developed the machine in the eighteenth and nineteenth centuries the machine raced like an engine without a governor, tending to overheat and its own bearings and lower its efficiency without any compensatory gain. This left the process of evaluation to groups who remained outside the machine milieu, and who unfortunately often lacked the knowledge and understanding that would have made their criticisms more pertinent.[8]

We are in a similar situation today. I recall a comment by the late anthropologist Edward Hall at a conference in Washington, D.C., many years ago. He was actually discussing a related issue, the paucity of social indicators to indicate the health of a city. "For all we know," he said, "New York may be dead already."

IV

Hall's comment is an excellent lead-in to the conclusion of this paper, where I will address two questions. The first is: what can designers contribute to the conversation about the quality of contemporary experience? The second is: what can they do about it? Do we know with certainty that our environment is alive or dead? If not, and I think the latter to be true, how do we gain a better understanding of our experience? How do we assess its value?

First, we can acknowledge the pressure to consume and ask ourselves how this pressure corrupts the public sphere. How do we feel about city buses and subways that are plastered with advertising for iPods or Target, thus obscuring any civic identity? How do we feel when we have to mouth the name of a large corporation in order to tell someone that we went to a baseball game at the U.S. Cellular Field? How would we feel if the names of the Chicago Transit Authority subway lines were sold to corporations, as was recently proposed, and we would have to buy a ticket for the Sarah Lee Line or the Motorola Line rather than the blue or brown line? And how do we feel when we in the developed countries are consuming twenty to thirty times more energy per person than anyone else in the world?

To begin an analysis of what interferes with living a humane life, I would have to say that materialism is a significant factor. It drives manufacturing and incorporates a sense of unreasonable entitlement into the design of many products. I am certainly not advocating a return to a life of sackcloth and ashes, but I believe the ideals of measure and proportion that were central to the highest stages of Greek civilization would be most helpful in rethinking our own values. Thus, moderation would be an important factor in any *calculus of value.*

As a counter to materialism, I want to introduce self-awareness, particularly the ability to use the self as a resource of invention, imagination, and critical insight. To know the self means to leave space inside to observe one's surroundings and to discover one's thoughts, abilities, and feelings. And certainly an exposure to the great minds of the past and present is essential. Many years ago at Columbia University, I had an extensive introduction to the great thinkers and writers of the Western and the Eastern world. I read Plato and Montaigne, Ibn-Khaldun and Rabindranath Tagore. While I do not hear the echoes of these authors' voices as clearly as I did when I first encountered them more than forty years ago, their texts left resonances that have continued to prompt my feelings and reflections since then. As a result of my education and other experiences I have striven to live a life of quality and to resist when possible those aspects of my environment that, according to my feelings, do not contribute to this goal.

Like all of us, I have had to come to terms with a world of opposing values. Like Morris, I believe that the world is run by the contemporary equivalent of his British plutocrats—the large national and multinational corporations—whose power transcends that of most governments and even that of the United Nations. But I have also come to recognize the power of an oppositional movement in which where citizens have found each other in person or online. If anyone is to clear a path to a better world, it will be these civil society groups working together. Whether culture jamming, global boycotts, or electronic petitions, new forms of protest are emerging that at the very least provide a social space for like-minded people to assert their own convictions about how life should be lived.

To this end, I want to introduce the concept of the citizen designer, which I first encountered in an anthology of essays edited by Steven Heller and Véronique Vienne. I see the designer as having three possible ways to introduce his or her talents to the culture. The first is by designing, that is, making things. The second is by articulating a critique of cultural conditions that elucidates the effect of design on society; and the third is by direct political engagement. Too much power that affects all forms of design is in the wrong hands and can only be countered with well thought-out strategies of action. I would also like to suggest that William Morris was one of the first citizen designers and can serve as an excellent example of how a designer can engage with the culture of his or her day.

To conclude, I can do no better than to evoke the same words with which Morris ended his lecture "Art Under Plutocracy" more than one hundred and twenty years ago. "One man with an idea in his head is in danger of being considered a madman," he said; "two men with the same idea in common may be foolish, but can hardly be mad; ten men sharing an idea begin to act, a hundred draw attention as fanatics, a thousand and society begins to tremble, a hundred thousand and there is war abroad, and the cause has victories tangible and real; and why only a hundred thousand? Why not a hundred million and peace upon the earth? You and I who agree together, it is we who have to answer that question."[9]

Notes

1. William Morris, "Art Under Plutocracy," in *Political Writings of William Morris*, edited and with an introduction by A. L Morton (New York: International Publishers, 1973), 58
2. Ibid.
3. Ibid., 64
4. Ibid,. 68
5. Ibid., 74
6. Ibid. 80
7. Oscar Avila, "Hotels Make Beds Cozier, But Maid's Day a Lot Tougher, "*Chicago Tribune* (August 23, 2005)
8. Lewis Mumford, *Technics and Civilization* (New York: Harcourt Brace & Co., 1934), 282
9. William Morris, "Art Under Plutocracy," 85

WHERE PUBLIC MEETS PRIVATE: THE LOS ANGELES WOMAN'S BUILDING

Teal Triggs

"Space provides an essential framework for thinking
about the world and the people in it."
—Leslie Kanes Weisman[1]

"The Woman's Building is the room of our own, the private
space where the community begins."
—Denna Metzger[2]

The Los Angeles Woman's Building (1973–91) has often been overlooked in historical or cultural discussions about the rise of feminism in the United States. While much was written about the activities of this remarkable space during its early days in the 1970s, little attention has been given to it since—in particular, its importance as one of the first cultural and educational organizations dedicated exclusively to the training and development of women as artists and designers. At the same time, historians have neglected the Building's role in facilitating the manner in which women's personal issues could be brought into a public arena. This despite the fact that many of the Building's participants were, and still are, well recognized within their specialist fields, contributing significantly to developments in art, design, and education.[3]

My own fascination with the Building is longstanding. With an interest in design history and feminist issues, I applied for a travel grant from the U.K. Arts and Humanities Research Board which would allow me to meet and interview those women (and men) who had actively been involved in the creation and development of the Woman's Building. As I made my way from the east coast of the United States to Los Angeles the network gradually unfolded, with women who, despite their own busy schedules, made time to speak of their own personal experiences while at the Building. This merely confirmed the generosity of spirit in which feminism has evolved. As I heard each woman's story, and the roles they

This essay first appeared in *zed.7 Public + Private* (2000). Guest Edited by the Women's Design + Research Unit (Project Team, Siân Cook and Teal Triggs with Zed Editor, Katie Salen). Research for this essay was made possible by a grant from the Arts and Humanities Research Board, United Kingdom.

played in its development, it became increasingly apparent that the building itself had provided a space in which women could openly discuss social, political, and personal concerns specific to their lives as women. The reasons they were drawn to the Woman's Building are as diverse as each woman herself. Some were looking for emotional support while others wanted to enroll in workshops in order to develop their ideas or learn new skills. Yet, in all cases, the Building provided a proactive environment where personal viewpoints could be explored through their work as artists, performers, writers, or designers. It is with this in mind that I have decided to focus not so much on the art that was produced there (this has been well covered elsewhere), but more specifically on the physical spaces of the Woman's Building and in the way that it actually functioned as a "house" (or home) for women working in the arts.[4]

PHYSICAL SPACES

The Los Angeles Woman's Building opened its doors in the autumn of 1973 on the crest of the second wave of feminist activity.[5] Founded by three prominent members of the American art and design community—Arlene Raven, Judy Chicago, and Sheila Levrant de Bretteville—the Building was established ". . . to provide a public arena for sharing and honoring the artistic achievements of women."[6] It was modeled on the Woman's Building of the 1893 World's Columbian Exposition held in Chicago, and also adopted an organizational structure consisting of the Board of Lady Managers.[7] The earlier nineteenth century version of the Woman's Building embraced almost every aspect of women's lives domestically as well as professionally. This was conveyed through its exhibition displays and equally in the way that women artists and artisans carried out the Building's decorative program. Eighty years on, the Los Angeles Woman's Building followed in this tradition, seeking to ". . . house a multiplicity of women's creative efforts."[8] From the outset, the Los Angeles Woman's Building became an important cultural venue for women and a focal point for ". . . a variety of private and collective enterprises."[9] By this time, of course, feminism had moved on and developed a political flavor all of its own.

During its eighteen-year existence, the Los Angeles Woman's Building occupied two locations within the city. Initially, the Woman's Building was housed on North Grandview in the old Chouinard Art Institute building—a property owned by CalArts. After the sale of the CalArts building in 1975, the Woman's Building moved to a warehouse space on North Spring Street. There were advantages to both spaces, as Sheila Levrant de Bretteville remembers: "The first Woman's Building site had a courtyard ringed by two storeys with ample rooms, a form, where everyone could come together . . . the second building was in a warehouse district . . . but we saw the advantages offered by three empty floors we could reshape as we came to understand their uses. . . . "[10]

In both locations, a range of organizations occupied the converted sites. The Feminist Studio Workshop (FSW), the Women's Graphic Centre (WGC), and the

Extension Program presented a range of classes and workshops. In addition, the Woman's Building hosted a series of successful conferences including *Women in Design* (1975), *Woman's Words* (1975), and *Woman's Culture at Work* (1980). They were also instrumental in bringing in guest lecturers ranging from women such as the philosopher Mary Daly to contemporary literary figures (e.g., Margaret Atwood, Adrienne Rich, and Alice Walker). Other spaces in the Building were, at various times, occupied by small businesses or professional women's organizations. These included offices for lawyers, a travel agency, the National Organization for Women, Women Against Violence Against Women (WAVAW), the Sisterhood Bookstore, a thrift store, a café, and various rental galleries.[11] By combining a range of activities and services, the Woman's Building created an environment in which women could freely explore the "intersection between private and professional lives."[12]

IMAGINING COMMUNITIES

"Context is all."

—Margaret Atwood, *The Handmaid's Tale* (1985)

Michel de Certeau writes in *The Practice of Everyday Life*, that space (espace) is ". . . actuated by the ensemble of movements deployed within it." In order to exemplify this point, de Certeau observes that the city streets defined by their geometrical planning are "transformed into a space by walkers."[13] He suggests that space is produced ". . . by the operations that orient it, situate it, temporalize it, and make it function. . . ." The Los Angeles Woman's Building as a space functioned in a similar manner. The buildings provided a "practiced space" for women, which "acted as a vehicle for physically uniting diverse aspects of the community, bringing women together at the same time in the same place."[14]

In terms of space and spatial relationships, the Woman's Building operated on several different levels. Firstly, there was the broader context of the neighborhoods in which the two buildings were located. These areas were selected partially as dictated by ever-tightening financial concerns. As a result, its founders were limited to renovating relatively inexpensive spaces or finding ways in which to barter: "The owners of the Old Chouinard Art Institute building in the Wiltshire area, for example, agreed to six months free rent, in exchange for the necessary renovations to take place."[15] The second building, located in a Los Angeles warehouse district, proved more problematic. Sheila de Bretteville comments, ". . . we couldn't afford the buildings which were next to other buildings as part of a context of life, so we ended up getting a building that was in a warehouse district . . . we were in the middle of two Latino gangs. We could have had big trouble as Judy Baca cautioned we might, except that never happened because they were perhaps too busy getting on each other's case to be bothered with us. . . ."[16]

The potential difficulties for locating an essentially "white, middle-class, totally female institution" in the middle of a highly ethnic, populated neighborhood, did not go unnoticed.[17] Lucy Lippard writes in a 1974 issue of *Art in America*,

"The Woman's Building is still primarily a white middle-class institution, although its groups are exploring ways to open it to more minority participation. . . ."[18]

One way to address the situation was to create opportunities for the Woman's Building to "reach out" into the local neighborhood as well as the greater Los Angeles area. For example, "consciousness-raising dialogues" were created with men and women from the Studio Watts Workshop, and there was the availability of the FSW Extension Program classes. In addition, special projects such as "Madre Tierra" (1982), involving twelve Chicana artists and writers under the direction of Linda Vallejo, were also encouraged. At the same time, the space of the Woman's Building needed to be accessible to the diversity of interested communities. Innovative use of exhibition spaces was one possible solution. Levrant de Bretteville comments,

> . . . [W]e tried to organize shows that would attract different communities so that they would meet each other. . .we'd have an art exhibit by a relatively well known artist like Ree Morton or Joyce Kozloff, a group show that highlighted a particular group of issues such as incest survival, or "Books, Posters and Postcards by Women" or "Las venas de la Mujer," taking place at the same time so that different groups of people would have to mix.[19]

Secondly, the Woman's Building provided a physical structure in which individual interests and personal concerns were nurtured. At the same time, it provided the space for artists and designers to present their work to a broader range of public audience. A key factor of the organization's intent was to take the private public, where women could actively affect social change. As if to punctuate this point, for the Building's fifth anniversary, the feminist and artist Kate Millet hoisted her Fat Lady onto the top of the Building. The sculpture announced the Building to the neighborhood but also globally, appearing on the front page of the *Los Angeles Times*. But publicity was not the only outcome that was beneficial to women at the Building. It was also the collaborative experience of community that Kate Millet felt to be crucial to the completing of the project.

> I had a wonderful time building the Fat Lady there. All sorts of women came to help. We put up a little sign "Volunteers Wanted." I bought everybody a cup of coffee. It was the only reward apart from each other's company.[20]

As feminism sought ways of establishing new and better sets of social constructs, the terms by which women defined themselves could be transformed. The configuration of the space itself within the Woman's Building facilitated change by orchestrating, under one roof, studios and more public galleries. Susan King, the past Studio Director of the Women's Graphic Centre remarks,

> There is a big difference in doing your work in a secluded studio and in a supportive environment that was experimental . . . and, it was a public thing. The Woman's Building changed all of this.[21]

However, it is also the relationship between feminist theory and its application to art and design practice in which the Woman's Building operated at its best. Feminism encouraged working at the Building to express as well as critique areas in which they felt victimized. They often shared their views and invited public dialogue addressing their feelings of victimization, alienation, or sexuality through a variety of mediums. This meant that projects—both individual and collaborative—tackled difficult and emotive issues such as violence against women, abortion, rape, and incest. In 1979, for example, Paula Lumbard and Leslie Belt curated *Bedtime Stories: Women Speak Out About Incest*, an exhibition of art, writing, performance, and video confronting the issue of incest.[22] Other performances, such as *In Mourning and in Rage* (1977), by Leslie Labowitz, Suzanne Lacy, and Bia Lowe raised awareness about violence against women; and issues of sexuality were addressed in an educational piece, *An Oral Herstory of Lesbianism* produced by the Lesbian Arts Project.

WOMEN'S GRAPHIC CENTER

"Feminist design reaches out, invites dialogue and strives to transform the
dominant culture."
—Sheila Levrant de Bretteville[23]

Social and personal issues were also communicated by those who were interested in developing their skills as graphic designers and typographers. Founded at the same time as the Woman's Building (1973), the Women's Graphic Center (WGC) offered classes to students who were more experienced as well as to those new to the areas of design, writing, graphic arts, and related production techniques. Workshops in typography, logo design, letterpress, artists books, and printmaking provided women with opportunities to develop their production skills as well as further their understanding of design as a vehicle for social change. According to the introduction of the *Women's Graphic Center Handbook*,

> The WGC offered classes that explored, through graphic works, the juncture, tension and flow between private and public perceptions, activities and involvements.[24]

The intent of the program was to empower women through a better understanding of communication based primarily upon a series of feminist design principles. Writers, for example, were able to "assume control of their work" by learning how to print and design their own publications. Employing strategies proposed by feminist design, women could also ". . . create a mutually caring connection with a larger public through their work and in making women's experience public, visible, and accessible to discussion and change."[25]

Typography, as well, played a role in the manner in which texts would be represented. Andrea Dworkin herself demonstrated this in her "Afterword" to

Woman Hating that the representation of texts also affects the reading and under-standing of texts.[26] Similarly, writing in an issue of *Chrysalis*, Julia Stanley and Susan Wolfe remark,

> Even typographical conventions and punctuation have political implications: they can be altered to transform old meaning or they can confine meaning and hinder expression.[27]

Faculty members, including some of the most prestigious women working in the field of graphic arts and design, were sympathetic to this aspect (e.g., Sheila Levrant de Bretteville, Frances Butler, Cindy Marsh, Susan King, Sue Maberry, April Greiman, Deborah Sussman, and Judith Hoffberg, and one of the few male contributors, Simon Toparovsky). For some, however, the development of personal issues through graphic design was problematic. Adrienne Weiss, an ex-student of the Woman's Building program and now a practicing designer in New York, reflects:

> I think the idea of doing something personal was that it was confessional. Like you would confess whatever was going on with you...that wasn't my mode. I think only in very kind of rare situations does that happen with graphic design.[28]

Yet, the professional world was also accounted for with, for example, the profit-making activities of the WGC Typesetting and Design Service. Clients, which included The Museum of Contemporary Art, LACE Gallery, YWCA of Los Angeles, Contemporary Health Systems, and the Municipal Elections Committee of Los Angeles, provided an opportunity for graduates and instructors alike to put theory into practice. It also visibly promoted women within the profession itself.

Ultimately, we're left with the question: how does the work of the Woman's Building relate to feminism today? The Building was without a doubt an important center of activity, bringing women together at a time when the feminist movement actually looked like a unified force. Women who worked and played there went on to develop its message in their later careers. In the year 2000, as the women's move-ment diversifies still further, one can only wonder whether it is possible for such a space to exist successfully again. Although there is much work still to be done, it does not seem that the same energy is there. The Woman's Building was a way forward for its time, and for that alone it deserves recognition and no small amount of praise.

Notes

1. Leslie Kanes Weisman. *Discrimination by Design: A Feminist Critique of the Man-Made Environment* (Urbana: University of Illinois, 1994), p. 9.

2. Denna Metzger as quoted in *The First Decade: Celebrating the Tenth Anniversary of the Woman's Building* (Los Angeles: The Woman's Building, 1983), p. 6.

3. Many of its participants, including Sheila Levrant de Bretteville, Judy Chicago, Arlene Raven, Terry Wolverton, Cheri Gaulke, and Suzanne Lacy, have written about the history of the Woman's Building.

4. Documentation and examples of work from the Woman's Building are housed primarily in the Archives of American Art, Smithsonian Institution and in collections held in the libraries at Otis College of Art and

Design and the California Institute of the Arts. I would like to thank, in particular, Judy Thorn, Sue Maberry, and Coco Halverson at their retrospective institutions for their time and invaluable assistance.

5. *The First Decade: Celebrating the Tenth Anniversary of the Woman's Building*, p. 2.

6. Judy Chicago. *Beyond the Flower: The Autobiography of a Feminist Artist* (New York: Viking Books, 1996), p. 35.

7. Sophia Hayden Bennett was the first female to receive a degree in architecture from M.I.T. in 1890. The decorative artist Candice Wheeler supervised the Chicago Woman's Building exhibitions and library interior. Most notably, the artist Mary Cassatt painted an interior mural. See Isabelle Anscombe, *A Woman's Touch: Women in Design from 1860 to the Present Day* (New York: Viking Penguin, Inc., 1984), p. 40.

8. Sheila Levrant de Bretteville. "The Woman's Building: Physical Forms and Social Implications" in *Building for Women*. Suzanne Keller, ed. (Lexington: Lexington Books, 1981), p. 49.

9. Ibid., p. 47.

10. Author's interview with Sheila Levrant de Bretteville (New Haven, Connecticut, May 1999).

11. *The First Decade: Celebrating the Tenth Anniversary of the Woman's Building*, p. 6. The Building also had its own community exhibition spaces and studios, a monthly newsletter, *Spinning Off*, and a journal titled *Chrysalis*. It also housed the Women's Graphic Center: WGC Typesetting and Design as well as various theatre groups.

12. Sheila Levrant de Bretteville. "Feminist Design: At the Intersection of the Private and Public Spheres" in *Design and Society*. Richard Langdon and Nigel Cross, eds. (London: The Design Council, 1984), pp. 86–93. Her essay formed part of the discussions instigated by the British Design Council's 1982 international conference on the political and social implications of design in society.

13. Michel de Certeau. *The Practice of Everyday Life* (Berkeley: University of California Press, 1988), p. 117.

14. Sheila Levrant de Bretteville. "The Woman's Building: Physical Forms and Social Implications," p. 59.

15. *Neworld* (fall, 1979), p. 33.

16. Author's interview with Sheila Levrant de Bretteville (New Haven, Connecticut, May 1999).

17. *Neworld* (fall, 1979), p. 33.

18. Lucy Lippard. "The L.A. Woman's Building'. *Art in America* 62, no. 3 (May/June 1974), p. 86.

19. Author's interview with Sheila Levrant de Bretteville (1999). However, the Building still had its critics. In 1979, a journalist for the *Los Angeles Herald Examiner* questioned the motives of the lesbian membership of the Woman's Building. He wrote, "fortunately for the future of feminism, the vast majority of feminists are heterosexuals with a far more tolerant attitude toward me. . . ." Letters to the editor followed, with a call for the newspaper to ". . . publicly apologize to all women—gay and straight. . . ." *Los Angeles Herald Examiner*, May 30, 1979.

20. Author's interview with Kate Millet (New York, May 1999).

21. Author's interview with Susan King and Simon Toparovsky (Los Angeles, September 1999). The Building represented the culmination of its founders' previous work in educational programs. For example, Judy Chicago was founder of the Feminist Art Program at Fresno State College (1970) and with the painter Miriam Shapiro, established the Feminist Art Program at CalArts (1971). Shelia Levrant de Bretteville founded the Women's Design program at CalArts (1971). In 1973, Chicago, Levrant de Bretteville, and Raven came together to form the Feminist Studio Workshop, Inc. (FSW) as a nonprofit corporation "for the purposes of starting an independent environment in which women in the arts could work." In the same year, the FSW moved to the Woman's Building as an intensive two-year educational program. Other programs, including the Center for Feminist Art Historical Studies and the Extension Program offered classes and workshops in areas such as art, literature, graphics, film, video, and performance.

22. Jan Alexander-Leitz. "The Woman's Building: Where Woman's Culture Keeps Growing From Anger to Activism." *Neworld*, no. 6 (1975), p. 22.

23. Sheila Levrant de Bretteville. "A Definition of Feminist Design." *The Women's Graphic Center Newsletter* (n.d.), p. 5.

24. Sue Maberry. *Women's Graphic Center Handbook* (Los Angeles: The Women's Graphic Center, n.d.).

25. Sheila Levrant de Bretteville. "Feminist Design: At the Intersection of the Private and Public Spheres," p. 87.

26. Andrea Dworkin. "Afterward: The Great Punctuation Typography Struggle," in *Woman Hating* (New York: E.P. Dutton & Co., 1974), p. 197.

27. Julia Penelope Stanley and Susan J. Wolfe (Robbins). "Toward a Feminist Aesthetic." *Chrysalis*, no. 6 (1978), p. 59.

28. Author's interview with Adrienne Weiss (New York, May 1999). Weiss was a FSW student from 1978–80.

FIGHTING THE IMAGE WARS
Steven Heller

If the U.S. army had its way in 1966, the image that made me into an anti–Vietnam War protestor would never have been published. Yet somehow this contraband snapshot taken by a grunt soldier sneaked passed the censors and appeared in a New York underground newspaper. The government rightly feared that, if leaked out, such nasty images would adversely influence America's hearts and minds and so made distributing them a court martial offense. Nonetheless photographic evidence of the war's horrors could not be hidden forever and the image that I saw, which predated the 1968 photograph of the My Lai massacre showing bodies of women and children along a roadside, was more than my imagination could conjure up. It was as graphic as Goya's *Disasters of War*, but an even more vivid slice of genuine inhumanity. The photo featured a squad of smiling GIs posing behind six severed Viet Cong heads whose open eyes stared directly into the camera as though their bodies were buried in sand on a beach. It was not the heroic image of American troops I was used to★ or wanted to see. Yet once this and other similar photographs were uncovered, the national media was compelled to publish more intense images that changed more Americans' minds about the war.

Vietnam was the first battleground in what is currently called the image war; Iraq has become the second. Recent video and photographic barrages in the press and on the Internet of mutilations, decapitations, and torture have become instruments in a propaganda battle on both sides that will determine how the war in Iraq is viewed throughout the world. With the widespread availability of imagery, it is important to understand how to process lurid and monstrous images without becoming blinded by them. And it is necessary to balance reality and propaganda. In the image war, pictures are double-edged swords.

Shocking imagery is a fact of twentieth-century life. The camera made it inevitable and irresistible. After World War I, for instance, a German book titled *War Against War* showed surreptitiously obtained official undoctored photographs of grotesquely disfigured corpses used to document and protest the lost war. Some critics argued it was treasonous or at least insensitive to exhibit this to a nation that had already suffered so much. During World War II, selected photographs showing Japanese soldiers beheading Chinese prisoners were published in U.S. magazines, including *Life*, as evidence of Japanese barbarity. At the end of the war, pictures of concentration camp

Originally published in *PRINT* 58, no. 5 (September/October 2004).

horrors testified to the unfathomable Nazi transgressions of the Final Solution. In anticipation of Allied war crime trials these images were purposely released to ensure the
public remained unforgiving towards the vanquished.

Such is the political power of negative imagery that during World War II
American war photographers were prohibited from publishing scenes of excessively
bloody battles, and drawings made by official "war artists" were eschewed as overly
gruesome depictions (at least those that saw the light of day). It wasn't easy, but U.S.
military propaganda experts sanitized the war images, and the news media faithfully
complied. While it was acceptable to show barbaric adversaries, dead enemy soldiers,
and even bedraggled allies, rare were otherwise alarming representations of our own
troops in physical peril, like the recreated orgy of brutal violence of those D-Day
landing scenes in the film *Saving Private Ryan*.

News coverage may have been distorted, but there was sound reasoning
behind this strategy. War is hell, but for public relations it is better to show clean, white
crosses than blood-soaked corpses. The projected rhetoric of such imagery is the simple idea that, although war costs lives, our troops nonetheless die with honor. Images
were used to perpetuate this idea during World War II and Korea, but Vietnam was
another story.

Despite its best efforts, the government lost this image war. It could not prevent
grunts from taking snaps or journalists from making pictorial documents. Photographs of Vietnam are so starkly etched on our collective mind that even today simple
verbal descriptions allow one to conjure the South Vietnamese police official shooting
a prisoner in the head at point blank range, the naked Vietnamese girl running
down a highway, the Vietnamese mother holding her lifeless baby (a *Newsweek* cover),
and of course, the bloated bodies along the My Lai roadside. For some, these were
the Guernicas of the time, yet they were also real, captured moments of this war. As
the government predicted, these images were used to influence surging public opinion
against Vietnam policy. Heroic photo-ops they were not.

PR lessons were learned from Vietnam. However, despite attempts at image
management that worked so well during Desert Storm, the second Iraq war has produced a surfeit of horrific images that will not be easily erased. Many of us have
actual or anecdotal memories of Daniel Pearl and Nicholas Berg's decapitations (that
appeared on the Internet), the charred remains of American contract workers killed
in Falluja and suspended on a bridge over the Euphrates River, and, of course, the
tortured naked bodies of dead and alive Iraqi captives as their jailers/torturers
proudly posed in Abu Ghraib prison. Who will forget the hooded man on a box
with arms outstretched and attached to electric wires? Already it has become an icon
of the antiwar movement. Depending on the news organization, these images were
released with some trepidation, but eventually all but the decapitations (deemed too
grotesque for the U.S. mass media but not for Al Jazeera) were made available
because they were "news."

Legitimate news-gathering organizations have been fairly circumspect about
how to present strong image-based stories. On April 2 the *Philadelphia Inquirer*

reported receiving 185 complaints for its front and inside page picture coverage of the charred bodies, while at the same time CNN refused to show the available video (the next day, however, they joined Fox News and MSNBC in airing some of the footage). *Inquirer* managing editor Anne Gordon told her staff in an e-mail, "We do our job when we give readers all the news—no matter how painful or ugly." Previously, on April 1, *Washingtonpost.com* had already posted a photo gallery of the images—many newspapers use their Web extensions to show difficult images. On the Poynter Online Weblog (a news and information site for the newspaper industry) one blogger, Steve Outing, offered suggestions in a post titled "How to Introduce Truly Disturbing Images Online" discussing the release of sensitive picture stories that "pushes the boundaries of acceptability" on the Web "when other media wouldn't dare." He suggested that printed warnings before every controversial image allow the viewer the freedom to skip over them. Yet free access to these kinds of images has certainly increased, and the more lurid, the more viewers are attracted to them. Anyone who has scanned the newswires or the Web knows that more vivid images of Falluja were available. Most newspapers chose only those few that represented the story yet did not sensationalize it (Michael Moore shows graphic uncut footage in his film *Fahrenheit 9/11*). In fact, anyone who has access to news photo services knows that anytime there is a suicide bombing the photos of body parts strewn everywhere are available but rarely published or aired.

In this image war, the U.S. government only sanctions publication of disturbing pictures when it suits propaganda needs. For example, after the killing of Saddam's two sons, their swollen, scarred corpses were deemed appropriate evidence that they were killed during a "virtuous" fire-fight. Conversely, photos of flag-draped coffins of U.S. troops are restricted, argues the government, on the basis of privacy concerns. After the Pentagon inadvertently briefly sanctioned the release of coffin images, all further publication was immediately halted. In *Fahrenheit 9/11*, Moore montages these coffins together with additional restricted imagery (presumably taken off satellite feeds) showing wounded and dying soldiers, edited together with disfigured and dead Iraqi civilians in a startling antiwar polemic. In the image war, it is easy to exploit sensitive imagery for any purpose.

Even in a purely news context, this footage triggers emotional responses that can have adverse political ramifications. After publishing the Falluja pictures, *Los Angeles Times* editors Elizabeth Jensen and James Gerstanzang said, "While showing the images could erode support for the war, not showing them could have an opposite effect." When the *New York Times* ran a layout of the most infamous Abu Ghraib atrocity pictures illustrating a story headlined "In Abuse, a Portrayal of Ill-Prepared, Overwhelmed G.I.'s," the images inflamed emotion, but for some it opened the door for sympathetic responses, since the victimizers were, arguably, victims of a flawed system. Pictorial truth can be interpreted many ways.

People will read into images what they hope to get out of them. Of course, some will deny them or turn away in disgust while others will forever remember what they've seen. People can and will choose. But should all images be accessible all the time? Was it necessary to show the decapitations of Pearl, Berg, and Kim Sun Il (the Korean worker captured in Iraq)? In this image war, where terrorists and insurgents derive power from streaming horrific imagery onto the airwaves, human casualties are reduced to mere ordinance. Should they be used as such? Should the media refuse to show images that aid an enemy? The video shot in Mogadishu in 1993 of two downed Black Hawk helicopter pilots' corpses dragged through the angry streets convinced President Clinton (and Americans in general) to retreat from Somalia. The power of images to change minds and policy is endemic to any image war. So the news media must walk a tightrope: While choosing to spare the public from grotesque visual details, it also must present fair representations. For me the definition of fair is "truthful."

Yet I don't need to see every last gory truthful nuance to form opinions about the war. I believe that editors have a responsibility to edit, and suitability versus accuracy is a component of responsibility. Frankly, I found the blurred yet saturated color video-capture of a terrified Kim Sun Il moments before his beheading, that ran on the front page of the June 23 *La Repubblica* (I was in Italy at the time), more emotionally charged than the death blow (which I would have avoided watching). It may not serve the terrorists as well, but seeing a frozen moment of Kim's last seconds alive is ghastly enough.

As long as there are so many media and Internet venues, the image war will continue to be fought. The U.S. Army is doubtless looking for ways to offset the damage of Abu Ghraib, and Al Qaeda is trying to outdo the World Trade Center (which admittedly was their biggest image coup to date). How we as designers contribute to the image war, and how we as people respond to the images, may help determine who wins, if anyone really wins.

Notes

★ Years later my then brother-in-law, a former grunt serving in Vietnam during the Tet Offensive, showed me similar snapshots that he had taken mixed among benign portraits and landscapes.

HUMAN DIGNITY AND HUMAN RIGHTS: THOUGHTS ON THE PRINCIPLES OF HUMAN–CENTERED DESIGN

Richard Buchanan

As I walked on the shore of Cape Town to the opening ceremonies of a conference on design in South Africa in the summer of 2000, I saw through the rain and mist a small sliver of land in the bay.[1] Naïvely, I asked my host whether it was part of the peninsula that extends south of the city or an island. With what, in retrospect, must have been great patience, she quietly explained that it was not *an* island, it was *the* island. I was embarrassed, but I knew immediately what she meant. I spent the rest of the evening thinking about the political prisoners who were held on Robben Island, human rights, and the irony of a conference seeking to explore the reshaping of South Africa by design, held within sight of Table Bay.

I was helped in these thoughts by the address of the Minister of Education, Dr. Kadir Asmal, who opened the conference by exploring the meaning of design, the need and opportunities for design in South Africa, and, most importantly, the grounding of design in the cultural values and political principles expressed in the new South African Constitution. I have never heard a high government official anywhere in the world speak so insightfully about the new design that is emerging around us at the dawn of a new century. Perhaps everyone in the audience was surprised by how quickly and accurately he captured the core of our discipline and turned it back to us for action. Many of his ideas were at the forward edge of our field, and some were further ahead than we were prepared to admit. For example, I believe we all recognized his significant transformation of the old design theme of "form and function" into the new theme of "form and content." This is one of the distinguishing marks of new design thinking: not a rejection of function, but a recognition that unless designers grasp the significant content of the products they create, their work will come to little consequence or may even lead to harm in our complex world.

I was particularly surprised, however, by Dr. Asmal's account of the creation—and here he deliberately and significantly used the word "design"—of the South African Constitution. He explained that after deliberation the drafters decided not to model the document on the familiar example of the United States Constitution, with an appended Bill of Rights, but rather to give central importance from the beginning to the concept of human dignity and human rights. Though he did not elaborate on

First published in *Design Issues* 17, no. 3 (Summer 2001).

the broader philosophical and historical basis for this decision, it is not difficult to find. Richard McKeon, co-chair of the international committee of distinguished philosophers that conducted a preparatory study for the Universal Declaration of Human Rights in the 1940s, explains that the historical development and expression of our collective understanding of human rights has moved through three periods: *civil and political rights* were the focus of attention in the eighteenth century; *economic and social rights* were the focus in the nineteenth century; and *cultural rights*—formally discovered in the preparatory work for the Universal Declaration—became the focus in the twentieth century.[2] The U.S. Constitution begins with a statement of political rights, and the appended Bill of Rights is a statement of civil rights protected from government interference. The document was properly suited to the historical development of human rights in the late eighteenth century, and in subsequent evolution the United States has gradually elaborated its understanding of economic and social rights as well as cultural rights. The South African Constitution begins with a statement of cultural rights, suited to the current historical period in the development of human rights. It seeks to integrate civil and political rights, as well as economic and social rights, in a new framework of cultural values and rights, placing central emphasis on human dignity. The result for South Africa is a strong document, suited to a new beginning in new circumstances. The opening article of the Constitution, quoted by Dr. Asmal, reminded me of the Preamble of the Universal Declaration of Human Rights, which announces "recognition of the inherent dignity and of the equal and inalienable rights of all members of the human family."

Dr. Asmal's account was both historically important and a conscientious reminder of the cultural context of the conference. However, the next step in his argument brought the room to complete silence. He made the connection between practice and ultimate purpose that is so often missing in our discussions of design, whether in South Africa, the United States, or elsewhere in the world. Design, he argued, finds its purpose and true beginnings in the values and constitutional life of a country and its people. Stated as a principle that embraces all countries in the emerging world culture of our planet, design is fundamentally grounded in human dignity and human rights.

I sensed in the audience an intuitive understanding of the correctness of this view, though the idea itself probably came as a surprise, because we often think about the principles of design in a different way. We tend to discuss the principles of form and composition, of aesthetics, of usability, of market economics and business operations, or the mechanical and technological principles that underpin products. In short, we are better able to discuss the principles of the various methods that are employed in design thinking than the *first* principles of design, those on which our work is ultimately grounded and justified. The evidence of this is the great difficulty we have in discussing the ethical and political implications of design and the consequent difficulty we have in conducting worthwhile discussions with students who raise serious questions about the ultimate purpose and value of our various professions.

The implications of the idea that design is grounded in human dignity and human rights are enormous, and they deserve careful exploration. I believe they will help us to better understand aspects of design that are otherwise obscured in the flood of poor or mediocre products that we find everywhere in the world. We should consider what we mean by human dignity and how all of the products that we make either succeed or fail to support and advance human dignity. And we should think carefully about the nature of human rights—the spectrum of civil and political, economic and social, and cultural rights—and how these rights are directly affected by our work. The issues surrounding human dignity and human rights provide a new perspective for exploring the many moral and ethical problems that lie at the core of the design professions.

What is important at the moment, however, is that we may recognize in Dr. Asmal's argument the major tenet of new design thinking: the central place of human beings in our work. In the language of our field, we call this "human-centered design." Unfortunately, we often forget the full force and meaning of the phrase—and the first principle that it expresses. This happens, for example, when we reduce our considerations of human-centered design to matters of sheer usability, and when we speak merely of "user-centered design." It is true that usability plays an important role in human-centered design, but the principles that guide our work are not exhausted when we have finished our ergonomic, psychological, sociological, and anthropological studies of what fits the human body and mind. Human-centered design is fundamentally an affirmation of human dignity. It is an ongoing search for what can be done to support and strengthen the dignity of human beings as they act out their lives in varied social, economic, political, and cultural circumstances.

This is why Robben Island remained in my thoughts on the first evening of the conference. It reminded me that the quality of design is distinguished not merely by technical skill of execution or by aesthetic vision but by the moral and intellectual purpose toward which technical and artistic skill is directed. Robben Island, site of the prison in which Nelson Mandela and other political prisoners were isolated for so long from direct participation in the national life of South Africa, is another symbol of twentieth-century design gone mad when it is not grounded on an adequate first principle. It is a symbol of the wrongful use of design to shape a country in a system that denied the essential dignity of all human beings. Robben Island belongs with other disturbing symbols of design in the twentieth century, such as that which my colleague, the architecture and design historian Dennis Doordan, chillingly noted: The Holocaust was one of the most thoroughly designed experiences of the twentieth century, with careful attention to every obscene detail.[3]

Dr. Asmal's argument carried an urgent message for the work of the conference and for everyone in the design community. Not only is design grounded in human dignity and human rights, it is also an essential instrument for implementing and embodying the principles of the Constitution in the everyday lives of all men, women, and children. Design is not merely an adornment of cultural life but one of the practical disciplines of responsible action for bringing the high values of a country or a culture into concrete reality, allowing us to transform abstract ideas into specific, manageable form. This is evident if we consider the scope of design as it affects our lives. As an instrument of cultural life, design is the way we create all of the artifacts and communications that serve human beings, striving to meet their needs and desires and facilitating the exchange of information and ideas that is essential for civil and political life. Furthermore, design is the way we plan and create actions, services, and all of the other humanly shaped processes of public and private life. These are the interactions and transactions that constitute the social and economic fabric of a country. Finally, design is the way we plan and create the complex wholes that provide a framework for human culture—the human systems and subsystems that work either in congress or in conflict with nature to support human fulfillment. These range from information and communication systems, electrical power grids, and transportation systems to managerial organizations, public and private institutions, and even national constitutions. This is what leads us to say that the quality of communications, artifacts, interactions, and the environments within which all of these occur is the vivid expression of national and cultural values.

We are under no illusion that design is everything in human life, nor do we foolishly believe that individuals who specialize in one or another area of design are necessarily capable of carrying out successful work in other areas. What we do believe is that design offers a way of thinking about the world that is significant for addressing many of the problems that human beings face in contemporary culture. We believe that conscious attention to the way designers work in specialized areas of application, such as communication or industrial design, is relevant for work in other areas. And we believe that general access to the ways of design thinking can provide people with new tools for engaging their cultural and natural environment.

As we work toward improving design thinking in each of our special areas of application, we also contribute to a more general understanding of design that others may use in the future in ways that we cannot now anticipate. The urgent message of Dr. Asmal is that we must get on with our work as designers in all of these areas if we are to help in sustaining the revolution that has been initiated in South Africa and the wider revolution in human culture that is taking place around us throughout the world.

Notes

1. This essay is based on a paper delivered at a national conference organized by the Design Education Forum of Southern Africa, "Reshaping South Africa by Design," held in Cape Town from June 22 to June 24, 2000.

2. Richard McKeon, "Philosophy and History in the Development of Human Rights." In Zahava K. McKeon, ed., *Freedom and History and Other Essays: An Introduction To The Thought of Richard Mckeon* (Chicago: University of Chicago Press, 1990).

3. Personal communication with Dennis Doordan, 1999.

SINCE THEN
Milton Glaser

What has happened to our field since our first conference twenty years ago cannot be considered without examining the more troubling question of how the world has changed—since I have less than twenty minutes, I will not attempt to objectively summarize that question, but say that, speaking subjectively, the world seems more fragile and imperiled than it did in the mid-eighties. Perhaps the world always seems at risk. In my lifetime, I've witnessed a world war, the Holocaust, McCarthyism, Vietnam, Korea, the threat of nuclear annihilation, the Cold War—and in these times, AIDS, genocide in Africa and Bosnia, 9/11, global warming, the war on Iraq, the acceptance of torture, the Patriot Act, the tsunami, the devastation of New Orleans and the gulf coast, and overshadowing everything else in our minds—the emergence of international terrorism.

The political exploitation of the fear of terrorism is as alarming as terrorism itself. It has caused me to examine my role as a citizen and to think about whether designers as a group have a dog in this fight, to use a pungent down-home cliché. Our dog in this fight may be human survival.

My personal response to this condition has led me to become more active in civic life. As designers, we've been concerned about our role in society for a very long time. It's important to remember that even modernism had social reform as its basic principle, but the need to act seems more imperative than ever.

After 9/11, I produced a poster that was distributed around the city by students from the School of Visual Arts as well as wrapped around a million copies of the *Daily News*. It seemed to reflect what all of us were experiencing after the tragedy. Of course, the design problem, in the case of personal interventions, is how to become visible . . . how to enter into the bloodstream of the culture.

About a year afterwards, I produced a series of buttons for the *Nation*—the magazine that is, not the country. They expressed ideas that I felt should be made explicit: dissent protects democracy, secrecy promotes tyranny, no to empire, surveillance undermines liberty, leave no CEO behind, and Oil/War.

Originally delivered at the AIGA National Design Conference, Boston 2005.

Images referenced in this article are marked by an asterisk and can be viewed at *www.miltonglaser.com/pages/milton/mg_index.html.*

I've been occasionally described as a left-leaning or liberal designer—which is certainly true within our current political atmosphere—but consider the elusive nature of words. A few weeks ago, the provisional government of Iraq was being criticized by our government spokesman for being too conservative in regard to women's rights with the hope that a more liberal view would prevail. In Iraq, conservative is bad and liberal is good. Here our government tells us that conservative is good and liberal is bad. How the word "liberal" became stigmatized and avoided by politicians is worthy of a doctoral thesis. I am also fascinated by the derision that accompanies the words "do gooders" as if only the naïve and inept would consider doing good a principle. I think artists tend to be liberal because their view of the world has to include doubt and ambiguity as well as generosity and optimism. In recent years, I've come to believe that the world is divided between those who make things and those who control things.

Recent behavioral thinking suggests that one's political stance, be it conservative or liberal, might be largely genetic. No wonder logic turns out to be so ineffective in political discourse. Our last election was won largely on the basis of fear and personality. If our political beliefs are driven by our instincts and not by our intelligence, we can all be a bit more generous to one another. Of course, the issue becomes, if we hold our beliefs lightly, can we still maintain our passion and indignation when our sense of fairness is violated?

During the last Republican convention, I distributed this proposal around the city in an attempt to deflect the violence that confrontation might produce. It reads in part:

> The Republicans have every right to meet and choose their candidate in our city without abuse. At the same time their convention creates an opportunity for all of us to express our disagreement with the culture of militarization and violence that our current leaders represent. It is time to change the mean-spirited and abrasive tone of our civic discourse. We need an alternative to the harsh and degrading words and images that have filled our consciousness since the war began. On August 30, from dusk to dawn, all citizens who wish to end the Bush presidency can use light as our metaphor. Imagine, it's 2 or 3 in the morning and our city is ablaze with a silent and overwhelming rebuke. . . Light transforms darkness.

Buttons, flyers, posters, postcards, T-shirts, and books. How primitive are the means we have to dissent. And yet I believe these modest tools can help change history. This spring, Mirko Ilic and I created a book for Rockport Press that we titled *Design of Dissent*, which documents the graphic resistance to institutional power over the last ten or fifteen years. It received a surprising amount of press and television coverage for a book that we thought would be of interest mostly to design professionals. In June, an exhibition opened at the School of Visual Arts that will travel across

America. In fact, there will be two shows in circulation. As you know, the *Graphic Imperative* is a survey of sociopolitical posters from 1965 to 2005, put together by Elizabeth Resnick, Chaz Maviyane-Davies, and Frank Baseman. This is not a coincidence. It's a case of breathing the same air.

Many of us have been troubled by the passivity of the American people towards the events of our time. Part of this condition must be attributed to the cynical use of fear our government has employed to control peoples' judgment after the trauma of 9/11. This was made possible in part by television, my favorite whipping boy, and the most persuasive means of indoctrination in human history. George W.S. Trow said this about television in a book called *Within the Context of No Context*: "The trivial is raised up to power in it. The powerful is lowered toward the trivial. . . . No good has come of it."

Perhaps the most obvious loss is what we call our sense of reality. Television combines news about the war, Paris Hilton's career, global warming, and Geico commercials into events of equal importance. The result is an enormous population that believes nothing matters.

Our discussion on the ethics of designers always gets impaled on the issue of whether a client's desire for profit can be reconciled with our ethical desire to do no harm or, put another way, can we serve a client and the public at the same time. The difficulty of these questions explains why the AIGA and other design-based organizations have found it so difficult to define a designer's obligations to the public. But this is not the horse I want to beat today.

I very much believe that whatever special respect exists for people in the design profession comes more from their relationship to the role of art and making things than their service to business. When I was five years old, I decided to become an artist. I had no idea where that decision came from, outside of the pleasure I experienced making things. In teaching, I've discovered that many students of design had a similar epiphany at an early moment in their lives. I became a designer, but like many of us, I've always struggled with the relationship of Art and Design, and the question of what precisely separated the two activities. "Can Design be Art?" is a question that has always obsessed me. Not long ago, I reread E.H. Gomrich's magisterial *Survey of Art History*, which begins, "There really is no such thing as Art. There are only artists." How liberating, the question is finally answered—if there is no Art, Design cannot be considered Art.

Then again, it is reasonable to imagine that there are many artists living undercover, in a kind of witness protection program, in the realm of design. I've carefully called myself a designer all my life in part because I fear being pretentious, and also because I realized I would never surpass Vermeer. But I feel ready for a conversion. I am thinking of changing my self-definition from a designer who occasionally practiced art to an artist who practices design. This is an easy claim to make because being an artist is a case of self-anointment, and there is no entry exam. More than anything else, the designation represents a view of life. History, of course, has its own standard.

If we need a definition of Art, the Roman literary critic Horace provided an elegant one. "The role of art is to inform and delight." Form and light are hidden in that definition. It's an idea I enthusiastically embrace. Of course, informing is different than persuading. When one is informed, one is strengthened. Persuasion does not guarantee the same result.

Delight is the nonquantifiable part of the definition that speaks to the role of beauty. What artists make is a gift to humankind; a benign instrument that has the possibility of affecting our consciousness through empathy and shared symbolism. We are affected not through logic but by a direct appeal to our limbic brain, the source of our emotional life. Although we don't fully understand how it functions, I'm drawn to this mysterious part of our work, which we frequently describe as metaphysical or miraculous. These words may simply mean that we still do not understand what our brain is capable of.

The most important function of art through history has been to work magic, to change the very nature of those who experience the work—in these cases beauty transforms as well as informs. Searching for the miraculous strikes me as being a good way to spend my time. I'll show you two examples of what I mean.

A woman interested in Buddhism asked me to design stationery for her. In the course of doing the work, I made a discovery. A folded piece of paper could operate like a printing press. There are three faces of the Buddha on the left hand side of the page printed in red yellow and blue. When folded the faces align to create a full-color head of the Buddha that smiles at you through the envelope. My client added the line at the bottom of the page, "when discarding please burn." After all, you don't want to throw the Buddha in the garbage.

About the same time, I received an assignment from the Holocaust museum in Houston to design a poster marking their tenth anniversary. "Don't make it too dark," they specified; "we don't want to frighten children." I took the assignment seriously but I must admit it took me months to deal with it. Discovering the meaning of the Holocaust is not designing a cereal box. Someone at the studio gave me a book called *Man's Search for Meaning*, by Viktor Frankl, a psychotherapist who lived through Auschwitz. At one point, he realized that though he had no control over any aspect of his life, what he ate, what he wore, what he did each day, or anything else, he did have one choice. The choice of how to react to his condition: to accept it and be crushed, or to transcend it and find meaning in it. This is perhaps the only meaning of the Holocaust, and it enabled me to design something that was not a reflection of despair but a tribute to the human spirit. Its intent was to elevate and enlarge consciousness in the way a work of art does through the use of light and form. I used a quote of Frankl's as the text for the design although it is not evident or readable until you are ten or twelve inches away. He describes the day he left the camp and how he progressed step by step, until he once again became a human being.

After finishing the poster, I had a realization. For years, I've wondered how most of the world ignored the Holocaust even though they knew terrible crimes were being committed against the innocent. How could people be so callous and unresponsive? I have contempt for such people. And then I realized with a chill that our time has been marked by events of incomprehensible brutality and evil, and I have done almost nothing. I'm speaking of events in Africa.

I must say that all the recent images we have been seeing from the Gulf Coast—the deaths, the inferno, the people who lost everything, the helplessness, the despair, the children—are all echoes of the horror in Africa. It is not coincidental that the victims of Katrina are the poorest members of our society. Both situations are a poisonous combination of natural disasters and political indifference.

I am embarrassed by the possibility that another generation will point at us and say, "How could they have been so callous and unresponsive?" That thought led me to create a poster that the School of Visual Arts produced to be distributed around New York. The telephone kiosk people voluntarily tripled the number of locations the school had paid for. I consider this a good sign. The campaign will be up for the next month all over the city. As I speak, the U.N. World Summit is in session in New York as well. My hope is that it will be seen by most of the delegates to that summit. Financial aid is essential, but what is even more significant is a change of human consciousness. We can participate in this change.

In the course of writing this piece, I've also changed my mind again about my self-designation. Designer/Citizen seems like a more satisfying description. There has been no better time for all of us to assume this role. We are all at risk, but like Viktor Frankl, we can choose how to react to our circumstances. We can reject the passivity and narcissism that leads to despair, and choose to participate in the life of our times. It's twenty years since the first AIGA conference. Things have changed and there is much work to do.

RAGING BULL

Rick Poynor

At *Design Observer*, the weblog I participate in, my colleague Michael Bierut recently asked what turned out to be a surprisingly provocative question: "What is the relationship of bullshit and design?" Bierut was inspired by the astonishing success of *On Bullshit*, a slender little volume by Princeton philosopher Harry G. Frankfurt. Public enthusiasm for the book, first presented as a lecture twenty years ago, suggests that the quantity of bullshit in our culture is an issue that preoccupies many people.

Bierut had some surprising confessions for anyone nursing the idea that a bullshitter is not the most positive thing to be. "Early in my life as a designer," he said, referring to his student days, "I acquired a reputation as a good bullshitter." The Pentagram partner expressed the view that every client presentation was "inevitably, at least in part, an exercise in bullshit." It was clear, even in these opening remarks (the online discussion, in which I participated, ran on and on), that Bierut was using the word "bullshit" in a particular way. "The design process," he noted, "always combines the pursuit of functional goals with countless intuitive, even irrational, decisions." Bullshit was the kind of explanation offered to clients to explain these intuitions. Simply admitting, "I don't know, I just like it that way," would be unlikely to do the job because most clients need to hear something that sounds like a rational justification.

This struck a chord with many designers who responded to Bierut's post. "Bullshit is one essential part of the selling process, particularly at the stage where we are trying to sell the idea to the client," ran a typical remark. A design educator, Greg Hay, said he tried to make his students realize that "the best artists are not necessarily the ones with the best talent or work . . . they are invariably the ones who bullshit the best."

The odd thing about the way people kept using the word was that they seemed to disregard the basic dictionary definition. *Merriam-Webster Online* defines the noun as "nonsense" or "foolish insolent talk." As a verb, to bullshit means "to talk nonsense especially with the intention of deceiving or misleading." There is no dispute among lexicographers about the meaning of bullshit. Robert Chapman's *New Dictionary of American Slang* describes it as "nonsense; pretentious talk; bold and deceitful absurdities."

This is all rather damning, but the collective view of design bullshit, as it emerged on *Design Observer*, was much more tolerant and forgiving. "Bullshit is not

Originally published in *PRINT* (September/October 2005).

necessarily bad and can function quite well in the design process until someone decides to call it," Bierut said as the argument unfolded. I began to suspect that my own distaste for bullshit, grounded in the dictionary definition, was more severe than that of many designers, especially those who had come to regard a degree of bullshit as an inescapable part of dealing with clients. Bierut pointed out that "charlatans have long been viewed with something verging on affection in American culture," and someone else mentioned the snake-oil salesman as a quintessential American character.

Whichever way you look at it, though, a too-ready acceptance of the idea of bullshit spells problems for design. From the way the word was bandied about, it seemed that any explanation dealing with the intangible esthetic aspects of designing ran the risk of being written off as bullshit. Using the word as a lazy synonym for rationalization does intellectual damage to design, suggesting that "fancy talk" offered in support of a design decision will always be suspect, no matter how apt or well-intentioned.

In fact, the meaning of bullshit is much more specific. The bullshitter speaks purely for effect. He cares only about the way his words influence the listener. For this reason, Frankfurt writes, bullshit is a greater enemy of the truth than an outright lie. The liar knows and accepts the truth but chooses to deny it. The bullshitter couldn't care less whether what he says is true or not.

Referring to the use of so-called bullshit in client meetings, Bierut notes the "desire to conceal one's private intentions in the service of the larger goal: getting your client to do it the way you like." But is this really bullshit? What, after all, is being concealed? It must be obvious to the client that the designer is trying to win acceptance for the design proposal. That's a given. It must further be obvious that anything the designer says, any rationale offered, has this aim in view. The designer would be guilty of misleading the client—of bullshitting—only if he knew that his preference would not serve the project's purpose and might even harm it, but he chose to hide this and make a case for it anyway.

It's quite possible that this happens all the time, though not a single designer owned up to such irresponsible behavior in the *Design Observer* discussion. However, if a designer sincerely believes that his preferences will serve a project's aims, then "bullshit" is the wrong word to describe any rationale used to support them. Moreover, it is inevitable, given the subjective component of so much design, that designers will sometimes realize only later why their intuitions were appropriate. "If you made something red because 'it felt right' and later realized that it evokes worker solidarity or sexual abandon or fire trucks or hot sauce," writes Gunnar Swanson, "it is neither lying nor abandoning truth to say 'the color red does x.'" Exactly.

What tended to be overlooked in this discussion was the far more serious problem of the pervasiveness of bullshit in our culture. If designers can accept bullshit as part of their working experience, as a selling technique they might legitimately use on clients, then how scrupulous are they about having a hand in communications that contribute to the avalanche of bullshit in advertising, commercial promotion, and the media? Frankfurt certainly believes that there is a connection between the two phenomena.

"The realms of advertising and of public relations, and the nowadays closely related realm of politics, are replete with instances of bullshit so unmitigated that they can serve among the most indisputable and classic paradigms of the concept," he writes. Frankfurt points out that these areas are staffed by "exquisitely sophisticated craftsmen"—designers, art directors, photographers, copywriters—who work tirelessly to perfect every word and image. If people are drawn to Frankfurt's unlikely best-seller, it's because contemporary life splatters them with bullshit and they want to know why. Bierut asked the right question: What is the relationship between design and bullshit? But by taking a purely professional view, he approached the issue from the less significant side.

Any sign of tolerance for bullshit in public life should concern us. The last thing we can afford is to view the bullshitter indulgently as a source of amusement. In communication, as in all our social relationships, there has to be a basis for trust, and trust is grounded in a sense of what is real or unreal, reliable or unreliable, true or false. Those who aim to create an effect on the listener or viewer without regard for the truth of what they say contribute to a climate of vagueness and confusion that eats into everything. The willingness to switch off our bullshit detectors and go with the flow of verbiage, nonsense, dubious claims, and even falsehoods shows that the bullshit habit is dulling our critical faculties and blunting our instinctive sense of why honesty and accuracy matter. Lost in a haze of wishful thinking there can be no sensible basis for action, no way of making a rational choice. Bullshit leads only to even more bullshit.

When words become overfamiliar, it's easy to take them for granted. This seems to have happened to "bullshit," especially when it's reduced to the milder sounding "B.S." So imagine yourself in a field where cattle are grazing. You trip over a clod of earth and fall headlong into a deposit on the ground. This is our subject. There is nothing sweet-smelling about it.

CASTLES MADE OF SAND
Lorraine Wild

In 1980, my friend Bill Bonnell, a very successful and elegant designer of the American-Swiss persuasion, was working as a consultant on a brochure about some sort of customer service offered by IBM. At the time, all design work for the company had to be approved by Paul Rand, who was also a consultant for IBM, though "consultant" doesn't begin to describe the command that Rand wielded over that organization and its designers, both in- and out-of-house. Bonnell, like so many others at that period, was exhilarated by the typographic moves of Weingart, Friedman, Kunz, and probably also by the Russian avant-garde (which, after all, was the root of Swiss revisionism). There was a big exhibition on the Russians in Washington, which was one of the first times you could actually see the work that had only really become available in publications a few years earlier,[1] and a lot of young designers were excited by it.

So Bonnell, hardly a rebel but alive to all this, made the tiniest formal move on his brochure—layering a plus sign, which was a meaningful part of the text—with its own shadow in the center of the brochure. The plus sign and its shadow (approved by his client, since it functioned within a design that adhered to the IBM identity guidelines) reverberated with a sprightly energy, with its allusion to the "deep space" of an El Lissitzky composition and the Basel revisionists.

Thousands of the brochures were printed, yet when Paul Rand saw them, he angrily demanded that they be put in the trash (which they were). Bill was told to do it over and scolded like a recalcitrant school kid. I vividly remember Bill telling me this story, and how incredulously funny the whole thing seemed. On one hand, how could a little old drop shadow damn a piece of print (and its designer) to the garbage can?[2] On the other hand, how could a guy like Rand, who knew so much about typography, be so brittle as to think that the minimalized modernism of the 1970s was the ultimate, perfected form of visual communication, never to be altered in the least little bit?

Sounds stupid, doesn't it? Well, if you think it sounds dumb now, can you imagine how stupid it all seemed if you were young back in the late seventies? Can you imagine a job interview where you were warned you would only be allowed to use four typefaces (with no idea of what the typefaces might be used to communicate)? Or how about being told in graduate school that correct typography consists

Originally published in *Emigre*, no. 65 (2003).

of using only one font with one weight change? This would happen despite trips to the library to see great books of the past, many of them typographic mélanges that would cause any of your professors to drop dead. Or what if every "good designer" you knew started projects with the mechanics of the grid, and concepts seemed to be something only advertisers worried about? What if you saw the daily evidence piled up around you that the world operated with thousands of visual codes, but somehow you would not be taken seriously if you used any of them other than the desiccated form that modernism had devolved into? Could you be forgiven, perhaps, for beginning to suspect that what you were being taught was not actually modernism at all, but habit? Or bizarre fraternity rituals? The similarities to frat hazing were alarming; if you did what you were told without questions, you would be let "in"; everything depended upon emulating the cool, older guys who had managed to convince everyone that they were in charge. If you asked questions, there were no sensible answers and you definitely risked rejection.

Personally, I decided in the face of all that I had already experienced as a young designer, with doubts, to escape to graduate school, where I thought I could recuperate some sense of design as a process, with a history, an ethos, etc., etc. That's another story,[3] but while I was there, perusing the paltry literature of graphic design, I assumed that it would be minutes, just minutes, until the art history students I saw around me discovered graphic design.

After all, art historians had recently discovered photography, and in just a short while, a time certainly no longer than the years Mr. Poynor documents in *No More Rules*, a rich literature of historical and contemporary photography had appeared. And I'm not just talking about picture books, but books with ideas attached to the pictures: historical documentation, analyses of contemporary work, exhibitions, and diverse interpretations.

Sure, there was an element of careerism in this. If you were a young historian of the visual, would you rather (a) count the angels standing on the head of, say, the French Impressionist pin, or (b) wade into the relatively uncharted waters of the most basic and ubiquitous visual documentation? The perennial lack of jobs for PhDs only stoked my own little professional paranoia; that is, before I knew it, thousands of historians who knew nothing about graphic design as I knew and loved it (no matter how screwed up it was) would be studying it, writing about it, and creating graphic design history, just as they had for photography. On one hand, what a relief: one less thing for us busy designers to worry about. On the other hand, the threat of the uninitiated commandeering the story was just too scary.

About as terrorizing, it turns out, as Y2K, and similarly groundless. For reasons that are obviously complex, if not mystifying, the story of graphic design is still pretty much below the general academic radar. I would bet cash that there are still more college seminars on Madonna (or, pathetically, Britney) than there are on graphic design. Poynor himself admits in *No More Rules* that though (some) designers have used critical theory, cultural historians and theorists have still barely recognized the existence of graphic design. Not that there is a shortage of books on graphic design, but most of them are picture books of interest to practitioners only (not that these do not play an important role in the field, but still . . .). And now we have blogs, and we do not have to worry about anyone coming up with new or original ideas about graphic design, despite the self-proclaimed rebellion in so much of the current digital "conversation." No documentation, no footnotes, no idea that anyone, designer or not, has ever said anything about graphic design before, other than what has just scrolled by on whatever thread you are reading. Every day is a new day on the blogs.

So I cannot be anything but grateful for the publication of *No More Rules*. I do not think it is widely understood just how difficult it is to pull a book like this together: to gather the material, clear the rights, substantiate and present the story with any sort of confidence at all. Let's just say that it is part of the reason that the literature of graphic design is evolving so slowly. Rick Poynor is one of our heroes; not a graphic designer, but a self-described "fellow traveler"[4] who, as the founding editor of *Eye*, reestablished (and reinvented) an international approach to graphic design journalism that transcended the dog 'n' pony show–ghetto into which most magazines had devolved in the eighties.[5] He is also responsible for one of the most important compilations of new typography to document the work as it was happening: *Typography Now*, published in 1991; and recently, *Obey the Giant*, a compilation of his own essays on graphic design that has become required reading in many design departments.

No More Rules is about graphic design produced between 1980 and 2000. In his introduction, Poynor claims that it really isn't a history as such, but an explanation of a period marked by new images, ideas, arguments, experiments, and technologies driven by the influence of postmodernism. I'm not sure this distinction will register with many readers, since Poynor's book takes the familiar form of a survey. He provides a clear definition of postmodernism as an ongoing cultural phenomenon (rather than a formal fad), and he describes fairly accurately the commonly overlooked (or denigrated) relationship between graphic design practice and postmodern theory. He wisely substitutes the usual cavalcade of geniuses with an exploration of the origins of the work, and then a set of themes: Appropriation, Techno, Authorship, and Opposition.

Poynor's selection of work for his survey is very specific: a narrow band of academic design work of all types (often not properly identified as student projects, not then, not now); some pop culture stuff (mostly record sleeves); some small-run magazines, club flyers, posters, and design used to speak to other designers, like AIGA announcements or paper promotions. Probably the most "mass-market" examples depicted are Benetton's *Colors* magazine, the *Wired* spreads, Brody's design for covers of the *Face* and *New Socialist*, and the infamous Swatch ad by Paula Scher.

Many of the original critics of the sort of work featured here excoriated it on the grounds that it was too marginal, not commercial enough, and ultimately unimportant (and oh, yes, "ugly"). Of course, the very reason this work is worth reviewing is that it turned out to be massively influential beyond its tiny scale. The vitality of the experiments spoke to an audience that was ultimately seen as a market. That work and its proliferation, along with the shift to digital means, burst the bubble of the self-satisfied design scene I described earlier. But the reader of *No More Rules* would never know that from what is actually depicted, since the work is shown in isolation, without any sort of mapping of the way that the production and proliferation and consumption of the new work proceeded. There are no examples of what these designers were visually reacting to; no cause and, equally, no effect.

And that's the problem with the book, to this reader who witnessed and participated in the scene. It's missing so much of the specific energy and texture, the seriousness and rebellion, the orneriness and fun. As far as the late eighties and early nineties goes, it certainly is the only time I've ever witnessed designers arguing overtly about graphic design as if it meant something. If you read the "Letters to the Editor" from *Emigre* during those years, you begin to get the idea. Another example is that people no longer accepted the blank judgments of design competitions. Jurors' comments were insisted upon—a new phenomenon at that point, believe it or not.[6]

Poynor describes a dialogue published in *Print* in 1990 between Tibor Kalman and Joe Duffy that addressed the issue of stylistic appropriation. What he omits is that *Print* was trying to capture a public argument that had boiled over between the two at the 1989 AIGA conference in San Antonio, after Kalman accused Duffy (by name! on the main stage!) of making what he deemed phony work. Can you imagine two designers almost punching each other out over anything at an AIGA conference now? Tibor's attack, correct or not, was fueled by the same sort of crazy enthusiasm on which the designers of the postmodern typographic experiments were running. One could sense the end of a bad old system, and it was time to take it down and/or reinvent it through a challenge to its visual language.

Poynor claims that he is not writing a history, but I wish he had spoken to more people and written his book as a reporter, because the story of the big generational change that ran alongside the technological one is going to be much harder to reconstruct, as time goes by, than the citation of theoretical influences. The reductive modernism that was advocated by a tough and powerful older generation was so insular that it offered very few openings or clues as to where design might go next (other than the emulation of where it had been). Younger designers desiring to explore other avenues were on their own. Poynor really focuses on the turn toward theory, but seems to miss that this was part, but not all, of a desperate search—which included design history and the investigation into vernacular—by young designers who had concluded that the only way to reinvigorate graphic design was to look beyond its conventional borders.

One of the problems with the themes of *No More Rules* and Poynor's insistence that they all be viewed through the scrim of theory is that he imposes an artificial order where there really wasn't much. This results in the work seeming more programmed and much more dependent upon the influence of theory than it really was. Some work included thus seems anomalous because it illustrates the author's theme, not because it

is particularly representative of what a given designer did before or after the production of a given piece.[7] I found myself wishing for more actual reportage, if not history,
wondering what the designers (or the clients!) would have said they were up to—or
would have revealed they were looking at—at the point of making or commissioning
the work. There are a total of four "reference images" in this book (images that are
there as illustrations of outside influences), all in the introduction, all book covers of
theoretical texts.

I just don't believe that Poynor really thinks that the graphic design he is
describing was instigated entirely by designers obediently reading and translating theory
(and in fact he does address the issue of the [sometimes creative] misunderstanding or
misuse of theory), but his concentration on theory as the primary engine of change
seems a misrepresentation. Without a fuller explanation of what was behind the formal
experimentation, the admittedly challenging design and typography of this period can
appear to be pedantic and/or pretentious. I mean, who wants to see theory illustrated,
anyway?

The graphic design in *No More Rules* was simply not as purely bred by theory
as Poynor describes. In the chapter "Appropriation," Poynor connects the practice of
visual quotation from either historical or vernacular sources with the critique (citing
Fredric Jameson) that essentially says that when stylistic innovation is impossible,
contemporary art (and by extension, design) becomes empty, and more about itself.
He describes the distinction between parody and pastiche (in a nutshell: parody is
meaningful/good, and pastiche is meaningless/bad). Then Poynor walks through his
list: Barney Bubbles, Neville Brody, Tibor Kalman, Peter Saville, Paula Scher, Art
Chantry, Charles Spencer Anderson, and on to Old Navy, describing their work as if it
was created by a reaction to the existence of a theoretical debate (Old Navy?) around
postmodernism, and as if "retro" was invented around 1978.

But—in the words of another genius of the postmodern eighties, Pee Wee
Herman, "There's always a big but"[8]—this ignores the fact that there was a vivid, commercial, pop-cultural phenomenon of visual eclecticism and stylistic quotation that
existed as an alternate universe to young designers being trained as modernists in the
1970s. The work of Push Pin Studios was so influential in the publication design world
of New York, for instance, that by the mid- to late-1960s, the cool modernist school
of design associated with art director Alexey Brodovich and his successors was replaced,
at least in the upscale mass market magazines of the time, like *New York* or *Ms.*, with
rampant historicist typography. Not to mention the underground press; that was almost
uniformly historicist as well.[9] It is important to recognize that that eclecticism was
already a reaction to the hegemony of the photographic, typographic modernism established by the fifties generation of designers, such as Sutnar, Beall, Rand, Burtin, and
Golden.[10]

In the seventies a graphic design student might be asked to study Jan Tschichold
or the classical "Swiss" books of Emil Ruder and Joseph Muller-Brockmann, but he or
she was also probably spending a lot of time flipping through the bins at the local record
store, which were a whole alternative typographic education in themselves. It is easy to

forget how full of nostalgia and "appropriation" the imagery of pop music was, even in the sixties (look at the typography of *Rolling Stone* to this day, which adheres to a love of the muscular advertising vernacular of the American Type Foundry circa 1920), or how detached and "ironic" the imagery of a lot of pop music already was, even before Peter Saville (though he was really great at it). Who can explain why those naked kids are clambering up rocks on the cover of Led Zeppelin's *Houses of the Holy*?[11]

Next to Poynor's theory books and the big pile of magazines and album covers I'm proposing, I'd add the ironic visuals of Warhol, Ruscha, Richard Hamilton, and pop and conceptual art of many kinds; comic books, especially the underground ones; psychedelia of all sorts; "ad hocism"; the playfulness of Letraset; the relative novelty of Xerox art and mail art; Monty Python; and the deadpan vernacular of the National Lampoon parodies; not to mention all of the campiness of so much sixties culture, high and low. Poynor does mention the postmodern architects. There's no doubt that Venturi was important, and that by the seventies young graphic designers thought architecture was pretty interesting for its debates. And people were already scavenging through the flea markets for vintage clothing, old furniture, and printed matter, too; of course. The preferred era was the stuff just on the cusp of modernism, the thirties and the forties, which was valued for its ironic contrast to the stripped down, bland version of modernism one was supposed to master.

And if you were a student at Cranbrook in the seventies, you already knew Ed Fella's "art design" (though he did not call it that yet), which was already anticipating the tsunami of change. It was obvious. You did not need theory or Wolfgang Weingart to know which way the wind blew. And forward to the eighties: there was punk, the free-for-all of the Dutch work that was so inspiring (which Poynor does include), and where in the world is Tadanori Yokoo? I could go on and on, the point being that young designers in the seventies and eighties let life into what was a closed visual system. Though Poynor translates this largely as a search for autonomy or self-expression, I strongly disagree that this is all that accounts for the energy and effort of that work. I think the desire to make work that participated with as much intelligence and vitality as the rest of the culture was what was at stake!

That certainly was what motivated me, along with so many other young educators later in the eighties, to begin to work by revising the way that design was taught; that, and using design history, understanding that the visual conventions of modernism were not timeless truths, but instead, the results of a visual response to social, economic, and technological change, and that we were facing a similar situation. My question back in 1991 was, "If the audience has changed and the production has changed, and the messages might change, wouldn't common sense suggest that the notion of form might evolve too?"[12]

Poynor documents a lot of work that came out of the schools, but the limitations of his survey format hinder his explanation. For a time, some of the design schools were more responsible for creating a space where a little perspective and independence about the practice and the "profession" could occur than anywhere else. The formal investigations produced by students and teachers were produced against this context, which utilized, and was enabled by, a reading of critical theory, and had large targets. However, the forms themselves, despite the early resistance to them by an older guard, were so alluring (and so specific to a younger audience) that, like every other formal expression of a cultural idea in our consumer-based society, they entered into the life cycle of visual style; that is, they were marketed. It was not only for the students' benefit that David Carson, for instance, regularly visited several graphic design programs in the early nineties. The designer who continues to make big claims for the mystical power of intuition certainly—and wisely—saw something worthwhile in the sort of surrogate graduate study that he could access though his travels.

Another weird omission from *No More Rules* is the impact of the digital tools for motion circa the mid-nineties. There are no images of Web sites or frames of motion graphics included in the book at all! There is some discussion in the "Techno" section of the postmodern "simulacra" and the now charmingly old-fashioned optimism attached to it all in the pages of *Wired*, etc. But, again, Poynor's survey creates greater distinctions than actually existed between things that were in fact working simultaneously. Certainly the new "techno" tools had a big impact on "authorship" and this was expressed, again, through content, process, and form, since the space between conceptualization and designing (and publication) had so rearranged itself as to make the functionalist paradigm of modernism useless.

It is the ingestion of experimental styles by the marketing world that seems to have condemned the designers of these experiments (as if anyone participating in the Western economic system could escape that fate) in the eyes of so many now, including Rick Poynor.[13] At the very end of his book, he reveals his contempt for graphic design and designers (heavily hinted at by Chip Kidd's pastiche of a cover) by dumping them into an impossible conundrum: that the "Purpose and meaning of graphic design . . . is to sell things" and that any possibility of design having meaning beyond this depressing shallowness is dependent upon "fundamental systemic change," but in the meantime, why not ponder "resistance?" "To what sustained uses, other than its familiar and largely unquestioned commercial uses, might graphic design be applied?"[14]

Well gosh, there's all sorts of work that designers do that falls somewhere in the spectrum between marketing and protest (*Emigre* magazine, for instance), and I would argue that some of it is critical to the existence of what culture we have, unless you cynically write off all culture within a capitalist society as simply serving a market.

That we can even talk today about corporate work, commissioned work, independent work, designers as authors, designers as entrepreneurs, or designers as socialist resistance fighters represents one small triumph of the "experiments" that Poynor describes: that design is not just *one* thing anymore, but many (maybe too many) things. Now we have the freedom to call ourselves designers or whatever, with no one acting as gatekeeper. It's true that there are *No More Rules*. Now you are to be judged on the quality of your work, period. Today the curious question is what constitutes the designer's mind, but it's a collective problem, one that you see playing out in a lot of contemporary dialogue, even if it's not very articulate. But the generational dissing so prevalent in, say, the recent responses to "Rant," reminds me of what it sounds like to hear young women denigrate feminism. They have forgotten that the very ability to "make choices" is the result of the work of their predecessors, and an unflattering caricature of the efforts of the earlier generation has somehow superseded reality. The design equivalent—and Poynor's narrative—is that all that postmodern graphic design was concerned with was supercilious theory play, or formal solipsism, and it all got used up to sell sweaters or shoes, so who cares? In "Context in Critique," Dmitri Siegel proposes that what "graphic design needs is an opportunity for all sides in the Legibility Wars to come clean, a Truth and Reconciliation Commission of sorts. Then maybe we can move on and begin to examine graphic design as a process that inscribes economic and social context."[15] I wholeheartedly agree with Siegel: I just wish that *No More Rules* had supplied denser, richer, and more informed evidence of what transpired during the last twenty-five years, so that those who were not there to experience it firsthand might be able to make some sense of it. In the meantime, my paranoia about the historians taking over the story of graphic design has faded away, and every week some undergraduate reveals to me that another chunk of the very recent past is floating out to sea, as well. . . .

Notes

1. The catalog for the exhibition *The Avant-Garde in Russia 1910–1930: New Perspectives* (shown at the Los Angeles County Museum of Art in the summer of 1980, then at the Hirshhorn Museum in Washington, D.C. in the fall of the same year) states that it was the first major museum survey devoted to the Russian avant-garde in the United States.

2. In a recent conversation, Bonnell pointed out that the typography of the brochure, in which he mixed Garamond with Univers, was also cited by Rand as an abomination.

3. For a partial account of my time at graduate school from 1980 to 1982, see "That was then and this is now: but what is next?" in *Emigre*, no. 39 (summer 1996), pp. 18–33.

4. *Eye* made its debut in 1990; Rick Poynor was the editor for seven years, from issue no. 1 through issue no. 24.

5. See "Chairman's Essay" by Katherine McCoy, in the *Fourteenth Annual 100 Show, American Center for Design, Design Year in Review* (1992), pp. 4–6. In this essay, McCoy describes her idea to adjust the common competition format by encouraging the jurors to "curate" their choices as individuals (instead of trying to reach a consensus) and asking them to describe and defend their selections for publication in the *Annual*. Under the influence of postmodernism, McCoy felt no single idea at that moment could represent design practice, and opening up the jurying to specific personal choice (while asking the jury to justify their choices, for the record) would admit idiosyncratic and experimental works into the *Fourteenth Annual 100 Show* that might not have made it in under the old and unarticulated system. These reforms were also meant to deal with an old complaint against competitions as often presenting bland work because the closed nature of the consensual jurying made the choices seem capricious. Despite the greater transparency of the competition process that her reforms produced, the selections—and the reputation of the jury—still came under attack. See Michael Bierut's introduction "Planetarium," in *Planetarium: The 100 Show, The Fifteenth Annual of the American Center for Design, Design Year in Review* (1993), pp. 5–7. Bierut's attack (which was published in *Statements*, the journal of the American Center of Design, the following year) engendered further debate over the "rules" and purposes of design competitions, but it is clear to this reader, looking back on it all, that Bierut's original attack on the results of the *Fourteenth Annual 100 Show* was as much about the inclusion of the sorts of postmodern graphic design work of which, at that point, Bierut did not approve, as it was about any qualms he had about the jurying of the *Fourteenth Annual 100 Show*. I offer this sketch of just one more of the many skirmishes over graphic design as evidence of the turmoil of the times (which is perhaps underrepresented in *No More Rules*).

6. The most glaring example of this is the *Night Gallery* poster by Art Chantry (p. 86). The prolific Seattle designer Chantry has always been extremely catholic in his use of a variety of graphic styles, and while the *Night Gallery* poster of 1991 has the right date, Chantry's ironic use of many vernaculars predates the "theoriz-ing" of the vernacular that Poyner describes, and seems to connect Chantry to debates to which I doubt he

paid attention. Following his discussion of Chantry, Poynor's description of Charles S. Anderson and his "bonehead" style seems to miss the deliberately anti-ironic (and completely antitheoretical) nature of his work. So while Chantry's work and Anderson's work look similar, they are still bodies of work that are quite different in concept, despite their creators' shared indifference to theory (and despite the fact that their work looks good together on a page).

7. *Pee Wee's Big Adventure* (1985).

8. For a discussion of eclecticism in publication design in the 1960s and 1970s, see "1968 and After: Underground and Up Again" in *Modern Magazine Design* by William Owen (Dubuque, Iowa: William C. Brown Publishers, 1991), pp. 102–113.

9. Visual boredom and generational contrariness are underacknowledged as motivators for formal mutation in graphic design. Two examples: years ago, while freelancing for Milton Glaser, I was telling him about some volunteer work that I was doing for the librarians at the Cooper-Hewitt Museum, to help them sort some studio archives that had been given to them by the heirs of Ladislav Sutnar. Glaser's response was to tell me how awful he thought Sutnar's work was; that it exemplified the kind of design (from the generation immediately preceding his) to which he and his fellow young designers of Push Pin Studios were in direct reaction. Edward Fella also describes his early Detroit fake-Art-Deco "shiny shoe" illustrative lettering work as a joke that he launched in response to the clean modern style that prevailed even in the advertising world of 1950s Detroit.

10. Apparently, not even the designer! Aubrey Powell (member of the British design group Hipgnosis, which was responsible for some of the most iconic and "detached" album covers of the 1970s) has said that when they were commissioned to design the sleeve for Led Zeppelin's *Houses of the Holy* (1973), they were given neither a title nor music as a reference, so the designers just went ahead and based their design on a science fiction novel that they were enthusiastic about. (Pity that they did not base it on Barthes.) See *www.superseventies. com/ac1.8housesoftheholy.html.*

11. Lorraine Wild, "Graphic Design: Lost and Found" in *The Edge of the Millennium: An International Critique of Architecture, Urban Planning, Product and Communication Design*, edited by Susan Yelavich (New York: Cooper-Hewitt, National Museum of Design, Smithsonian Institution, and Whitney Library of Design, 1993), p.101.

12. Even this is not a new argument. For instance, here is Sheila de Bretteville writing in 1973: "The rigid separation between work and leisure, attitudes and values, male and female—which, we noted above, is reinforced by the tradition of simplification in the mass media and it also operates in product and environmental design. A few new voices were raised in the sixties who appreciated, not only complexity and contradiction, but the value of participation in the popular vernacular. However, the connection and response to the multiplicity of human potential was lost as their attitude became style and fashion.[. . .]" from "Some Aspects of Design from a Woman Designer" first published in *Icographic* 6 (Croydon, England: 1973), reprinted in *Looking Closer 3: Classic Writings on Graphic Design*, edited by M. Bierut, J. Helfand, S. Heller, and R. Poynor (New York: Allworth Press, 1999), p. 145. In this passage, de Bretteville raises the possibility that it is impossible for any critique that is offered via form to retain its legibility once it has entered the inevitable life cycle of style.

13. *No More Rules*, p. 171.

14. Dmitri Siegel, "Context in Critique." *Adbusters* (September/October 2003), archived at *www.typotheque.com/ articles/rant_reviewed.html.*

15. Ibid.

MY COUNTRY IS NOT A BRAND
William Drenttel

Branding was originally an approach for creating reputations for commercial products. Over time, it has come to be applied to almost everything, from high school sports to school meal programs; from universities to research centers; from art museums to ballet companies to cultural institutions; from political campaigns to cities to states. Today, even nations have become brands.

Item: Last month, we flew to Toronto to attend the Ontario Design Conference. The weakest presentation came from the global director of a large branding firm. Among other objectionable tactics, a canned PowerPoint presentation displayed, at a certain point, three brand logos simultaneously: Kodak, the Bay (a leading Canadian retail brand), and the American flag. I was outraged, and all I could think was, *my country is not a brand.*

Item: That same week, Robert George wrote a cover story for the *New Republic* titled "Conscientious Objector: Why I Can't Vote for Bush." This is how he ended his indictment: "At crucial points before and after the Iraq war, Bush's middle managers have failed him, and the 'brand' called America has suffered in the world market." According to his argument, U.S. officials should be summarily dismissed because they have let their shareholders down and the *brand* has suffered in the marketplace.

Item: In the most recent issue of *Eye* (no. 53), devoted to "Brand Madness," Nick Bell cites the example of Charlotte Beers, former CEO of Ogilvy & Mather, who was hired by the U.S. State Department to "combat rising tides of anti-Americanism." Bell quotes Naomi Klein: "Secretary of State Colin Powell dismissed criticism of the appointment: 'There is nothing wrong with getting somebody who knows how to sell something. . . . We need someone who can re-brand American foreign policy. . . . She got me to buy Uncle Ben's Rice.' "

Item: Not long ago, in a *New York Times* magazine interview, Bruce Mau urged designers to embrace "the richness of the marketplace." By way of example, he described his own approach to this Herculean task: "We are being asked to work on a vision for the future of Guatemala. How can we design Guatemala over the next ten years?"

What's most troubling here is the deeply inappropriate vocabulary we choose to deploy as we randomly penetrate such allegedly foreign disciplines as politics and

Originally published on *www.designobserver.com* (November 25, 2004).

international diplomacy. The decision to vote for George Bush based on his handling of the American brand? Defending a State Department foreign policy hire because, "SHE GOT ME TO BUY UNCLE BEN'S RICE"? A designer who believes that, based on his own knowledge of the marketplace, he can re-design the future of a country, albeit just a little one in Central America? While we're at it, let's not forget Rem Koolhaas designing a bar-coded flag for the capitalistic future of the European Union, or Landor setting out to "brand" entire countries, including Jordan and Hong Kong.

Nick Bell's discussion of "The Steamroller of Branding" in *Eye* is a thoughtful critique, which examines the process of creating identities for art museums and performing arts centers. Bell notes in particular the way branding has crept into the *experience* of the art—how it has actually invaded the space of the gallery and performance locale—rather than focusing solely on the commercial activities of these cultural institutions. I agree wholeheartedly with this assessment—yet I find this singular focus on the branding of art and performance institutions somewhat vexing, as it inherently leads back to an impenetrable dichotomy between *art* and *commerce*. Weren't the signatories of the *First Things First Manifesto* attacked for privileging high culture above commercial culture? Ultimately, this minimizes the importance of this essential critique of "brand madness" that makes the newest suite of *Eye* essays so imperative.

The problem with "Content" is that it risks becoming a fundamentally generic concept: in this way, it's not unlike the way "the brand" has become simply "Brand," sometimes invoked with an almost religious-like tone. (Whenever I hear these terms used in this way, I'm reminded of Goethe writing about the Sublime.) Content should not be an abstraction for designers, but rather something to be evaluated in specific and differentiated terms. It is in its specificity that designers need to begin making distinctions—distinctions that are not merely programmatic or pragmatic, but that carry with them implicit moral dimensions.

There is, for instance, a difference between helping an NGO to fundraise and helping an NGO to disseminate information about the state of the world in a crisis zone. Given the requirements of capitalism and communication in a branding-laden culture, such overtly divergent goals are, oddly, being subsumed under the same umbrella of *branding*. And yet they could not be more different.

The CARE identity program—its logo and its branding applications—are not the same as its challenge to the United Nations to take strong action in the Sudan. Its project no.SDN099 funds reproductive and psychosocial health services for abducted children and survivors of sexual violence in South Darfur. Meanwhile, through its corporate partners, Cisco Systems is helping to feed widows in Afghanistan, and Starbucks and CARE are "Winning Together" to fight global poverty, especially in major coffee-growing areas of the world. Of course, you cannot find CARE in Iraq because they have withdrawn after "the apparent death of Mrs. Margaret Hassan." But right next to the "Donate Now! Sudan Crisis" button, you can "Click here to voice your sympathy for her family."

This is but one instance in which the muddled notions of branding are communicated, and even here there are multiple types of content revealed: some tragic, some critical to the future of a geopolitical region, some involving genocide, some abjectly promotional. What is missing, however, are distinctions: distinctions between marketing efforts (CARE fundraising for hunger) and promotional initiatives (Starbucks feeding hungry laborers in Columbia); between communication (CARE reporting on a crisis zone) and advocacy (CARE trying to persuade the UN to intervene in Darfur); and between news feeds (Margaret Hassan's brutal murder) and community (at the push of a button, send her family your heartfelt condolences now). The future of peace in entire regions of the world is the *topic*, and yet the *form* for our experience is fundamentally filtered and branded—just as in Nick Bell's example of the filtered and branded experience of art in museums.

Branding, of course, has its value, its place in commerce and its confirmed role in the implementation of certain design initiatives. At its best, it leads to better commercial communication, to understanding the needs of an audience, or to building long-term relationships with consumers. And yes: wouldn't the world be a better world if more countries understood (and by conjecture, respected) the perspectives of other countries? Wouldn't America be more successful in the Arab and Muslim world if it were a little less interested in cheap oil and a little more interested in their culture, their interests, and their needs? Wouldn't it help if the United States had more people in its State Department who spoke fluent Arabic? (As of last year, there were only 54, according to the Advisory Group on Public Diplomacy's report, *Changing Minds, Winning Peace.*)

Meanwhile, we set our sights on branding the war, with sound bytes and promotional bumpers like "Operation Desert Storm" and "Operation Iraqi Freedom." In England, "Britain TM" is created for the Blair administration by Demos, based loosely on the premise of "Cool Britannia." There are also studies giving legitimacy to the "Branding of Britain in relation to the Brand South Africa." In Iraq, even before it had achieved independence as a sovereign nation, branding experts had a plan for a new Iraqi flag, a design that today might be characterized as either a failure of process or of research. At the end of the day, it was neither: it was a failure of intent. The symbol for a country should not be created by branding experts.

When the vocabulary of a nation's foreign policy is the vocabulary of branding, then it is, in fact, selling Uncle Ben's Rice. This transaction, with the vocabulary of the supermarket counter, is not how I envision my country speaking to the rest of the world.

SECTION V:
GRAPHIC DESIGN AS PASSION

THE CULT OF GRAPHIC DESIGN

Adrian Shaughnessy

Graphic design used to be homogeneous: everyone agreed about the fundamental principles, even if they disagreed about what was good design and what was bad design. But that's changing. In fact, in recent years design has begun to separate into two distinct strands. On the one hand we have mainstream graphic design; this is the professional practice of graphic design in all its myriad forms. Everything from the activities of big, brand-fixated design groups to socially important tasks like designing leaflets for the local hospital. Or, to put it another way, graphic design fulfilling its traditional role as a conveyor of information and a transmitter of commercial messages.

On the other hand, we now have another sort of graphic design. It is mostly done by small groups or individuals. Stylistically it is usually radical, adventurous, and sometimes even downright purposeless. It includes self-initiated activities like publishing books, magazines, and Web sites, and designing and selling items of graphic paraphernalia—T-shirts, posters, and DVDs. You might almost describe this as "design for design's sake." But perhaps a more accurate description is "design-culture graphics."

Not much new in this, you might think. Graphic design has always had its mainstream, and it has always had its maverick offshoots. But there's a new twist in all this. In many ways, both strands—mainstream graphics and design-culture graphics—are remarkably similar: both are done for money and both take their origin from a brief. What differentiates the two is that design-culture graphics caters to a new audience: it caters to the followers of the cult of graphic design.

The emergence of a nonprofessional cult—or culture—around graphic design is new. Until recently, graphic design was a well-kept secret that remained within the professional realm. Explaining to elderly (and not so elderly) relatives that you were a graphic designer was hard work: so you're a printer, they'd say. It got a bit easier in the eighties and nineties. Design became sexy and no business could afford to ignore the blandishments of big design groups offering business-nirvana via the medium of professional design—especially if they wore big glasses with bright red rims. More recently, another leap forward occurred when PCs became ubiquitous. Suddenly,

Originally published in *Creative Review* (April 2004).

nondesigners had fonts, drawing tools, and graphics packages, enabling them to combine images and text in a passable approximation of professional work. Graphic design was becoming less invisible.

One of the first signs of this new visibility was the explosion in the number of design books and magazines. Design books have been around almost since the start of graphic design, but they were usually published by small publishers for a strictly professional or academic audience, and were famously hard to find. Now you can buy them in mainstream bookshops. Design magazines and academic journals have also been around for a while. But a new generation of magazines in the eighties and nineties played a crucial part in promoting design awareness and creating the beginnings of a nonprofessional culture of design. It did this by chronicling the work and ethos of groups like Tomato and individual designers like Peter Saville. The impact of Tomato was a major factor in the rise of design-culture graphics. They avoided the jargon of the red-spectacled design consultants; they talked about "process" and not about "solutions." They were doers, and their work had a signature. In fact, they behaved like artists—but they were unquestionably graphic designers.

It has always been a fundamental belief of graphic design that the designer must never become the story; it would get in the way of the client's message. In America, David Carson and Stefan Sagmeister ignored this nostrum and promoted themselves ruthlessly. They published monographs and they were endlessly profiled in magazines. In the end, they become more famous than the work they produced. At the same time, other designers were stretching the boundaries of graphic design. By flaunting sacred rules such as legibility and clarity, and by promoting notions of design-authorship and the development of signature styles, design began to attract the attention of people interested in contemporary culture in the widest sense. Today, the result of all this is the emergence of the cult of graphic design. Like other cults, it has its celebrities and it has its own magazines. And it is undoubtedly fuelled by the vast numbers of design students that the government is shoe-horning into universities, sadly without the requisite number of jobs for them when they graduate.

An insight into design-culture graphics was given to me by Marc Valli, who runs the enterprising chain of Magma bookshops. There are now three Magma stores—two in London and one in Manchester—selling design books and graphic paraphernalia. This fact alone tells us something about the rise of design culture, but Valli has gone a step further and has launched a magazine called *Graphic* ("not after graphic design," he stresses, "but after the expression 'graphic culture'"). *Graphic* is unlike the other more professionally focused design magazines. It is really a fanzine for design culture.

Valli is uniquely well-placed to comment on trends in design outside of the professional sector, and he's convinced there is a sea-change taking place. "In my opinion," he notes, "graphic-design has stopped being just a specialist discipline to become a culture. Design book publishers keep describing the market for graphic-design books as being a 'professional' market. But when you look at our Covent Garden and Manchester shops on a Saturday afternoon you will find that they are filled with young people who are interested and passionate about design but whose jobs have nothing to do with design. There is nothing very 'professional' about the whole thing."

There are other places to see design culture at work. Try the online discussion group on The Designers Republic Web site. Called "Speak/Discuss," it is a vibrant exchange of views, tips, moans, and noisy outbursts. It's hard to tell who the contributors are: most seem to have some connection to the professional design world (there are lots of anguished riffs about employment prospects), and many appear to be design students. Yet others are clearly just design fans, united by a fan-like interest in the doings of fashionable design groups, and a highly informed interest in the subject of graphic design.

You can also look at the interest surrounding a group like Airside. Helped by their links to Lemon Jelly—just as Tomato's links to Underworld helped them—Airside have plugged themselves into the wider arena of music. Their self-published calendar has become a cult buy. It probably hasn't outsold Justin Timberlake's posters, but it's a hot, sought-after design-culture artifact.

Next year the Barbican launches an exhibition called *Communicate: Independent British Graphic Design since the Sixties*. The Barbican (which, in my experience, is a more commercially minded organization than its often radical programming schedule might indicate) are doing this, you assume, to appeal to a wider audience than a purely professional audience; to do this they will need to tap into the design-culture audience.

There are many other examples of graphic design coming out of its professional shell. Lots of design groups sell posters and T-shirts from their Web sites, and many young designers appear to regard being featured in books and magazines as highly as—if not more highly than—they regard the traditional designer activities of winning jobs, earning fees, and building stable practices. It's not that they don't do these things, it's just that the other stuff is now hugely important.

And although we're still a few years away from the design-culture world becoming self-sustaining, the old professional-world hegemony is being challenged. It is being forced to accept a new offspring: a lively, kicking baby. It is a tiny market, but it will grow. In many ways it mirrors the split that has existed for the past few decades in the record business. The music industry is dominated by big global labels supplying music to the mass market. But there is also a vast web of tiny labels—often run by one person—releasing music to specialist audiences. As the big labels become more and more conglomeratized, the difference between the two strands is sharper than ever before. In fact, the world of small labels is almost totally disconnected from the world of the major labels. They barely occupy the same universe.

Is this rupture likely in graphic design? Probably not. Design-culture graphics needs to stay within the commercial sphere. But increasingly it looks as if there will be a branch of graphic design separated from the professional world. We're not talking about airy notions of "design as art" here, either—it's definitely graphic design, and part of its attraction to a young audience is its roots in commercial world activities. To this audience, the world of branding and commercially rooted imagery is as attractive, if not more so, than art. Or as Marc Valli describes it, "the visual culture we all float in, an environment densely populated with digital technologies, but also an environment in which people express themselves in a language and a style that is very vivid, direct, bold, basic, devious, dangerous—well, graphic."

GRAPHIC FANTASIES:
REFLECTIONS IN THE GLASS CEILING
Véronique Vienne

Recently, in a book of short essays, I came across the description of a man fantasizing about a woman he met in a train. He imagined running his hand through her chestnut hair, caressing the back of her neck, and sliding his hand inside the sleeve of her sweater. Oh, that again, I thought. But I was startled out of my complacency when the hero began to speculate that the mysterious woman might be a graphic designer.

Wait a minute. The writer's comment felt like an intrusion. Graphic design is one of the few professions that's free from sexual stereotyping. Even though there is a glass ceiling—in the design field, women are still a minority in top managerial positions—their femininity is not the issue. Girls who can tell Bodoni from Helvetica are not typecast. Not yet, at least. Even though their medium is visual, their physical appearance has never been objectified.

But maybe it's time women in the graphic field claim their sexual identity instead of denying it. After all, women designers are increasingly more visible as cultural icons. Last time I checked, there are 5,770 Google entries for Deborah Sussman, 5,240 for Ellen Lupton, and 2,970 for Paula Scher. Not bad when compared with formidable women architects Maya Ying Lin and Zaha Hadid, for instance, who have respectively 2,110 and 6,710 Google entries.

But for female designers, visibility doesn't translate into influence. Because they do not want to be labeled as "women," these accomplished practitioners are reluctant to affirm their uniquely feminine perspective. Case in point: a typical meeting I was part of recently where a dozen design and marketing professionals, mostly women, were discussing the design direction of a popular product for women. All the solutions proposed

Originally published in *Graphis*, no. 340 (2002), p. 12.

by the team embraced as gospel the feminine clichés of the moment—sensuality, softness, "organic" shapes, pastel colors. Whenever one of us strayed from the accepted norms, proposing a less sugar-coated approach, you could feel reprobation from the group, as if we were under oath not to challenge hackneyed notions concerning gender.

An hour into the meeting, I noticed one of the attendees, a quiet young man who had been sketching on a pad all along. Peeking over his shoulders, I realized that he was turning every single idea proposed by the group into a slick rendering. But all his drawings looked the same. Rocket-shaped variations of the feminine form, they reinforced the assumption we all took for granted: that women are attracted to shapes that reflect masculine fantasies of the idealized female body.

I looked around the room: all the women took great pride in being mature, professional, and marketing savvy. Yet no one—including myself—was ready to give the kind of authentic feedback that might upset the client. When you are paid a four-figure day-fee as a consultant, you choose your battles carefully, and I didn't feel that taking what would be perceived as a strident feminist stand would be constructive.

But the next generation of designers, it seems, will be less cautious when asserting their gender perspective. In a recent design criticism exercise, graphic design students of a class I teach at the School of Visual Arts in New York—the majority of them female in their early twenties—bluntly assessed the design of an architecture magazine as being "not feminine enough."

"What exactly do you mean by 'not feminine enough'?" I asked, amused and delighted by their candid appraisal. They needed no soul-searching to come up with answers.

"Feminine means subtle, not obvious."

"Feminine means less goal-oriented—more open-ended."

"Feminine means more complex, and more insightful."

"Feminine means 'Don't tell me what to think'."

You can always count on students to teach you a valuable lesson. When refusing to be labeled as women designers, the smart women of my generation unwittingly embrace an oversimplification that's typically masculine. Enough already. We are not images reflected in a glass ceiling.

EXPERIMENTAL TYPOGRAPHY.
WHATEVER THAT MEANS
Peter Bilak

Very few terms have been used so habitually and carelessly as the word "experiment." In the field of graphic design and typography, experiment as a noun has been used to signify anything new, unconventional, defying easy categorization, or confounding expectations. As a verb, "to experiment" is often synonymous with the design process itself, which may not exactly be helpful, considering that all design is a result of the design process. The term "experiment" can also have the connotation of an implicit disclaimer; it suggests not taking responsibility for the result. When students are asked what they intend by creating certain forms, they often say, "It's just an experiment. . .," when they don't have a better response.

In a scientific context, an experiment is a test of an idea; a set of actions performed to prove or disprove a hypothesis. Experimentation in this sense is an empirical approach to knowledge that lays a foundation upon which others can build. It requires all measurements to be made objectively under controlled conditions, which allows the procedure to be repeated by others, thus proving that a phenomenon occurs after a certain action, and that the phenomenon does not occur in the absence of the action.

An example of a famous scientific experiment would be Galileo Galilei's dropping of two objects of different weights from the Pisa tower to demonstrate that both would land at the same time, proving his hypothesis about gravity. In this sense, a typographic experiment might be a procedure to determine whether humidity affects the transfer of ink onto a sheet of paper, and if it does, how.

A scientific approach to experimentation, however, seems to be valid only in a situation where empirical knowledge is applicable, or in a situation where the outcome of the experiment can be reliably measured. What happens when the outcome is ambiguous, nonobjective, not based on pure reason? In the recent book *The Typographic Experiment: Radical Innovation in Contemporary Type Design*, the author, Teal Triggs, asks thirty-seven internationally recognized designers to define their understandings of the term "experiment."

Originally published in *Items* 1 (March/April, 2005) (and published in Dutch under the title "Grenzen aan vernieuwing"), this English version was first published in the book *We Want You To Love Type* (Den Haag: Typotheque, 2005).

As expected, the published definitions couldn't be more disparate. They are marked by personal belief systems and biased by the experiences of the designers. While Hamish Muir of 8vo writes "Every type job is experiment," Melle Hammer insists that "Experimental typography does not exist, nor ever has." So how is it possible that there are such diverse understandings of a term that is so commonly used?

Among the designers' various interpretations, two notions of experimentation are dominant. The first one is formulated by the American designer David Carson: "Experimental is something I haven't tried before . . . something that hasn't been seen and heard." Carson and several other designers suggest that the nature of experiment lies in the formal novelty of the result. There are many precedents for this opinion, but in an era when information travels faster than ever before and when we have achieved unprecedented archive of information, it becomes significantly more difficult to claim a complete novelty of forms. While over ninety years ago Kurt Schwitters proclaimed that to "do it in a way that no one has done it before" was sufficient for the definition of the new typography of his day—and his work was an appropriate example of such an approach—today things are different. Designers are more aware of the body of work and the discourse accompanying it. Proclaiming novelty today can seem like historical ignorance on a designer's part.

Interestingly, Carson's statement also suggests that the essence of experimentation is in going against the prevailing patterns, rather than being guided by conventions. This is directly opposed to the scientific usage of the word, where an experiment is designed to add to the accumulation of knowledge; in design, where results are measured subjectively, there is a tendency to go against the generally accepted base of knowledge. In science a single person can make valuable experiments, but a design experiment that is rooted in anticonventionalism can only exist against the background of other—conventional—solutions. In this sense, it would be impossible to experiment if one were the only designer on earth, because there would be no standard for the experiment. Anticonventionalism requires going against prevailing styles, which are perceived as conventional. If more designers joined forces and worked in a similar fashion, the scale would change, and the former convention would become anticonventional. The fate of such experimentation is a permanent confrontation with the mainstream; a circular, cyclical race, where it is not certain who is chasing whom.

Does type design and typography allow an experimental approach at all? The alphabet is by its very nature dependent on and defined by conventions. Type design that is not bound by convention is like a private language: both lack the ability to communicate. Yet it is precisely the constraints of the alphabet that inspire many designers. A recent example is the work of Thomas Huot-Marchand, a French postgraduate type designer who investigates the limits of legibility while physically reducing the basic forms of the alphabet. Minuscule is his project of size-specific typography. While the letters for regular reading sizes are very close to conventional book typefaces, each step down in size results in simplification of the letter-shapes. In the extremely small sizes (2pt) Minuscule Deux becomes an abstract reduction of the alphabet, free of all the details and optical corrections that are usual for fonts designed for text reading. Huot-Marchand's project builds upon the work of French ophthalmologist Louis Emile Javal, who published similar research at the beginning of the twentieth century. The practical contribution of both projects is limited, since the reading process is still guided by the physical limitations of the human eye; however, Huot-Marchand and Javal both investigate the constraints of legibility within which typography functions.

The second dominant notion of experiment in *The Typographic Experiment* was formulated by Michael Worthington, a British designer and educator based in the United States: "True experimentation means to take risks." If taken literally, such a statement is of little value: immediately we would ask what is at stake and what typographers are really risking. Worthington, however, is referring to the risk involved with not knowing the exact outcome of the experiment in which the designers are engaged.

A similar definition is offered by the *E.A.T. (Experiment and Typography)* exhibition presenting thirty-five type designers and typographers from the Czech Republic and Slovakia, which coincidentally will arrive in the Netherlands shortly. Alan Záruba and Johanna Baluaíková, the curators of *E.A.T.*, put their focus on development and process when describing the concept of the exhibition: "The show focuses on projects which document the development of designers' ideas. Attention is paid to the process of creating innovative solutions in the field of type design and typography, often engaging experimental processes as a means to approach unknown territory."

An experiment in this sense has no preconceived idea of the outcome; it only sets out to determine a cause-and-effect relationship. As such, experimentation is a method of working which is contrary to production-oriented design, in which the aim of the process is not to create something new, but to achieve an already known, preformulated result.

Belgian designer Brecht Cuppens has created Sprawl, an experimental typeface based on cartography, which takes into account the density of population in Belgium. In Sprawl, the silhouette of each letter is identical, so that when typed they lock into each other. The filling of the letters, however, varies according to the frequency of use of the letter in the Dutch language. The most frequently used letter (*e*) represents the highest density of population. The most infrequently used letter (*q*) corresponds to the lowest density. Setting a sample text creates a Cuppens representation of the Belgian landscape.

Another example of experiment as a process of creation without anticipation of the fixed result is an online project Ortho-type. (*www.ortho-type.it*) The trio of authors, Enrico Bravi, Mikkel Crone Koser, and Paolo Palma, describe ortho-type as "an exercise in perception, a stimulus for the mind and the eye to pick out and process three-dimensional planes on a flat surface. . . ."Ortho-type is an online application of a typeface designed to be recognizable in three dimensions. In each view, the viewer can set any of the available variables: length, breadth, depth, thickness, color, and rotation, and generate multiple variations of the model. The user can also generate those variations as a traditional 2D PostScript font.

Although this kind of experimental process has no commercial application, its results may feed other experiments and be adapted to commercial activities. Once assimilated, the product is no longer experimental. David Carson may have started his formal experiments out of curiosity, but now similar formal solutions have been adapted by commercial giants such as Nike, Pepsi, and Sony.

Following this line, we can go further to suggest that no completed project can be seriously considered experimental. It is experimental only in the process of its creation. When completed, it only becomes part of the body of work that it was meant to challenge. As soon as the experiment achieves its final form it can be named, categorized, and analyzed according to any conventional system of classification and referencing.

An experimental technique that is frequently used is to bring together various working methods that are recognized separately but rarely combined. For example, language is studied systematically by linguists, who are chiefly interested in spoken languages and in the problems of analyzing them as they operate at a given point in time. Linguists rarely, however, venture into the visible representation of language, because they consider it artificial and thus secondary to spoken language. Typographers, on the other hand, are concerned with the appearance of type in print and other reproduction technologies; they often have substantial knowledge of composition, color theories, proportions, paper, etc., yet often lack knowledge of the language that they represent.

These contrasting interests are brought together in the work of Pierre di Sciullo, a French designer who pursues his typographic research in a wide variety of media. His typeface Sintétik reduces the letters of the French alphabet to the core phonemes (sounds which distinguish one word from another) and compresses it to fifteen characters. Di Sciullo stresses the economic aspect of such a system, with an average book being reduced by about 30 percent when multiple spellings of the same sound are made redundant. For example, the French words for skin (*peaux*) and pot (*pot*) are both reduced to the simplest representation of their pronunciation—*po*. Words set in Sintétik can be understood only when read aloud, returning the reader to the medieval experience of oral reading.

Quantange is another font specific to the French language. It is basically a phonetic alphabet that visually suggests the pronunciation, rhythm, and pace of reading. Every letter in Quantange has as many different shapes as there are ways of pronouncing it: the letter *c*, for example, has two forms because it can be pronounced as *s* or *k*. Di Sciullo suggests that Quantange would be particularly useful to foreign students of French or to actors and presenters who need to articulate the inflectional aspect of language not indicated by traditional scripts. This project builds on experiments of early avant-garde designers: the work of the Bauhaus, Kurt Schwitters, and Jan Tschichold.

Di Sciullo took inspiration from the reading process when he designed a typeface for setting the horizontal palindromes of Georges Perec (Perec has written the longest palindrome on record, a poem of 1388 words which can be read both ways;

see *http://graner.net/nicolas/salocin/ten.renarg//:ptth*). The typeface is a combination of lower- and uppercase and is designed to be read from both sides, left and right. (This is great news to every Bob, Hannah, or Eve.) Di Sciullo's typefaces are very playful and their practical aspects are limited, yet like the other presented examples of experiments in typography, his works point to previously unexplored areas of interest, which enlarges our understanding of the field.

Although most of the examples shown here are marked by the recent shift of interest in European graphic design from forms to ideas, and the best examples combine both, there is no definitive explanation of what constitutes an experiment in typography. As the profession develops and more people practice this subtle art, we continually redefine the purpose of experimentation and become aware of its moving boundaries.

DESIGN AS RELIGION
Nick Currie

Showing a graphic design student around my hometown of Edinburgh, Scotland this Christmas, I happened to choose a route that led from one of the city's oldest and most sacred interiors, Saint Giles Cathedral, consecrated in 1243, to one of its newest, a design and contemporary culture store called Analogue, opened in 2001.

Analogue strikes me as a sacred space: calm flagstones and pebbles surround low minimalist tables; lecterns bear beautiful, illuminated books, CDs, DVDs, and magazines. Whereas the Saint Giles gift shop betrays a syncretistic and somewhat confused hodgepodge of beliefs—pots of honey jostle for shelf-space with Russian icons, aromatherapy scents, and books of Scottish ghost stories—Analogue has an admirable clarity of purpose, a spiritual focus, even a whiff of severity about it. Ghost stories and other tourist trinkets would not be tolerated here. A Zen modernist atmosphere prevails. People speak in whispers.

I leaf through some Gasbook creators' specials, then pluck up the courage to speak to Analogue's bearded "high priest," founder Russell Ferguson. He tells me he was inspired to open the place by reading about Colette, the curated "select shop" in Paris. He's still never been to Colette, but he's made pilgrimages to Magma in London and Zakka in New York. Inspired by them, he intends to transform his back room into an art gallery soon.

Originally published in *Voice: AIGA Journal of Design* (January 2005).

I'm impressed. Edinburgh never had a store like this when I lived there. If it had, it might have changed my life. I ask Russell (who didn't go to art college, but opened Analogue after managing Edinburgh's arthouse cinema, The Filmhouse) whether he thinks the design bookshop boom is a product of the nineties. He tells me that it probably is; Colette was founded in 1997, Magma in 2000. Russell chose the name "Analogue" because, in a postdigital culture, "analogue" is exactly what books are: they're objects, but made special by our immersion in electrons. The analogue and the digital complement each other.

Right now, Analogue is doing okay thanks to the fact that intelligent lay people as well as art students and professional designers come in to buy books about design. But Russell thinks that the cult may be played out within five years; he fully expects to move on to something else.

Analogue has a selection of music CDs and creative magazines; I open electronica bible *The Wire* and glance through some year-end surveys by music journalists. A paragraph by someone called Richard Henderson catches my eye. "Irony and solipsism have supplanted the visceral intelligence that, not so long ago, was the stuff of music," Henderson complains. "We inhabit, after all, a landscape where digital typefaces carry the cultural purpose once accorded hit singles."

Aha! That's a very telling grouch, a jealous snipe at design from a music journalist. As a musician turned design commentator myself, I can't help wondering whether the sanctity of 1970s rock music (with its fiercely vocational, charismatic, illuminated gurus, its passionate converts and adepts) has now passed to design. Do aspirational, spiritually minded people now turn to "contemporary visual culture" to fill their god-shaped holes?

Conservative blogger Michael Blowhard seems to think so. In a recent column he ponders what he sees as design's pretentious spiritual tendencies:

> As far as I can tell, for many graphic-design people, "good design" is a crusade. They get worked-up about "good design"; for them, the "good" in "good design" is a moral "good" and not just a cool or snazzy "good." Graphic design can save the world! I find this attitude so bewildering that I wonder whether graphic designers are initiates in a cult I know nothing about.

Blowhard (a conservative who hides his barbs behind impeccable politeness) finds the source of design's questionable cultishness in a book by Alain Weill, *Graphic Design: A History*:

> I feel like a dimwit for having been so clueless. Wouldn't you know it: the idea of "graphic design" was born with our old friend and curse, modernism. It had—and in the eyes of many graphic designers still has—a revolutionary program. Which means that, by my standards anyway, "graphic design" really is a bit of a cult. Evidently you either believe in the program and you draw your energy from it, or you aren't a real graphic designer.

It's certainly true that many modernist creators had high-flown spiritual rhetoric to match their utopian political agendas. Architect Mies Van Der Rohe, for instance, said "Architecture is the real battle of the spirit," and believed that "God is in the details." According to Mies, "the battle for the New Dwelling is only a part of the larger struggle for new ways of living."

The tone is strikingly similar to the Magma Web site. "Once books were carriers of light and knowledge," Magma solemnly informs surfers. "They were worshipped and they were feared. They were recognised as a rich and reactive substance, a highly nourishing and volatile matter. . . . A powerful source. Our hope is that when people walk into Magma they will realise something, something will have changed in the way they perceive things. . . . We hope Magma won't be just a place that sells books, magazines, brochures, CD-ROMs, DVDs, objects, toys, T-shirts. . . . We hope that Magma will become a way of watching the world change and evolve."

Well, here's my credo. I'm not a designer, but I love design. I love stores like Analogue, Magma, and Zakka. I enter them as reverently as Philip Larkin entered a church, removing his bicycle clips and doffing his hat. To me they're temples to human creativity, places dedicated to higher values, yes, even spiritual values. In a world that knows the price of everything and the value of nothing, these stores and the curated, inspirational printed matter they contain reaffirm my belief that beauty really is elevating and that every "creator" is a kind of god. However pompous, pretentious, trendy, vain, empty, elitist, or silly it may appear to non-initiates, our cult does contain values I'd call "spiritual." I hope it continues and expands. If we spread the word, the congregation will rise.

URLs
Analogue Books, Edinburgh: *www.analoguebooks.co.uk*
Colette select store, Paris: *www.colette.fr*
Magma Books, London: *www.magmabooks.com/content/service/about.asp*
Zakka, New York: *www.zakkacorp.com/home.php*
Michael Blowhard on graphic design:
www.2blowhards.com/archives/001798.html#001798

DESIGNING UNDER THE INFLUENCE
Michael Bierut

The other day I was interviewing a young designer, just nine months out of school. The best piece in her portfolio was a packaging program for an imaginary CD release: packaging, advertising, and posters. All of it was Futura Bold Italic, knocked out in white in bright red bands, set on top of black and white halftones. Naturally, it looked great.

Naturally, I asked, "So, why were you going for a Barbara Kruger kind of thing here?"

And she said: "Who's Barbara Kruger?"

Okay, let's begin. My first response: "Um, Barbara Kruger is an artist who is . . . um, pretty well known for doing work that . . . well, looks exactly like this."

"Really? I've never heard of her."

At first I was speechless. Then, I started working out the possibilities. One: My twenty-three year old interviewee had never actually seen any of Barbara Kruger's work and had simply, by coincidence, decided to use the same typeface, color palette, and combinational strategy as the renowned artist. Two: One of her instructors, seeing the direction her work was taking, steered her, unknowingly or knowingly, in the direction of Kruger's work. Three: She was just plain lying. And, finally, four: Kruger's work, after have been so well established for so many years, has simply become part of the atmosphere, inhaled by legions of artists, typographers, and design students everywhere, and exhaled, occasionally, as a piece of work that looks something like something Barbara Kruger would do.

Let's be generous and take option four. My visitor isn't alone, of course. Kruger, who herself began as a graphic designer, has created a body of work that has served as a subtle or not-so-subtle touchpoint for many designers over the past two decades. Occasionally the reference is purposeful, as in my own partner Paula Scher's cover for *From Suffragettes to She-Devils*, which uses Kruger's trademark typeface for a book that surveys a century of graphics in support of women's rights, although in this case the Futura is turned sideways and printed in shocking pink. Similarly, the late Dan Friedman's square logo for Art Against AIDS deploys Futura (Extra Bold) and a red and white color scheme in a way that is both effective and evocative.

Further afield, the brand identity for the Barbican Art Gallery uses the same typeface and, controversially, applies it (usually at an angle to render the italic strokes

Originally published on *www.designobserver.com* (February 26, 2005).

dead vertical) to every exhibition that appears there. Sometimes it seems appropriate: when the subject is the work of Daniel Libeskind, the onrushing italics seem to evoke his urgent, jagged forms. Other times, the connection is more remote, or downright nonexistent. But, of course, searching for any connection at all is purely a parlor game. The goal of the One Gallery, One Font philosophy is not to serve any particular exhibition, but to create a unified identity for the Barbican Art Gallery, which it certainly does. I wonder, however, what would happen if the Barbican ever *mounted an exhibition on Barbara Kruger?* Would the collision of typographic matter and antimatter create some kind of giant vortex as the snake eats its own graphic tail?

We've debated imitation, influence, plagiarism, homage, and coincidence before, and every time, the question eventually comes up: is it possible for someone to "own" a graphic style? Legally, the answer is (mostly) no. And as we sit squarely in a culture intoxicated by sampling and appropriation, can we expect any less from graphic design? I remember my disorientation several years ago when I first saw the new American Apparel store down in Greenwich Village. A banner bearing the store's resolutely hip logo hung out front: the name rendered (American Airlines style) in cool Helvetica, paired with a stripy star symbol that effortlessly evoked the reverse hip of seventies American style. And no wonder: it was the very logo that Chermayeff and Geismar's Bruce Blackburn had designed for the American bicentennial back in 1976.

Today, Blackburn's logo is gone from the American Apparel identity. A lawsuit? Or, more likely, the great zeitgeist wheel has turned once again, rendering the 1976 logo too outré to bother plagiarizing? No matter. We've arrived at a moment when all that has preceded us provides an enormous mother lode of graphic reference points, endlessly tempting, endlessly confusing. Does Barbara Kruger own Futura Bold Italic in white and red? Does Bruce Blackburn own stripy five-pointed stars? How much design history does one have to know before he or she dares put pencil to paper? Picture a frantic land-grab, as one design pioneer after another lunges out into the diminishing frontier, staking out ever-shrinking plots of graphic territory, erecting *Keep Out*! signs at the borders: This is mine! This is mine!

I remember seeing an *Esquire* cover about ten years ago: the subject was radio personality Howard Stern. What a rip-off, I thought, seeing the all-too-familiar Futura Italic. To my surprise, it turned out to be a Barbara Kruger cover illustrating a Barbara Kruger article. Who would have thought: she's a Howard Stern fan. And the lesson? If anyone can rip you off, you may as well beat them to the punch.

PART NOTES
Rob Giampietro

L ate in the evening, with a glass of wine, I'm sitting in a dark room trying to consider the packaging of an album by an Estonian composer named Arvo Pärt that will include a piece of his called "Fratres," which is nearly twelve minutes long. Mine is an imaginary job, a problem for thinking through after dinner. But suppose I were to be faced with it. Suppose I were to try to contain this piece of Pärt's, a piece that arises from design and vanishes from it just as quickly. How could it be done?

Memories strike first and hardest, and I begin to sort through them. The first time I ever heard Pärt was Thursday, March 12, 1998, on a cold night at the Basilica of Saint Mary in Minneapolis. That night, the sun set at 6:16 PM according to the almanac, but new snow and a full moon kept the city looking bright and blue well after nightfall. Earlier that day I had been at the Walker Art Center to see a show by the artist Robert Gober, and, by chance, I picked up a brochure that said "Sound Visions Spring Music." I still have the brochure in my files today, and getting out of my red chair, I set down my glass to find it.

In my hands is a CD-booklet–sized, 16-page brochure printed in black and cyan only. The typography is neurotic—four weights of Akzidenz Grotesk including the Condensed and Bold Condensed weights, a rounded vernacular gothic, and close-set Clarendon caps. Looking at it today, I think what it said was more important than how it looked. A "rare opportunity," a "hypnotic vocal tapestry" in an "acoustically superb sanctuary." The language now sounds as clumsy as the type. But at a time in my life when I thought Minneapolis to be so provincial that any rare opportunity was one worth taking, here was a promise to hear something beyond hearing. I remember walking to the box office to buy tickets immediately. Hours later, sitting in the Basilica, the singers' voices started the "Kyrie" of the *Berlin Mass*. There were no words for these sounds, nor shapes to give them form. The music existed as an encounter with thresholds, like standing on the firm earth over a void. The encounter was thrilling.

Once I was aware of him, I began to encounter Pärt more and more often. I remember finding him in the listening library at college by accident when someone had left a CD in the wrong tray. Then again at a friend's debut recital in New York City. His music seems to inhabit the films I watch: Denys Arcand's *The Barbarian Invasions*, Gus Van Sant's *Gerry*, Michael Mann's *The Insider*, Bernardo Bertolucci's *Little*

Originally published in *DotDotDot9* (Winter 2004/2005).

Buddha, Julie Bertucelli's *Since Otar Left,* and Terrence Malick's *The Thin Red Line.* You will find him in the films of Jean-Luc Godard, of Werner Herzog, of Mike Nichols, and of Michael Moore. I fell in love with a girl as I watched Tom Tykwer's *Heaven,* where Pärt plays more than once.

As I consider the package, trying to bring a form from facts, I consider the process of listening itself. It is a process of building and unbuilding. The music I hear is first built for me, note by note, and I simply apprehend it. Then, with more listening and repeated playings, I break the shimmering thing back into pieces in an effort to understand its whole. There is, must be, a reason the filmmakers I watch, the designers I work with, the people I love, hear these sounds of Pärt's and respond as they do. We all want to know: Is what we're hearing about Pärt or about us? Who is this package for, and what do its contents yield?

Part of me thinks of "Fratres" as a design. Its structure exists independently from its orchestration. It exists already as a piece for strings and percussion, winds and percussion, eight cellos, string quartet, violin and piano, and MIDI sequencer. Its phrases of four, six, and eight notes are voiced in three voices—high, middle, and low—over nine variations, or three triads of three. "Fratres" has three beginnings, three middles, and three ends in each of its three movements, and the arrangement of the three phrase-sets in the three different voices of each of these three movements creates first one, then two, then—just barely—three tonal centers to the piece. More than a third of the tonal experience of "Fratres" comes from the overtones that result from the three perfect intervals played—the octave, the fourth, and the fifth. So nothing exists: no given orchestration, no single experience, not even all of the notes on the page. This is fitting: Pärt often tells the story of a Russian monk he met, who, when asked how to improve oneself, said he knew of no way. Pärt said he tried by writing prayers and setting them to music. The monk shook his head. "You are wrong," he said. "All the prayers have been written. Everything has been prepared. Now you must prepare yourself."

This preparation comes from transcendence. In Pärt's music, what is unknown is summoned from what is known through the natural variance of incantation—of reciting something over and over—like the casting of spells and the saying of prayers. With no preordained thematic drive to obey, the music literally goes nowhere and operates with great drama by placing you where you are, intoning the same tones again and again to create a world of very few parts, a space that holds only the players, the sounds they play, and the person listening.

Though I am describing the music to myself now, the package I'm trying to design is no closer. Here is what I hear: "Fratres" begins quietly. A beat maps the space, a pulse. Then, a breath, the drawing of bows, timed with the beat. Four notes, arching like a sunrise, then six in a similar pattern, then eight. The four return again, slightly different but hopeful, then six, then eight. The players are quiet and find the pulse again. Now four tones dipping like a valley, more labored on their journey uphill. The same pattern of six then eight. Four. Six. Eight. The sound is broadening, rounder. The pulse. The beats are a rhythm, an organizer for the arrangement of the notes, sounding as they did before, but more insistently now. Two forces in opposing directions. The movements in this interval are labored and driving forward. At last, the sound rings. The pulse returns and the first third is complete.

More falling than rising, the opera is greater. The drama of the second third. Beat, beat, beat. Beat, beat, beat. The music insists and refuses to resolve, simmering, then vaporizing the structure it found before. Now it finds itself in two states at once. Beats and then the weather. A thunderclap and air fronts inside and out. The music hall trembles, tensing for the storm.

The final third begins. The warmest sounds so far, like a folk dance or children running in a ring, yelling with joy. The pulse of nighttime beats with the regularity of vespers. A hushing when the sounds resume. The quieter of the two voices is found lower down. On the refrain, it is quieter still, sounding as if, in an icy forest, someone has just stopped walking. The pulse trails off, drifting. Now, after the storm, the wind settling, the intensity of resting after a hard day, of releasing breath. A good job. The pulse, calm, falls silent.

Ideas from Pärt of a typographic sort: the tabula rasa (or blank slate)—his name for a skittering piece written for the violinist Gideon Kremer. The package is empty. When I was younger, learning to play the piano by ear, I would play intervals that made the best shapes. The beauty of a perfect interval is more than sonic. The Estonian alphabet has thirty-two letters. Bracketing those that are only used in foreign words,

A B [C] D E F G H I J K L N O P [Q]
R S Š Z Ž T U V [W] Õ Ä Ö Ü [X] [Y]

twenty-seven letters remain. Three nines, each of three threes. Pärt's process for composing much of his music, including "Fratres," is one he calls "tintinnabulation," which takes a certain chord and inverts it several times over to evoke the pealing of bells, modulating its register in a manner that suggests overtones. This is the beauty of well-chosen arrangements. The sound is simultaneously static (the chord is not changing) and in flux (the chord is permuting). The triad sounds over and over again as instruments trade its notes, passing them through the auditorium as other, quieter voices wander afield, uprooted. These bell-like overtones are slippery, toning and overtoning and changing between the soundings. Something happens when metal is struck with that kind of force, I think to myself. Something else resonates.

I am searching for answers by considering form. I pour another glass of wine. Digging through a pile of articles I've made on the floor, I find Pärt searching for answers, too:

> Tintinnabulation is an area I sometimes wander into when I am searching for answers—in my life, my music, my work. In my dark hours, I have the certain feeling that everything outside this one thing has no meaning. The complex and many-faceted only confuses me, and I must search for unity. What is it,

this one thing, and how do I find my way to it? Traces of this unimportant
thing appear in many guises, and everything that is unimportant falls away.

I am frustrated by the answers I am getting. Maybe it's enough just to enjoy the music.
As quickly as I can ask, "Is Pärt a designer?" I am asking myself, "Should I try to be
claiming him as one?"

With "Fratres" on the stereo, I am on the noisy Internet, and it is getting later.
I find I can type *F-R-A-T-R-E-S* with one hand. When I translate a French interview
with Pärt, the word for "composer" comes out "type-setter." I find that Pärt's birthday
is September 11, 1935—sixty-six years (two thirty-threes) before the towers fell. In his
music, he says, the second iteration of the triad represents "terror." I find the moment
of Pärt's musical transformation from his early serialism to his later minimalism coincides to the month with my own birth. I find a quote about the packaging of his music
that coincides with this coincidence: Alex Ross of the *New Yorker* writes, "Even the
packaging of the disks, all crisp lines and monochromatic fields, is a beautiful exemplar
of minimalist style." I find each of the package designs and note the typefaces: Palatino,
Palatino Titling, Trajan, Gill Sans, stretched Avant Garde, Garamond Bold, Akzidenz
Grotesk, Times Roman, Frutiger, Rotis Serif. These facts refuse me.

Pärt says,

> We must count on the fact that our music will come to an end one day.
> Perhaps there will come a moment, even for the greatest artist, when he will
> no longer want to or have to make art. And perhaps at that very moment we
> will value his creation even more—because in this instant he will have
> transcended his work.

We reach a consensus on things, and these things should be noted down. Here is one:
the Estonian composer Arvo Pärt. Here are my notes. The wine is done. The room is
quiet. As I get ready for bed, I remind myself that there is, in fact, no problem here to
be solved.

DESIGN OUT OF BOUNDS?
Dan Nadel

I magine the book you are now holding, subtract the text, delete the design, enlarge the images to full-bleed size, project them onto coated paper, and square bind them. Flip through the pages of lone images and ask yourself, Is it liberating to look at all those pictures without the commentary or art direction? Die Gestalten Verlag thinks so. DGV, a Berlin-based graphic design publisher started by three designer friends in 1995, has flourished during the millennial design boom, producing designer monographs, design overviews arranged by location or theme, and occasional visual culture magazines. These publications showcase primarily young European graphic design and illustration influenced by pop culture, vector graphics, and ambient imagery. Commentary or writing of any kind is kept to a minimum, usually in the form of a short, pithy introduction. There are other publishers in this niche but the output of DGV, which includes books like *Pictoplasma, Swiss Graphic Design*, and *72-dpi*, is, for better or worse, the most concentrated record of this phenomenon.

DGV's work represents an odd cultural moment, somewhat akin to the sudden burst of metawriting spawned by *McSweeney's* a few years ago. The same sentence structures and tones applied to any topic inevitably flattened meaning. Likewise, the volume and sameness of DGV's brand of imagery has flooded the market and deadened whatever (questionable) meaning was once held in flat, pixilated graphics of babes in bikinis, slick dudes, cars, graffiti, skateboarding, and other youth culture du jour. Firmly rooted in style and trend-based culture as fleeting as last season's fashion accessories, the work is meant to communicate a simple feeling: "cool," "hot," "now." Unlike the more articulate, idea-based design prevalent in the United States for the last few years, it is not delivering a message in paragraph or even sentence form.

The speed at which the imagery is created and then packaged into books constitutes a relentless barrage of similar styles, discouraging actual thinking beyond immediate, trend-based instinct. Unfortunately, the immediate canonization of the material in book form gives it easy legitimacy, which can become insidious because it constitutes a nonverbal but de facto message: "this is how graphic design is today." Watching the phenomenon in action—books dominating design sections in stores, frantic postings on community sites—makes me wonder about its effect on a generation of students simply overwhelmed by the stuff, or a design world mistaking

Originally published in *Metropolis* 23, no. 3 (November 2003).

style or one-word communications ("cool") for what excellent design is really capable of: elegant, functional, and at times beautiful and surprising communication.

The DGV style has evolved out of the colorful ambiguity of rave graphics and the grit and hipster spirit of David Carson–esque collage (the last major graphics trend) into the realm of the digital. Having absorbed the stylistic lessons of both—that is, that style can equal substance, and legibility may not be that important—it has now literally flattened out, favoring slabs of color, silhouetted figures, and ambiguous gesture. It has absorbed Japanese cartoon graphics (increasingly related to Takeshi Murakami's Superflat movement), graffiti lettering styles, and faux images of blueprints, buildings, space ships, and other objects easily generated in Adobe Illustrator. The most important factor in the global dissemination of the flat style is the almighty vector graphic. Vector graphics (computer images created with the use of programs like Illustrator) have risen to dominance because of their compact file sizes, which mean they are the fastest loading images on a screen, the easiest to transmit via e-mail, and also the best way to make even the most ragged draftsman look like a pro.

Just as the DGV visual material favors style over traditional content, the formal construction of the books is based on imagery instead of commentary. Büro Destruct's eponymous monograph is a portfolio of the Swiss firm's work featuring only a written foreword. The book has no grand design scheme or solid organizational principle. Instead it consists of examples of their vector art in all its permutations. Flyers, exhibition posters, CD covers, and illustrations all flow into one another. Editor-in-chief Robert Klanten sees "no need for commenting in the traditional 1980s pre-digital way. I try to let the designers explain themselves in *their* language and not in the teacher's voice," he says. "This teacher-like narrator would like to explain A to Z while all he can mostly capture is his very own A to Z, rather than the language of the work he describes—which means that most of the time it is hot boiled, self-serving bullshit."

But a lack of context does not divorce DGV publications from their own b.s. factor. One artist is nearly indistinguishable from another because they are all using the same tools and all operating from the same set of visual clichés, learned in, most likely, the same places. Rather than heightening the mystery, the effect is to deaden the work, sealing it off from the curious onlooker.

With the exception of recent contributions to the new, pocket-book sized *Emigre*, the once prolific exponents of theory and passionate argument in graphic design seem to be on an extended hiatus. Eliminating words all together is a fine way to stifle even the thought of an articulate response. The work gives the viewer nothing to respond to—no extra design foothold. Again, the lesson for the audience is intellectually deadly: don't bother thinking—you don't need to. That's a poor, unworthy example to propagate at any time, and particularly now, when it's so *easy* to just lay back and let your chosen entertainment or medium sweep you away.

Watching the designs move from sameness to blandness proves to be an unexpected lesson in the effects of design's globalization, for the Web now carries styles from one end of the planet to the other, for quick and easy absorption. Tapping into that one style is certainly an issue of taste among the editors, but it also demonstrates the empty sameness of the books. There is nothing beyond the immediate "now" of design, so the viewer can only gaze at one nonsensical image after another, gathering indistinct impressions and forming no articulate conclusion. The books are basically graphic ephemera to be glanced at and stored for future use—this is disposable style, not necessarily essential design. With a couple of exceptions, the quantity and sameness of the images don't allow for or necessitate interpretation beyond a split second of feeling.

The quick hit of recognition followed by a fading impression jibes too well with the usual business of culture these days. Whereas culture, pop or otherwise, sometimes provides a window into another imagination and alternate possibilities, these days the dominant picture windows just reflect back at us, like funhouse gags. The Whitney Museum of American Art recently staged an exhibition called *The American Effect*, which featured non-American impressions of America, consisting mostly of one-liner gags about our culture. Meanwhile, film is caught in a relentless (and relentlessly commented on) recycling of old TV shows and other licensed properties. The dramatic conclusion would be to say the order of the day is art and culture that lead back into themselves in a soft loop of meaninglessness.

So the temptation is to simply ignore the stuff as you might bland pop music, but that would be ignoring an influence and risking being out of touch.

It's almost easy: The substance and packaging of the flat ambient style, as represented by DGV and other houses, may "only" be pop style, but pop always matters—it's popular—and its lessons can be harmful. In this case, the material refuses thorny, hard thinking in any direction, leaving a void where ideas should be. This void is insidious because it represents a basic misconception about the potential of graphic design. By thinking and representing beyond our media-saturated lives, it can communicate unexpected and unhindered thoughts to an intelligent, active viewer.

In other words, design can be more than just style and quick, gut reactions.

So, ignoring lousy but influential pop—losing touch—would mean not understanding why this work appeals to its audience, missing the point of it. And in some sense, it means missing the point of a more intelligent vision of design. If whole sections of the design medium can simply be cordoned off, then what does that say about the medium in general? If a more intelligent vision is not worth shoring up, then why bother? Questioning what it is, what's appealing about it, and whether or not those elements can be mined in an intelligent, rigorous way, remains essential. Peering over that void, and approaching a style echo chamber with a new voice will allow insight into a fairly opaque area. That activity will give those curious (and those furious) insight and the conceptual tools to argue and engage with this and any material, rather than just changing the channel.

DESIGNING THE REAL WORLD
Al Robertson

At a mundane level, what practitioners usually mean by the "real" of the "real world" is money. Time is money and there isn't any of it for "pussyfooting around," for empty talk, for fancy idealism. "A job in industry," "making a living," and paying off a student loan or a mortgage—these are real, in the "real world." In the "real world" your ideals will turn to custard before the might of money and even you, the original talent, the precocious rebel, the cool designer, will be corrupted. Dollar ranks big time, and no one, it seems, can stand up to it.

Yet there must be more; surely there must be a "real" meaning for the "real world" which is at once representative of something deeper and yet also accommodates the glib certainty of economic determinism. If one view of the "real world" is that it is the place where "reality" is the black and red of profit and loss, then such an unbalanced and limited vision itself represents an implicit failure of the dominant reductionist outlook of the past two hundred years. Life, even in the real world, cannot be that simple. In fact, is not life so complex in reality that the reductionist tendency must be viewed with the suspicion that it actually serves more as a tool for concealment and denial than of understanding?

Yet typographic design serves to reduce the complexity of visual communication into accessibility by way of an apparent simplicity, to eliminate conceptual confusion and visual "noise" from a focused clarity of intent. But the character of that simplicity is deceptive. Not only does it belie all the effort and process—complexity of research, conceptualization, synthesis, and realization—but it reduces all the complexity of the cultural landscape of the everyday (which it plunders for the purpose) to a self-serving and instrumentally simplistic "message." This process also purports to deliver meaning (albeit as the graphic hegemony of the commonplace) to a "target audience" in the "real world."

Hitherto the "real world" was implied to be where self-interest dominates because "survival" depends on it. In the "real world" (of commerce, business, and self-interest) it is suggested that there is no room for ideals or for ethics. In the "real world" there is no room for anything except the relentlessly amoral drive to profit. This apparently is why the "real world" is so tough. An unmitigated, mono-directional drive to self-interest is a hard row to hoe. It's risky in the real world because you might "lose

Originally published in *TypoGraphic Writing: Selected Writing from Thirty Years of* TypoGraphic, *the Journal of the International Society of Typographic Designers.*

your shirt" unless you're "realistic," "pragmatic" and "hard-nosed"; unless, in other words, you take more than you give, on a "me-first" basis. This is curiously narrow and conveniently indulgent because one critical paradox of "reality" is that, as a social construct, it is contingent on other-interest as well as self-interest.[1] Relationship is all. But admittedly it is tough working at relationship. Listening is hard work; as is integrating your needs and wants (ambition and greed) with others. It is a struggle reconciling with others the ambiguity, uncertainty, and indeterminacy of real world contradiction and confusion. So it follows that if the real world is contingent upon relationship, then self-interest is bound to seem an easier option over the short-term. A handy ideology indeed!

"Praxis" means practicing critically and responsibly within the public sphere. The personal process of designing involves all the conceptual, reflexive, visual, and technical activities of doing, making, and knowing. In the public sphere, however (and all visual design performs in the public sphere), praxis necessarily involves others. "*Praxis* may not even exist without others for it is fundamentally exoteric, other-seeking, dialogic."[2] Praxis is the transformation of practice into a more responsible form of cultural production. Through their capacity to reflect on their actions in/on the public sphere, and through the purposefulness of their reason, intellectual professionals like designers become free to intervene in their own reality.[3] Design praxis means making oneself accountable to others in the public sphere. But is this place called the public sphere the same place as the "real world"?

The "real world" is not just private, it is public too; and as such, it cannot be a place governed by self-interest. Rather, the public sphere is where "disinterest" must be exercised with critical responsibility for the good of all. "Disinterest" is not lack of interest, or indifference, or apathy. "Disinterest" means an absence of self-interest, an impartiality in which one is not influenced by one's own advantage—as in "the shared disinterest known as the public good."[4] If we remember Victor Papanek's version of the "real world" in *Design for the Real World*, it was diametrically different from what we have described above. We have here an interesting contradiction. The implicit meaning of the phrase "real world" seems to have shifted from a place where real (ordinary, poor, powerless) people live to a place where money and self-interest govern everything. In his seminal book, Papanek points out the iniquities of useless, low-quality, unsafe, expensive design as it impacts society. For him, most designers—especially graphic designers—were more committed to designing for other designers than for ordinary people (the "audience"). The real world is poor, uninformed, exploited, disadvantaged, unwired, and home to 5 of the 6 billion inhabitants of spaceship earth. Thus only 5 percent of the world's population owns a phone, only 4 percent owns a personal computer, and only 2 percent is connected to the Internet.[5]

The real world, then, is about six times larger than the "real world" of design practitioners. The latter is an almost wholly owned corporatist subsidiary, concerned more with squeezing maximum profit out of its one billion overconsumers by selling them things they don't need, they can't afford, and from which globalized manufacture and branding further damages both the natural and cultural environments on which the majority of planetary citizens, who are not able to "participate," depends for their sustenance. As Eric Hoffer puts it, "You can never get enough of what you don't really want."[6] And this money roller coaster is called success! It seems that the real world is very badly designed indeed.

Clearly then, there is plenty of opportunity for design praxis in the real world. There is an enormous "market" for the design of communication ecology and an emancipatory visuality of social change. In fact, it would seem that the real world not only needs design praxis, but also itself needs designing from the garden up! But Papanek's critique of graphic design focuses on the social products of design and the social role of designers, not on the processes of designing. He was quite correct to criticize "the profession" because the profession pursues profit with every bit as much single-minded zeal as the next businessperson. The profession is reluctant to engage in real world praxis and to examine critically its central role in the perpetuation of an ideology of corporatist domination and consumerism, which is antithetical to democracy and planetary life. Notwithstanding that, surely the process and practice of designing is a fundamental human activity worth preserving, even if the "profession" as it stands is not. As Papanek puts it so appositely: "Design is a basic human ability to help autonomous self-realization."[7] This is why I believe more in the real world of design education than the unreal world of professional design. It is way past time for the design profession to get real. Design might well be too important to leave to designers.

Notes

1. See Berger, P. and Luckmann, T., *The Social Construction of Reality: A Treatise on the Sociology of Knowledge* (London: Penguin, 1971).
2. Taylor, P., *The Texts of Paulo Freire* (Buckingham and Philadelphia: Open University Press, 1993), p. 46.
3. Freire, P., *Cultural Action for Freedom* (London: Penguin, 1972), p. 52; and Goulet, D., "Introduction," in Freire, P., *Education: The Practice of Freedom* (London: Writers and Readers Publishing Cooperative, 1976), p. ix.
4. Saul, J.R., *The Unconscious Civilization*, (Ringwood Victoria: Penguin, 1997), p. 76.
5. This article was first published in 2000, before the proliferation of cell phones as we know it today, and when Internet take-up was still in the low hundreds of millions (perhaps 2–3 percent of global population).
6. Hoffer, E., quoted in Saul, J.R., *The Doubter's Companion: A Dictionary of Aggressive Common Sense* (Toronto: Penguin, 1995), p. 71.
7. Papanek, V., quoted in Poynor, R., "Disobey the Giant: A Kind of Manifesto" (Transcript of a talk given to U.K. design educators, 2003).

INNOVATION AND RESTRAINT:
THE BOOK DESIGNS OF RICHARD ECKERSLEY

Roy R. Behrens

Graphic designers who work for university presses too often go unheralded in a profession that tends to gravitate toward high profile, more glamorous venues like magazine and corporate design. However, sometimes a designer of scholarly books does such extraordinary work that it isn't possible to ignore him.

A case in point is Richard Eckersley, senior designer at the University of Nebraska Press, whom Robert Bringhurst (author of *The Elements of Typographic Style*) has lauded as "a brilliant designer of books," while designer Richard Hendel writes (in *On Book Design*) that Eckersley's prize-winning layouts are models of "how books ought to be designed."

Most of Eckersley's book designs are characterized by typographic subtlety and restraint, the lineage of which can be easily traced to Jan Tschichold, Eric Gill, Paul Renner, and other Modern-era masters of what Geoffrey Dowding called (in the title of his famous book) the *Finer Points in the Spacing and Arrangement of Type*. His best covers and page layouts are at once unobtrusive and exacting—they have, as Beatrice Warde would say, the functional "transparency" of a crystal wine goblet.

"Book design," writes Robert Bringhurst, "is a subtle art, in which the greatest achievements are apt to draw little attention to themselves, while the things that do draw attention to themselves may be unrepeatable tours de force." It is symptomatic of our time, however, that the work for which Eckersley is primarily known is anything but transparent. It is his provocative layout for Avital Ronell's *The Telephone Book: Technology, Schizophrenia, Electric Speech*, an unorthodox scholarly study of Jacques Derrida, Martin Heidegger, and the philosophy of deconstruction, that was published by Nebraska in 1989. The first book he designed by computer, it is louder and hence more startling than any of his other projects, and unquestionably a masterpiece.

In postmodern criticism and philosophy, deconstruction takes apart familiar forms, writes historian Jeremy Musson (in *Key Ideas in Human Thought*), "as one might disassemble a jigsaw puzzle, not looking for correspondences which would help to fit pieces together to make a single unit, but concentrating on individual elements and on

---

Originally published (with slightly different wording) in *PRINT* 55, no. 6 (January/February 2002).

Editor's Note: Richard Eckersley passed away in 2006.

the gaps, dislocations and disjunctions between them." Although it appeared more than fifteen years ago, Eckersley's design for *The Telephone Book* is still radically innovative, even shocking, because of its highly unusual use of deconstructivist strategies to convey (and, in some ways, to confound) a labyrinthine point of view.

If only in a superficial sense, the book's layout threatens to upstage the text, by calling attention to itself and to tricks-of-the-trade that designers employ to enable—or, at times, to complicate—the act of reading. In page after page, there are outrageous, deliberate gaps, dislocations, and disjunctions. On one page, for example, is a backwards mirror image of the page that faces it. On others, the snakelike trails of space that come from careless word spacing (called "rivers") are intentionally used as a means to disrupt conventional word clusters. On still others, the words in a passage on deafness are blurred to the point of being indecipherable; one line runs into another because of the exaggerated use of negative linespacing; and a text is interrupted by sudden pronounced jumps in the size and style of a typeface or the position of its baseline.

Type compositor Charles Ellertson, who has worked with Eckersley for many years, refers to the methods used in *The Telephone Book* as "hammer blows" when compared with his lighter, implicit approach. Yet this book "in a quirky sense, pays attention to classical form," Ellertson adds. "It is an important book," agrees Scottish book designer George Mackie, "appearing as it did in 1989, as an article of faith almost, showing resolutions of type undreamed of in the past, showing the greater muscle the designer now had, for better or for worse." At the same time, cautions Mackie, Eckersley's work "must be seen across his scores of less idiosyncratic books where his touch invisibly makes the passage of thought from author to reader the more precise, the more congenial."

While *The Telephone Book* is unique, it would be wrong to see it as inconsistent with Eckersley's other work. Many of the same methods can be found in his layouts for Derrida's *Glas* (1986) and its companion volume *Glassary* (1986); and, to some extent, they are revisited in his designs for Warren F. Motte's *Questioning Edmond Jabes* (1990), Derrida's *Cinders* (1991), Blaise Cendrars' *Modernities and Other Writings* (1992), Eyal Amiran and John Unsworth's *Essays in Postmodern Culture* (1994), and L.C. Breunig's *The Cubist Poets in Paris* (1995). One need only look at the title pages of these or any of his other books to see how he toys with the tensions among form, function, and invention; or at the copyright pages, which are often so disruptive and unusual that, as Bringhurst recommends, "a collection of his copyright pages could in itself serve as the syllabus for a good design course."

Eckersley was born in England in 1941, and spent his earliest years in a London that was being bombed during World War II. To keep him and his older brother out of harm's way, his parents sometimes sent them to northern England to the comparative safety of their grandparents' home, where Eckersley may have embarked on a path that led to his lifelong commitment to books.

Among his most vivid memories is the fastidiousness of his paternal grandfather. The latter, a Methodist minister and diabetic, doled out life's small pleasures as exactly as he weighed his food intake. Fortunately, he delighted in words and books, so reading was one of the few activities he permitted young Richard on the Sabbath. Eckersley recalls that not until he washed his hands would the books he asked to see be placed ceremoniously in front of him. "I was taught to open the covers gently," he recalls, "and to turn the pages by their top corners." It was in his grandfather's house, on those Sundays, that Eckersley began to develop a passion for words, typography, and book design. He appears to have inherited his grandfather's strict and unwavering eye for detail, a trait that would later prove critical to Eckersley's achievements as a typographer.

Another important influence was his father, Tom Eckersley, a well-known poster designer. Often cited in design history texts (along with Hans Schleger, F.H.K. Henrion, and Abram Games) as one of the "Famous Foursome" of World War II–era poster design, he was eulogized when he died in 1997 as "the quiet giant of British graphic design."

Eckersley's two brothers, Anthony and Paul, immediately followed their father's career path and became graphic designers. Richard, however, took a more circuitous route. He attended Trinity College, Dublin, where he earned a degree not in design but in English and Italian literature. It was through his editorship of a literary magazine and related student activities that he became involved in magazine and poster design. "I discovered that I liked design very much," he remembers, so much so that, when he graduated from Trinity, he signed up for classes in art and design at the London College of Printing. There, however, he was not the only Eckersley: His father was head of the graphic design program, and both his brothers, at various times, received their degrees from the school.

After college, Eckersley was hired by Percy Lund Humphries, a famous London publishing house that had earlier employed such design legends as Jan Tschichold and Edward McKnight Kauffer. (Eckersley recalls how he found, in a storeroom, odds and ends from the drawing board of Kauffer, who had worked there in the thirties.) After a few years, he began to teach at the London College of Printing while also doing freelance work.

It was during this period that he lived and worked in the United States for the first time, when in 1972 he traded jobs for four months with American book designer Richard Hendel, an arrangement whereby Hendel taught in London while Eckersley designed books at the University of Massachusetts Press. Throughout their exchange, recalls Hendel (who is now senior designer at the University of North Carolina Press), Eckersley "brought fresh ideas to the design of scholarly books." His finest works, he adds, "are devoid of typographic trickery, with every detail considered."

In the late 1970s, Eckersley was senior graphic designer at the Kilkenny Design Workshops in Ireland, a daring government-funded attempt to improve design standards in industry. He left in 1980, when the Irish economy nose-dived and the government had to withdraw its support from the enterprise. He returned to the United States to teach at the Tyler School of Art in Philadelphia, but it was only a one-year appointment and he soon was unemployed. His design portfolio at the time, he remembers, "was an omnium gatherum; an Irish bouillabaisse heavy on saffron, light on garlic." It was then that he applied for the job of staff designer—the first such position— at the University of Nebraska Press, where he still works.

Eckersley, his Swedish-born wife, Dika, and their three children moved to Lincoln, Nebraska, in 1981, where Dika also became a book designer at the same press. In the past quarter of a century, he has designed dozens of volumes for Nebraska and other academic presses. Throughout that period, he has also been active in the Association of American University Presses and other organizations; has taught as a visiting lecturer at prominent schools in both the United Kingdom and the United States; and has had his work selected for the design profession's most prestigious competitions. Among his various book awards is a silver medal from the Leipzig Book Fair and the Carl Herzog Book Design Award. Perhaps the most gratifying of his honors was his designation several years ago as a Royal Designer for Industry by the Royal Society of Arts, an award that his father had also received in 1963, making them the only father-son duo to achieve that distinction.

That same year, in 1999, when Warren Chappel's *A Short History of the Printed Word* was revised and enlarged by Robert Bringhurst, it included two of Eckersley's books as distinctive examples of current design. In addition, his work was featured in *Typography Now* by Rick Poyner, *Design Writing Research* by Ellen Lupton and J. Abbott Miller, *On Book Design* by Richard Hendel, *Emigre, Eye*, and other periodicals.

Eckersley's lifestyle is a lot like his layouts: structured and restrained, but enlivened by interesting detours. When I last visited him, he was deeply involved in the painstaking work of laying out a new book by Avital Ronell, titled *Stupidity*, promoted as a scholarly work on "ignorance, dumbfoundedness, and the limits of reason." Committed first and foremost to the challenge of designing, Eckersley seems wholly oblivious to the prospect of awards or fame: "The prize of recognition for a book designer," he wrote in a recent essay, "is to be allowed to design more books."

SECTION VI:
GRAPHIC DESIGN AS IDEA

DUMB IDEAS
Mr. Keedy

Design theory: Is it back? Since the thrill of digital technology has become an agony of endless upgrades, dot-com millionaires have come and gone, and everyone has a roadside stand on the information highway or has published a self-promotional SUV of a book, maybe now is a good time to think about what's going on.

Reading design theories from the past, you can't help but be struck by how many times the same issues are discussed. It is as though every generation has to have essentially the same conversation but in a new way. Weblogs (blogs) are the new way that designers are having that conversation now. They range from Design Observer, which reads like the Op Ed pages of a design journal, to Speak Up, which reads like *Chicken Noodle Soup for the Designer's Soul*. As one of the many sporadic "lurkers" of design blogs, I of course enjoy hearing what other designers have to say, but it comes at a cost. You must be willing to wade through a seemingly endless recitation of dumb ideas that have already been refuted long ago. The only thing more annoying than having your ideas ignored or forgotten by the next generation is watching them make the same stupid mistakes you made. So as a kind of public service, I thought I would start a list of some of the most popular but dumb ideas in design. Ideas that are popular because they seem to provide an answer, but dumb because they're wrong.

- Designers just talking to other designers and "preaching to the choir" is a waste of time.

     Yeah, if only plumbers, acupuncturists, and nuclear physicists were allowed to talk about design, that would be soooo helpful. A similar cliché is that "a broader range of voices needs to be heard," as if there were some malevolent force at work silencing a multitude of insightful design critics and theorists. How they manage to do it now that any nitwit who can work a keyboard is free to opine on any and all topics on the Web is a real mystery.

Originally published in *Emigre*, no. 66 (2004).

We need to have more designers talking about design honestly and intelligently without the usual self-promotion and moral posturing. There are about 150,000 designers in the United States alone; a couple of them are bound to have a few good ideas. Obviously you can always learn something from other disciplines, but are we unable to learn anything from each other?

- Design theorists and lecturers should refrain from using big words and quoting academic intellectuals. It just serves to obfuscate (see what I mean) their ideas, alienate the audience, and cover for the fact that they don't really have any ideas of their own.

This is the anti-intellectual's lament. If you can't say something quickly and simply, then you can't expect a simpleton to understand it. There is no shortage of small-worded, anecdotal, *Readers Digest*–style accounts of design in "these United States" as far as I can tell.

It's a big country and an even bigger world. Next time you find yourself assaulted by flagrant verbosity and misguided citations, turn the page or turn up your iPod. This too shall pass. Or get a dictionary, read some books, and take some classes, dumb ass. Or take the offending pontificators to school and teach them by your own concise yet intricately nuanced example.

- Content is good, style is bad.

Don't get me started. This is a dumb idea that is deeply ingrained in design. I, of course, blame modernism, and am confident that we will get over this idiotic notion in this new century, as it has done entirely too much damage in the last. It was helpful in the beginning for modernists to make the point that making meaning is an important part of why we make things at all. But it's not the only reason we make things. Meaning and content are contextual anyway, so what exactly would a styleless context look like? Who said style has no meaning or content anyway? Everyone should read *The Substance of Style*, by Virginia Postrel, the best design theory book by a nondesigner in years. It may help designers get over their style phobia: The first step is facing your fear and recognizing you have a problem—with style.

- Designers should always try to do work that is experimental.

I don't even know what that word is supposed to mean in design anymore. It used to mean work that is provisional, not complete or refined; a work in progress that is created to test a hypothesis. A student effort. Something you do to test an idea or technique, not something you do to publish or show off. Not that there is anything wrong with a kind of gratuitous showing off, but you shouldn't try to justify it by calling it experimental. The idea that experimental work is complex or obtuse and cutting edge is really cornball. We should be much more critical of anything labeled experimental. After all, that is the point of an experiment: to see if it worked. Legitimately experimental work is part of the design process and goes on all the time, a process that most designers started in school, and many continue with. It's a means, not an end.

Mature designers often don't need to experiment very much anymore, as they know what they are after and are working on refining and improving their vision and craft. For the most part they keep their experiments to themselves and just show us the good stuff.

- Designers should strive for timelessness.

Yes, it's still with us, and probably always will be, because dumb ideas are timeless. But we won't know for sure, of course, until the actual end of time. Maybe if designers stop using that word, they will have to use other words that have a sensible meaning, giving people the impression that designers are sensible people. A similar variant of the timeless malarkey is the equally dumb idea of "transparency" or zero-degree design. It's like Santa Claus and democracy: It seems to work as long as we pretend to believe in it.

- Designers should develop their own personal voice; originality and authenticity should be their goal.

This idea is so last-century. The assumption here is that personal voice, authenticity, and originality are all good things, which they often are but just as often are not. Everyone has a personal voice but not everyone can sing. If you have an authentically bad personal voice, you should leave the singing to someone else. And there is no shortage of stupid original ideas. It still makes for good advertising copy, but originality doesn't count for much in design because design isn't very original. Design is about organizing and making, but not from scratch and always in the context of use.

If people design an original typeface, for example, they don't invent new letters; they invent new shapes for letters that we understand only because they are so similar to the shapes of letters that already exist. It is not so much the originality of the particular shapes that are important, but rather the ingenuity of the letter forms in the context of all the other letter forms that existed before, and the meaning or significance they convey in that context. Uniqueness in and of itself is not very significant, nor is it as pervasive in design as we claim it is. Invention and imagination are very important to design but they don't come out of thin air, they come from the context they were created in, not from some self-taught genius.

- Designers need to redefine their context.

The concept of context seems to have gone from something you are already a part of, to something you simply invent. Unfortunately, just because you say something doesn't mean it is true (even if it is on talk radio or a blog).

Context isn't something you make; it's something that is. You can have any idea about design you want, but that idea won't necessarily have any effect on design, because design is in the world—not in you. The idea of re-contextualizing design is like playing a game in which you get to make up the rules as you go. You are only to be judged by your own criteria. And guess what? You win!

Design has become way too decontextualized as it is. How many times have you read a designer profile in which absolutely no designer is mentioned other than the one under review? As if he or she was the only designer that ever designed anything, and everything he or she says is accepted as gospel "straight from the horse's mouth." What's the point? Must everything be a self-promotion? Do we really get to invent our own relevance?

- Designers should be more autonomous.

The idea here is that autonomy will give designers coherency through self-definition and a separation from the demands of the market-place. This self-proclaimed autonomy is supposed to rally the troops because they get to make up their own job description. But an autonomous com-munity is a bit of an oxymoron, isn't it? You can only get away with being autonomous as long as someone else is picking up the garbage and making sure the trains run on time. Sounds a lot like being an artist. At a time when designers can't even agree on what to call themselves, or what exactly it is that they do, it is not hard to see why an "every man for himself" attitude is popular. When I think of the autonomous designer, I imagine a self-taught ten-year-old with a laptop.

- Design criticism and theory are just personal opinions, not facts.

Well, duh! But opinions and so-called facts are not mutually exclu-sive. Facts start as opinions first. If they pass muster, they become facts. Opinions are as valuable as facts in the development of knowledge. The sentiment above implies that one person's opinions are as valid as and equal to anyone else's. In spite of what you may have been told in kindergarten, or a lit crit class in grad school, that is (in fact) not true. However, uninformed opinions do serve to illustrate how not to think about something. That is why discernment and the critical process are important, and why opinions are important, not just facts (which should be contested from time to time as well).

People get good at what they do by working at it. Discussing, study-ing, and writing are all part of the work that is essential to understanding what constitutes the primary issues, values, and criteria of a discipline, and develop the strategies that move it forward. The dictionary says that an opinion is "a belief stronger than an impression and less strong than personal knowledge, and it is a formal statement by an expert after careful study." What's wrong with that?

- Design theory is for making sense of design practice.

I think of theory as coming in three flavors: methodology, criticism, and "pure" theory. Methodology is probably the most directly related to practice because you first have to know "how to" practice. Criticism happens after the fact and is a bit more removed from practice by a "critical distance." And finally, "pure" theory may not be related to practice at all. Most design theory consists of a mix of these three flavors in various combinations and often has a bit of history, philosophy, and politics thrown in, as well.

When I first started teaching design theory at Otis Parsons in 1987, I put a lot of effort into making connections between theory and practice for the students, as if to justify the need for a theory class at all. By trying to "connect the dots" for them, I was teaching theory as a critical methodology for use in practice. Although critical and methodological thinking is really useful, probably the most useful thing a designer can get from theory is inspiration. By insisting on direct and (often obvious) relevance to practice, theory becomes less useful as an idea because it loses its ability to inspire. I think that is why designers who insist that "design is about ideas" don't seem to ever have any. They think it is enough to be for the idea of having ideas. Who isn't? But they lack the inspiration to find them.

In the theory classes I teach at CalArts now, it is up to the students to "connect the dots" between theory, the studio, their own work, and the world. Tibor Kalman said "We need more why and less how." I think we need more why, how, and why not?

• You can't separate form from content.

Yes, you can. You can separate form from its "original" content and attach it to a new content (pastiche), but it always retains some vestige of its "original" content. For example, Raymond Loewy's pencil sharpener looks like it is going to take flight, because its streamlined form was separated from the aerodynamics of airplanes. Things get even more complicated when you mix multiple forms and contents together (eclecticism). You can separate a form and content from each other, but you can't have content without form or form without content. Even though designers talk about "empty formalism," forms are never completely devoid of content, because forms come from somewhere, and they bring with them vestigial content.

Designers play in the space between form and content all the time, but they are pretty lax about articulating the subtlety and complexity of the relationship between them, and words like "pastiche" and "eclecticism" are too sweeping in scope to be much help.

• What is needed in design is a new. . . .

You can fill in the rest of the sentence with almost anything, and it will probably still qualify as a dumb idea. Past favorites have been new rules/context/wave/ resistance/sobriety/complexity/autonomy/paradigm for the new desktop/digital/ interactive/web/motion/virtual/corporate/cultural, whatever. Usually championed by someone who didn't really know much about the "old" whatever, other than the fact that it desperately needs replacing.

I, for one, have certainly not been immune to the charms of the new, and its pal "the next big thing." They are full of promise, but seldom deliver. Try this little experiment: every time you read, write, or say the word "new" in relation to design, replace it with the word "good."

It is a lot easier to be new than it is to be good. The criteria for being new are only based on the past few years, but the criteria for being good are based on every-thing we have learned since the beginning of time. However, you actually have to know history before you can use it as a criterion for judgment. By working "intuitively" rather than intellectually, designers can convince themselves and their clients that they are creating "new" work, and newness is exactly what clients want to make boring products seem interesting. In this respect designers are rewarded more for their igno-rance than for their insight. That's why many designers don't bother with the past beyond what they have experienced themselves. When was the last time you heard a designer bragging about doing the "oldest" thing?

Designers enjoy being the arbiters of fashion, and ignorance is a small and easy price to pay for the privilege. The idea that "there really is nothing new under the sun" is an old one, but do we really have to insist that everything be new? It is a lot more likely that a useless piece of crap will be new than old, because the test of time tends to throw most of the crap out. I'm willing to settle for just good.

WONDERS REVEALED:
DESIGN AND FAUX SCIENCE
Jessica Helfand and William Drenttel

0.001. REAL SCIENCE

From global warming to genetic cloning to persistent threats of bioterrorism, science—perhaps more than any other discipline—is revolutionizing the world. As a cultural influence its reach is pervasive: from stem cell research to sustainable agriculture, it affects what we eat and breathe, and where and why and how we behave the way we do. In a very real sense, science is the connective tissue linking past to present to future, and in this context, its relationship to visual communication is

Originally published in *Emigre*, no. 64 (Winter 2003).

critical. It is through graphic design that the complexities and wonders of science are revealed.

So why are there so few designers participating in the articulation, expression, and dissemination of these new ideas? Why isn't there a more central, intellectually relevant, and creatively meaningful role for designers—one that revolves less around aestheticizing preexisting content and is based, instead, on inventing new ways to visualize these new ideas?

Remarkably, there has been little evidence of any significant response from the design profession, other than the superficial appropriations of the visual language of science that suddenly seem to be springing up in every design annual, in every monograph, and in every design school critique. Science is the new style idiom of choice, with designers everywhere parroting its visual currencies, adopting its formal vocabularies, and stealing its lingo, its acronyms, its cool, cryptic code. But these are cosmetic enhancements, visual conceits that by and large lack a fundamental knowledge of the underlying discipline itself. For design—a profession that once prided itself on translating form into content—such ignorance is alarming, and the false piety is disturbingly disingenuous. Consider the frequency with which periodic tables have recently been graphically revived, harmoniously constructed graphic tropes that invoke the visual language of Mendeleyev's classic grid, to codify everything from hardware to cereal to Strathmore's guide to cultural elements. It is as if science offers a kind of credibility that design itself lacks, an instant validation and a seriousness of purpose that, quite possibly, design never had in the first place.

This new seeking after scientific style—let's call it Faux Science—is the antithesis of modernism: it's form awaiting content, or worse, serious form retrofitted with interchangeable content. So DNA is used as a paradigm for business strategy; our genetic legacies are reborn as branding schemes for bran flakes. Petri dishes are procured as objects of desire, inhabited by blurry bacteria used to metaphorically represent everything from bus schedules to bleach advertisements to the end of civilization itself. Designers document and chronicle and organize and record and list and process and craft endless diagrams with carefully plotted line weights and meticulously managed color specs, but what do they really know about enzymes or molecules or the structure of an atom? What do they really know about the world?

Filtered through design's brutally neutralizing style engine, contemporary design is anesthetized and stripped of its indigenous qualities: Science, in this context, is a graphic placebo. Meanwhile, designers conceal their intellectual weightlessness and flex their stylistic muscle, producing work that strikes just the right tone of Lab Chic.

And there they stand, positioned ever so meekly at the periphery of this new century, contributing nothing of substance to these, the most critical communication needs of our time.

And designers ask why design doesn't matter.

0.002. FAUX SCIENCE

"Science," wrote Heidegger, "is one of the most essential phenomena of the modern age." It's hygienic and objective, rational and finite, grounded in numerical certainty and cosmological reason. Science is all about clarity and specificity and rationalism, about charting DNA strands and analyzing chemical compounds, about physical density and gravitational pull and a reality that is anything but virtual. And in a world in which design has not only gone virtual but, in the process, become overtaken by catastrophically invasive degrees of public interaction, "science" itself has become unusually tantalizing. Gone are the days of thick eyeglasses and plastic pocket protectors, of nerds and slide rules and chemistry sets. In today's anything-goes world of relentless self-expression, science has become the designers' safe haven. It's the new "look and feel."

And it's an easy one to imitate. We grasp its formal conceits—its systematic language of documentation, its methodical alignments—and parlay them into a visual language that resonates with kick-ass authority. It's a safe, if counterfeit, posture for design, redolent of an aesthetic mindset that seems permanently lodged in the visual gestalt of circa-1965 Ciba Geigy pharmaceutical ephemera. Clean and lean. Formulaic. New and improved.

It's the DamienHirstization of everyday life.

0.003. FALSE AUTHORITY

The appeal of information design is that it offers instant credibility. This is the domain of numbers and bullets and charts and graphs, ordered lists that visualize the obvious. Information design is rational and authoritative, classified and controlled to within an inch of its life: everything in its place and a place for everything. Label it information design and it looks serious. Number it and it looks scientific.

But it's a false authority, particularly because we buy into the form so unquestioningly. Perhaps this is why so much information design looks alike, ratified by an alarmingly robust strain of Swiss modernism that obliterates the chance for a more expressive design idiom, a more content-driven form. It's also annoyingly ahistorical—unconcerned with earlier sources and ignorant of alternative models that would, arguably, introduce a more original point of view.

Information design has become its own legitimizing force, regardless of its content or context. It's modernism run amok: form *masquerading* as content.

0.004. PANACEAS

In biology, the term "morphology" refers to the basic form and structure of organisms without consideration of function. And that is precisely what the morphology (or shape) of elliptical forms seems to be. Yet if the lozenge shapes we see everywhere bear little resemblance to the content they frame or to the function they are intended to illuminate, then what meaning do they have, and what purpose, if any, do they actually serve? Unlike the tangible and quantifiable world of biology, here in the graphical realm such "organisms" are not only function-free, they are little more than ornamental. They're graphic panaceas: a visual cure-all.

Biology, of course, isn't the only discipline in which morphology plays a central role. In the language of numbers, there is *mathematical* morphology, which concentrates on stochastic geometry, random set theory, and image algebra. In the lexicon of infertility, there is *reproductive* morphology, or shape (along with mobility, or speed, and motility, or motion). Finally, in *linguistics*, morphology is the study of the form and structure of words. Here, it can include deviations and inflections, random detours from the essential "shape" of things.

Nevertheless, the preponderance of lozenge-shaped *objects* in contemporary graphic matter suggests that it is this very deviation that has perhaps superseded everything else, celebrating form—perhaps even at the expense of content itself.

0.005. DOCUMENTING

Combine the urge to collect with the inclination to organize, and the resulting activity offers a unique assortment of scientific pretensions. In documenting, designers dutifully observe the minutiae of their efforts, recording with a detail-consciousness bordering on the absurd.

Not long ago, we attended a graduate design thesis review featuring several months' worth of lint recovered from a clothes dryer. The cumulative, color-coded evidence of this rather bizarre little odyssey in textile hygiene was presented, like a rare archaeological specimen, in an oversized glass vase located—where else?—on eBay. (Jesse Gordon's portrait, *The Oldest Piece of Dust*, offers a slightly more ironic, though equally detailed, study of the design of detritus.[1])

This is navel-gazing raised to new and rather worrisome levels: The designer is so busy organizing that it is unlikely s/he will have the time, distance, or objectivity to transcend the work through insight, observation, scrutiny, or point of view, any of which might celebrate the power of an original idea. God forbid that anyone should have an original idea. We're just too busy documenting it all.

0.006. CATALOGUING

Do we strip visual information of its natural scale and emphasis, and in the process, streamline form to negate design's meaning and message? Or do we just make it look good by making it look clean, orderly, and cross-referential?

The popularity of the full-bleed photographic tome is based upon an exhaustively micromanaged cataloging of, well, pretty much anything. This inclination to make 300-page books of endless (and often word-free) photographic sequences is science gone astray; for where the scientist analyzes, the designer merely amasses. The poor reader is left to make sense of it all, to locate some hidden narrative or excavate some

profound meaning as a consequence of meandering through interminable juxtapositions of intentionally nonlinear thinking: so Times Square (turn the page) becomes
Beijing (turn the page) becomes a little girl's hand poetically situated against a cloud
(turn the page) becomes a wad of colorless chewing gum stuck to the bottom of a
chair. Full-bleed image saturation abounds: It is an attempt to create an immersive context which, upon closer inspection, is little more than a theatrically staged set of aggres-
sively cropped images meant to create an indelible impression of Real Life or Drug
Trafficking or Parked Cars in The Rain. This is not science. This is not even design.
This is artifice.

Hegel once posited an inevitable transition of thought, brought about through
contradiction and reconciliation, formed along a trajectory of thinking that began from
an initial conviction and evolved to its opposite. In the thesis/antithesis/synthesis model
of Hegelian dialectics, we easily locate the scientist, who migrates from observation to
analysis to discovery. Meanwhile, the designer catalogs the everyday, making thick,
wordless books with pictures that jump the gutter.

0.008. THE NEW VERNACULAR

Designers have long been drawn to the vernacular, appropriating found artifacts and
celebrating the texture of the street. Over time, the vernacular became a way to create
instant nostalgia, a surface style that looked authentic but was anything *but*. From appropriation came inspiration, a postmodern culture of juxtaposition and pastiche. Because
the vernacular belonged to everyone, it resonated as real, familiar, and accessible. It was
the art of the everyday, beautiful in its ugliness: design within reach.

Faux Science is the new vernacular, a methodology that, while highly disci-
plined in a formal sense, is still all about appropriation. Arguably, perhaps, the landscape
has shifted, too, from grit to grid. It's not so much a tension of form versus content as
a favoring of style over substance.

Science represents an enormous opportunity for designers, but not if their
contributions remain fundamentally restricted by what they know. At the core of this
critique lie serious questions about the role of education. Why don't design students
study music theory? Why aren't they required to learn a second language? And why,
for that matter, don't they study science? "The difficulty lies not in the new ideas,"
writes John Maynard Keynes, "but in escaping the old ones." In other words, design
beyond reach.

Note
  1. Jesse Gordon and Knickerbocker, in Peter Buchanan-Smith (ed.), *Speak: A Curious Collection of Uncommon Things*
      (Princeton Architectural Press, 2001).

ED WORDS: RUSCHA IN PRINT

Michael Dooley

I dismounted my bike at the entrance to Ruscha's studio and greeted him with, "Hey, Ed: what's the good word?"

His answer was direct, emphatic, and open-ended. "The good word is here—and now!"

Sure, these were two words—maybe even three. But Ed Ruscha isn't limited by graphic design strictures of precise communication. He's a fine artist who's earned a monumental reputation by carving out a vocabulary all his own, one in which economic means are put to generous ends. In *The Works of Edward Ruscha*, an early 1980s retrospective catalog, Peter Plagens, currently *Newsweek*'s art critic, called him "Robert Irwin's equal as the most important West Coast artist in the wake of Abstract Expressionism." And he has long been an inspiration to contemporary graphic designers: Rudy VanderLans cites his bookworks and P. Scott Makela cites his paintings among their major influences.

Interest in Ruscha's printed pieces brought me to his studio on Electric Avenue in graffiti-tagged Venice, California. I'd noted, in a 1991 *Print* magazine review of the Museum of Modern Art's *High and Low* exhibition, that his Absolut howling coyote was possibly the most mysteriously downbeat liquor ad ever created. And now I was meeting him to investigate his record, book, magazine, and exhibition catalog covers, his posters, and his little "artist's books."

He speaks in an amiable southwestern drawl, often punctuated by a wise and hearty *hunh hunh* of self-reflective amusement. In conversation, his eyes rivet you with a stare of steely attentiveness that lets you know he's with you, here and now. But he's not one for grand pronouncements about his work; he's most at ease relating anecdotes.

If I wanted the full story on his reproductions, I'd need to stare into his original paintings. Their smooth surfaces—with words that seem like echoes and images like ghostly apparitions—evoke a distance, a there and then.

The foregrounding of text is now a commonplace art practice, ubiquitous in the works of Jenny Holzer, Barbara Kruger, and Christopher Wool. But this wasn't the case in the early 1960s, when Ruscha began doing oil paintings of words set against backdrops that suggested sunset vistas or enigmatic voids. If simply printed on a page,

First published in *PRINT* (September/October 1994).

these images could be taken for headlines; on canvas, the words were alienated from human conversation and brought into an eternal now. They became absurd paradoxes, at once majestic and humble, seductive and elusive.

The first paintings were of short words and cartoon noises. *Electric. Pressures. Honk. Smash. Damage. Oof.* His choice of typestyles varied from standard sans- to slab-serif. Sometimes he'd use condensed, squared-off, bevel-edged letterforms of his own design that resemble the landmark Hollywood Hills sign, a word/object that often appears in his work. "It's nothing new; sign painters have used it for years. I call it 'Boy Scout Utility Modern' because it's just so elemental. Curves are hard. Reduce everything to straight lines and you've got something."

By the late 1960s, though, his words were all curves: script rendered to resemble puddles. *Oily. Pool. City.* In the seventies his vocabulary expanded to pastel drawings of clipped phrases. *Those of Us who Have Double Parked. Another Hollywood Dream Bubble Popped.*

Ruscha thinks of his paintings as covers for books that haven't been written. He's even lettered the sides of his canvases as though they were spines. But if the books existed in fact, they'd be mysteries with countless clues and no solutions. A work like *Now Then, as I Was about to Say. . .* seems to be asking a story rather than telling one. As he put it in the title of a painting of a stone fireplace, there's "no end to the things made out of human talk."

Sometimes these nonexistent books acquire new chapters when they're sold. *Invasion of Privacy* went to publicity-prone tennis terror John McEnroe, *I Don't Want No Retro Spective* to permanently typecast *Harold and Maude* costar Bud Cort, and *He Enjoys the Co of Women* to Woody Allen. Allen does not, however, own *I Plead Insanity Because I'm Just Crazy About That Little Girl*, a work Ruscha also happened to produce that same year.

Art directors are fond of adapting Ruscha's canvases as literal covers for art and lifestyle publications. *Sand in the Vaseline*—a 1974 painting with fly-in-the-erotic-ointment phrasing that acquired dire connotations in the age of AIDS—was used as part of the cover composition for a 1992 retrospective CD set by Talking Heads, the art school band that became famous for singing in spastic strings of sentence fragments about buildings on fire.

And then there's his own design work.

When artists such as Robert Rauschenberg and Jasper Johns were quick to dissociate themselves from their commercial art backgrounds once they began to achieve a modicum of fine art recognition, Ruscha expresses no embarrassment about his occasional forays into design, which date back to his training at Chouinard Art Institute, now CalArts. Dave Hickey, a Las Vegas–based art critic and friend of Ruscha, believes, "Ed's not slumming when he's doing graphics. He doesn't regard high art as inextricably, dialectically opposed to low art. He sees the difference between them as more a gradation than a polarity.

"Ed pretty much maintains his own autonomy," Hickey continues. "He doesn't just function within the parochial realms of the art world, which is a very small world,

I can assure you. Doing covers is a way for him to maintain a place in the larger culture, for him to not be some sort of elitist, ivory-tower twit."

Richard Marshall, an independent curator formerly of the Whitney Museum of American Art, who has organized Ruscha exhibitions, sees Ruscha's designs as works of art in themselves. "He's a master at combining graphic design and fine art. If there are such separate categories, he's made them one. He's blurred the boundaries between them. His so-called formal artwork reads as graphic design and his so-called graphic design reads as formal artwork. That's part of the intrigue of his work, and I think he likes that ambiguity."

Ruscha himself is quick to make a distinction between his commercial work, with its requisite committees and compromises, and his fine art. "I'm a painter. I paint pictures. I use paint on canvas, and that's the essential business of my work. I'm not a graphic designer. It's not even a part of my life. It's just that it's influenced me to the point where I paint with those tools and that imagery. I do things with typography. *Hunh hunh.* In my paintings."

What he does is take bold, straightforward typography and slick, illustrative surfaces—the vocabulary of graphic design—and filter these elements through his unique sensibility to produce works radically different from—and often anathema to—traditional commercial art. His indeterminate, open-ended messages play against and undermine standard conventions.

Peter Plagens, who's written extensively on West Coast art, considers Ruscha a "viewer-friendly" artist who maintains wide popularity by cloaking his subversiveness with "good, honest, important commercial art values. When you look at the deliberately crude silkscreens and the garish colors of Andy Warhol—another former commercial artist—something is being pushed in your face and daring you to say, 'This isn't art.' And then the art seems to ask, 'Okay, if I'm not art, why? Come up with some reasons.' But Ed always has this wonderful ability to go against the grain. Most everything he does is attractive. They look nice, they're well made, they're clean. There isn't anything in an Ed Ruscha work of art that's off-putting on the face of it."

Hickey sees significance in the secret shushes of Ruscha's *She Sure Knew Her Devotionals*, a pastel on paper, and the violations of standards and norms implicit in his paintings of a Standard gas station and Norm's restaurant in L.A., both set ablaze. "Ed's interested in the non-discursive aspects of language—the sound and the look—and how they get involved in the act of communication. In terms of information theory, he's interested in the noise that accompanies the message as much as the message itself. He cares what it means but he's more concerned with the oddities of what it means than some sort of linguistic content."

In Oklahoma City in 1950, when the thirteen-year-old Ruscha would pedal his bike from house to house on his paper route, bringing people the news, something was in the air beyond papers tossed, something that had to do with the physical material of printed words.

Three years earlier, a neighbor down the street who drew little cartoons introduced him to Higgins India ink. He was captivated by the black liquid, by how it smelled and how it looked when he'd spill it, making blobs on white paper. "For some reason, India ink was like a precious substance to me. And I loved this little bottle they had it in. And it just got me into drawing and I thought, well, maybe someday I'd like to grow up to be a cartoonist. It's one of those little side dreams you have. That seemed to be the first opening for me as an artist. And then it took different courses as I grew up."

So Ruscha—the man who'd go on to use a Harold Gray *Orphan Annie* comic strip and a George "Lichty" Lichtenstein *Grin and Bear It* comics panel in his art before Pop Art's Roy Lichtenstein even thought of doing his first Popeye painting—began with this idea that he wanted to be a cartoonist. Then he wanted to be a sign painter, or maybe some other kind of commercial artist. In 1956 he drove to Los Angeles to pursue his dream, accompanied by Mason Williams, a buddy since the fourth grade who'd go on to become a songwriter/poet. He moved into an apartment on Sunset Place and began taking design courses like lettering, typography, and layout at Chouinard.

At the time, he had no interest in fine art. "I didn't study to be a classical painter, and I'm not one. *Hunh hunh.* To go to a museum. . ."—he pantomimed a yawn. "And I never really appreciated the art they were pushing at us anyway, like Degas and Monet."

But in 1957 Ruscha changed direction. He can pinpoint the precise moment he decided to aim his career toward fine art. He was in the school library and he came across a picture illustrating a magazine article. The magazine was the February/March *Print*, the article was a cover story exploring "the landscape harbors of inspiration," and the picture was Jasper Johns' *Target with Four Faces*.

Johns had rendered his target in encaustic over newsprint on a square canvas, and set it beneath a row of cast plaster reliefs of identical faces, cropped nose-to-chin, with closed mouths. These faces were partitioned in a wooden box, hinged from above so it could be shut. A year later, this artwork would appear on the cover of *ARTnews*.

"*Target with Four Faces* was hot. It was a very threatening, challenging work. The teachers at Chouinard didn't like this unconventional kind of art. They took it as an offense. It went against everything they taught us. They taught us asymmetrical art, and that thing was symmetrical. I was overwhelmed by this contrary work of art. I was so disarmed and puzzled by it that it gave me strength. And I loved it for that. Now I've seen the work many times—the actual work—but it all began with that reproduction. So isn't that kind of living by second nature? Second-hand influence?"

Considering Johns' target is itself a second-hand object in the inverse sense—a painted version of what normally would be printed on paper so it could be fired upon—Ruscha's response was the completion of a circle. But before he went on to blow that circle wide open with his own puzzling, challenging works—using materials as unconventional as axle grease, gunpowder, blood, and semen—he made his living doing commercial jobs. After leaving school in 1960, he painted For Sale signs. He spent what he describes as a hellish stint doing layouts for an ad agency. Then he was hired by Sunset House to personalize mail-order ceramic gift items. He'd letter names in script on the roofs of birdhouses that held kids' school supplies. "And there was a thing called a chopper hopper, it was for old folks' false teeth. It had a lid on it, and I'd letter their names on there. *Hunh hunh hunh*. In enamel."

He'd do tens of thousands of these things, birdhouse after birdhouse, hopper after hopper—from September to the end of November for the Christmas market— for a couple of years. "It was piecework. I could get a nickel for one of those bird-houses. I could make enough to live on for the whole year. And I liked it better than doing layouts at some advertising agency."

Sunset House allowed him time to paint, and his work began to be exhibited locally. In 1962, he shared wall space with Lichtenstein and Warhol in a group show at the Pasadena Museum, now the Norton Simon, called *New Paintings of Common Objects*. He also "designed" the announcement poster, a work he considers pivotal. In what would now be labeled as a Conceptual Art gesture, he selected the Majestic Poster Press, a commercial outfit, from the yellow pages, then dictated the information over the phone. Majestic set the copy with bold wood type and printed the poster in black and red on yellow, a standard format for boxing matches but hardly the norm for museum exhibitions. "I didn't want to put too much art in this thing. *Hunh hunh*."

By 1965, he'd produced several of his most important paintings and had become well respected among California's and New York's inner art circles, but he still needed to earn a living. He moved to a studio on Western Avenue with a view of the Hollywood sign, and began a two-year stint doing layout and production for *Artforum*. "They'd come in once a month, give me a pile of photographs and press proofs and I'd align them and do the paste-up." The masthead listed him as Eddie Russia. This was Ruscha's touché to people who mispronounced his name.

In 1968—the year Ruscha completed an eleven-foot-wide painting of the Los Angeles County Museum of Art looking as though it had caught fire—fellow artist Billy Al Bengston asked him to design the catalog for Bengston's LACMA exhibition. Ruscha chose flocked sandpaper for the covers, nuts and bolts for the binding, and a Bible-like satin ribbon bookmark. He then hired people to assemble all 2,500 copies by hand, screwing bolt after bolt. "The bolts fit this guy's personality very much. And I was intrigued with the idea of doing this thing without having to send it to a bindery. I like the idea of handwork. That's why I liked Sunset House."

Ruscha also sized the photos, spec'd the type, checked the color, and oversaw construction. He's still pleased with the results, but it was his last commercial book design job. "I couldn't do that today. I don't even know what the typeface names are now. I'm certain the whole industry has changed enormously since I used to do this. Then you had to count picas carefully and get exact measures. Nowadays, it's completely different. Macintosh and all that. They're much better today, aren't they? You can do everything. You can say, 'Take this story and put it here! On this page!' And it just goes *Rzzzztt!*"

For his 1982 solo exhibition catalog cover, he got the idea to use a work he'd done three years before, *I Don't Want No Retro Spective*. It was a pastel drawing of a Pepto Bismol–like smear overlaid with white letterforms staggered with a suggestion of the stop-and-start rhythm of the Rolling Stones' hit song "Satisfaction." He set the drawing in a black frame flecked with yellow spots that seem to have both micro- and macrocosmic scale.

Ruscha has a few standard approaches to magazine cover design. Sometimes he'll adapt works in progress. *Anchor Stuck in Sand* was originally intended as a print to raise money for the *Paris Review*, but Richard Marshall, who was then the magazine's art editor, thought it would lend itself perfectly to a wraparound cover. Some of the editorial staff objected that the front half, an anchor tip jutting out of the sand, was too suggestive, but Marshall says he "loved that it could be seen as a big dick. I encourage reading into imagery."

Sometimes Ruscha will take photos for cover designs. For the cover of the first—and only—issue of *PUSH!*, in 1991, he photographed his brother's Studio City swimming pool at the request of the design director, Lloyd Ziff. Ruscha had already designed the tiles at the bottom of the pool to resemble a sunken registration form request for name, address, and phone. At one point, he'd considered making the tiles wavy so the rippling water would actually straighten out the words. "That would have been an expensive experiment. *Hunh*."

Back in 1966, when Ruscha was freelancing for *Artforum*, he was commissioned to design the cover for a special issue devoted to the Surrealist movement. He carved letterforms out of balsa wood, set them on glass with colored lights underneath, added soap bubbles, and photographed this tableau of sudsy "Surrealism."

His early association with *Artforum* made him an obvious choice to design the cover of its thirtieth-anniversary issue in 1993. The resulting photo is a decidedly less ambitious effort. Dowel sticks, laid on linen and *pffffed* with a few shots of red spray paint, are arranged to form a receding "Etc., Etc." Editor Jack Bankowsky detects an accusation of redundancy. "I read it as a good-humored dig that opened up the question of how an art magazine becomes an institution. When Ed Ruscha was *Artforum*'s designer, it was a fresh new publication that was just discovering its identity. Now the magazine is in a completely different moment in its history."

Hickey sees the cover in an even larger context, as "a comment on Ed's whole idea of history, which is that it's basically not going anywhere, it's just some sort of ongoing cumulative activity. He has a very Postmodern idea of history: 'Then there's one and then there's another one and then there's another one, etc., etc., etc.' He would probably say that about his own work."

Sometimes Ruscha's approach to creating a cover image is to interpret the magazine's name. In 1969, when Mike Salisbury was art director of *West*, a supplement inserted into the Sunday *Los Angeles Times*, he asked Rushca to create a cover that spelled out the magazine's title. Ruscha, who was doing his liquid letterforms at the time, painted an image that seemed to capture a momentary, arbitrary arrangement of puddles in a loose approximation of the word, overlaid onto a Rothko-like abstract background with colors that suggested the western sunset.

Ruscha remembers being "mildly disturbed" that the cover was printed with "(west)" added in bold black type. "They actually had more freedom to do what they wanted than a magazine that has to face the customer at a newsstand. It was probably one of those committee things, don't you think?"

"Yeah, in a way," admits Salisbury. "That was at the tail end of me getting away with murder doing all these far-out things with the cover logo, putting it into the bottom of the page, hiding it in the background, changing it—we even had a skywriter do it. By this time, everybody felt that it had just gone too far. So the parenthetical afterthought made the cover idiot-proof. But he's right; it was disturbing to have to put that type in there. I felt really guilty about having to do that."

Ruscha had run into a similar situation five years earlier, when he created a painting of a five-letter word meant as an album cover design for his friend Mason Williams, who'd become famous for his Grammy-winning tune "Classical Gas." "Warner Bros. wanted to print stuff all over it at first," Ruscha recalls, "but I said 'the whole point is not to do that.' So they shrink-wrapped it and put a sticker on it that said 'Mason Williams' and such and such. And that's fine, because when the shrink-wrap comes off, the label comes off, and then it's just an album that says 'Music' and that's what I like about it."

Although Ruscha views his design work as an adjunct to his fine art career, in 1963 he began to produce several inexpensive, unpretentious-looking softcover books—about one a year for fifteen years—that he considers as much fine art as his paintings. "When it comes to a magazine cover, it's a cooperative effort. But every time I did a book, I took care of everything. I labored over the letterspacing on these things. It all meant something to me, the selections, the cropping of photographs. These are strictly my own publications. The core to these books is the same thing that's in my paintings, the same thing that's in all my art."

The books came out of Ruscha's interest in typography and printing. In 1958, he worked as a printer's devil at Plantain Press, run by Saul Marks. "Saul Marks was a letterpress printer, but he also did halftones. He did offset, too, finally. He'd do small editions. He was well respected as a fine-arts printer. He did a catalog once for a Degas exhibit at the L.A. County Museum. He taught me how to set type, and I worked on the presses and I did just about everything that had to do with making a book, outside of the actual stitching of the binding.

"Somehow the concept of books has been strong in my life. And his shop was like a candy store to me, seeing books being printed, seeing presses and ink and the works. I just bought it lock, stock, and barrel."

The layouts of his books—with their generic typefaces, symmetrical composition, and casual sequencing—seem as though they don't have too much art in them, and the photos—mostly black-and-white—have a banal matter-of-factness, as simple and direct as mug shots. True to his contrary nature, pictures dominate Ruscha's books as words often dominate his paintings; the books can be "looked at" the way the paintings can be "read." Shots of vernacular architecture are corollaries to his vernacular phrases. Sometimes page after page will be left empty. "I liked the idea of leaving pages blank in between as a kind of pacing. You'd go from one to the other; pretty soon you'd think there's nothing more in the book, and then suddenly there's a picture."

Ruscha's first book, originally printed in an edition of 400, carries the deadpan descriptive title *Twentysix Gasoline Stations*. "I travel a lot between here and Oklahoma, so I started taking pictures of gasoline stations and they seemed to completely dominate my interest. There's something mystical happening there with me and gasoline stations."

Since his desire was to make a book rather than reach an audience, he was surprised that *Twentysix Gasoline Stations* had a favorable reception. It's sold thousands of copies in subsequent printings and is acknowledged as a prototypical contemporary "artist book." "I didn't actually think it was going to sell out. I was into the esthetics of making a book. It was the idea of 'I gotta make a book,' and so, instead of a book of photographs, it's almost like photographs were a support for the concept of the book. The subject matter of some of my books is almost less important than the books themselves."

Mason Williams recalls, "Ed and I had this philosophy, 'You need to have products in the marketplace.' Ed designed the cover for my first book of poems, *Bicyclists Dismount*, and I had it printed myself, and I'd give away copies. And we were just in love with the book form and this idea of seeing several hundred of the same item sitting there."

In 1965, Ruscha made *Some Los Angeles Apartments*. "Architectural subjects grab me. There's something about them I find riveting, possibly the abstractness, the boxes. It was like being a reporter, going in-depth on a subject and then coming back and telling people about it." Most of the apartments have vacancy signs in front.

For 1966's *Every Building on the Sunset Strip*, he mounted a motorized camera onto a pickup truck to shoot both sides of the street, building after building, for over two miles. Then he butted the black and white photos together in a 25-foot long, accordion-folded strip. The north side runs along the top of the page and the south, upside down, along the bottom, separated across a white middle divide.

"Sunset Strip was the hot spot of the city. I was intrigued by it. There were Hell's Angels types and music types and artists and the movie people. People would be driving along about five miles an hour, people in the back seat would have their tambourines. . ."—he makes *k-chika chika chika* sounds and gestures. "They used to do that back in the sixties. There was a lot of police brutality up there and a lot of kids on drugs. It was beginning to be a toilet bowl, but it was still a curious place." Even more curious is that he chose to document not the wild weekends of revelry but the quiet, mundane morning after, practically stripped of human presence.

In the aerial photos of Ruscha's next book, *Thirtyfour Parking Lots in Los Angeles*, not only aren't there any people to be seen, there are hardly any cars. Telltale traces of life are found in the splotches and streaks of oily residue between the hatched and herringboned lines that designate parking spaces.

Los Angeles Times art critic Christopher Knight, who considers Ruscha "the visual poet laureate of spiritual displacement and psychological homelessness," equates the oil stains with fingerprints found at the scene of a crime. "You can tell by the size of the stains who goes where more often. Patterns of migration are identified in those photographs, but there's no one in them. The people have moved on. And if that ain't modern American life, I don't know what is."

Ruscha and I are now in a room off to the back of the studio. He's showing me his other books, like *Real Estate Opportunities*, with lots of photos of lots, "lots" of "nothing" with For Sale signs. I've been noticing various visual elements that link together his books, his designs, and his paintings. Wood. Fire. Water. Gas. Food. Lodging. Vehicles. Etc. I mention how the rugged road texture that finds its way into so many of his photos echoes the speckle patterns in other works he's accumulated to show me. He shoots me his here-and-now stare, breaks into a wide grin, and says "See, it all connects together, doesn't it?"

Hunh hunh.

VISITATIONS

Denise Gonzales Crisp, Kali Nikitas, Louise Sandhaus

The following are excerpts from a series of online chats that took place in September 2002 between Louise Sandhaus in California, Kali Nikitas in Minnesota, and Denise Gonzales Crisp in North Carolina. Together, these three designers/educators had taken a two-week trip in June to Holland and London to visit designers and design programs, museums, and fashion houses. These chats reflect

Originally published in *Emigre*, no. 64 (Winter 2003).

on the state of graphic design as they encountered it, and were also meant to help inform the three as they returned to teaching and developing curriculum at California Institute of the Arts, Minneapolis College of Art and Design, and NCSU's College of Design, respectively.

Denise: Okay getting started. What motivated you two to organize this trip?

Kali: As the chair of a graphic design program, it was important to reacquaint myself with the European design community, both for my own growth and to set up potential relationships with studios and schools for study abroad, internships, visiting artists, etc.

Louise: I work with an astounding faculty, but I still felt I needed to expand my scope of influence and be exposed to the ideas and issues that designers in other countries are dealing with.

Kali: I was reminded how a different political and social climate affects designers and their work philosophy and formal expression. I noticed a lot of simple, clean work and the need to make design be more than just pretty. Particularly in the exhibition we saw at the Design Museum in London, curated by Emily King and Christian Kusters.

Louise: I wrote a review of that show for *Eye*. It was based on the book *Restart*, which was about the response by designers to an exhausted postmodern chaos through creative use of systems or sets of rules to define the process . . .

Denise: . . . that can also control the outcome of the form. My sense is that design studios, and education programs—or maybe the more progressive design programs— are starting to ask how designers might contribute more deeply to the process of design. How they can find themselves both at the core of developing systems that continue to generate form, as well as making the end product, and understanding how these forms work in the culture.

Louise: Yes, but in some of these programs it seems that the more designers get involved in the "product," the more the development of the visual form as a significant contribution to the function of the work gets diminished or overwhelmed.

Kali: Which is a big mistake.

Denise: Right. Can you say Jacob Nielsen?

Kali: When you believe that form is not important, you are being naïve or lazy.

Denise: What about the form we encountered in Holland and England? Are the designers we talked to developing systems at the expense of the form?

Kali: Depends on the designer. Take Foundation 33. They stick to systems so much that the form does not vary much from project to project. The form suffers. Experimental Jet Set, Graphic Thought Facility (and the list goes on, also in the United

States), have made some interesting systems that have generated some interesting forms, but by now it's a bit trendy and predictable.

Denise: Would you say Experimental Jet Set was among the originators of this trend though? I ask, because I do think some of their work is attempting to find intelligent counters to style mongering. Unfortunately, the forms their systems generate are borrowed from the "unemotive" universally minded sixties.

Louise: Some of their work reminds me of sixties conceptualism, of Sol Lewitt's manifesto. Lewitt said that "Banal ideas cannot be rescued by beautiful form."

Kali: I'm thinking about the "Conceptual Art" show we saw at the Stedelijk Museum in Amsterdam. The work in that exhibition was beautiful and rooted in new ways of thinking. The form that those artists created was not boring, maybe because the form was a natural expression of the times.

Denise: It's no accident that this show was curated now. Clearly there's a trend toward, or back to, a type of conceptualism filled with thick and juicy ideas. Graphic designers seem to have adopted the look too, though. Which is why I think the trend toward sixties and seventies modernism is as much about mining the past (pomo) as it is an attempt to redirect our values.

Louise: I wonder if sixties-style conceptualism really ever went away in Europe. I'd also like to point out that there are two kinds of conceptualism. There's the conceptualism that tries to get the material object out of the equation. For instance, Shoot, the 1971 performance by artist Chris Burden, where he had someone shoot him in the arm, was about an experience as a work of art rather than an object. And then there's the conceptualism in which the system is the idea, which finds its expression in a particular visual form.

Denise: I'm thinking of Karl Gerstner and his modular systems, which generated and regenerated form like a machine, and new form at that. This isn't what we saw in Europe, though.

Kali: No, it's not. We saw designers who were either ignoring history, or were unaware of history.

Denise: Right. Remember, Experimental Jet Set even said that in Europe Helvetica is just a typeface, and doesn't mean what it might in the United States. I guess that does indicate they're aware though.

Louise: From what I could tell, very little history, design or otherwise, is taught in the schools we visited. "Now" seems to be a blank slate that arrived from nowhere.

Kali: And look at how few of the designers we visited were interested in what we are doing or what is happening in the United States.

Denise: Did anyone ever ask about our work, our programs?

Kali: That's my question. Maybe my expectations of the profession are too high. Since school, I have been interested in what is happening on both coasts as well as across the ocean. I think everyone should look beyond their backyard. It seems natural to have a dialogue with designers in other countries. But maybe our education was unique. And maybe the Europeans we met are content, and aren't looking elsewhere for any answers.

Louise: I also want to bring up Hal Foster's new book *Design and Crime*, which is this melancholic reflection on design. He talks about Rem Koolhaas—a designer who generates unique, well-researched descriptions of contemporary cultural conditions into which his designs are supposed to function. For instance, the project on China and the one on shopping that he did with the Harvard students where they create these over-the-top comprehensive doorstopper compendiums of the history and circumstances of an existing cultural situation. Rather than imagine utopic or idealized conditions instead of the realities of shopping and development, he and the students are more interested in describing a condition that actually exists. I'm guessing that it's to get a better grasp on what to design before considering what the designed thing looks like. But there doesn't seem to be a consideration of the social or political agendas that these situations he's describing represent. And so there's no response in the "design solution" to that part of "reality," including the possibility of saying, "This isn't the future I want to live in," and perhaps offering some viable, alternative proposal. Some of the graphic design work we saw had a similarly partially blind agenda. And unlike Rem's project, there seems to be little knowledge of the past; no vision of the future, no reason for why anything is being made.

Denise: This lack of a greater context is the true issue for me. And as you suggest, it is what seemed to have gone missing in what we saw in Europe. So many designers were attempting to find something meaningful. And I applaud that. Yet the result seemed to still end up being capital "D" design. For me, much of what we saw still comes back to a wholesale acceptance of what graphic design is supposed to look like. No one we visited, except maybe Goodwill and Graphic Thought Facility, was attempting to challenge D-esign.

Louise: Design versus design?

Denise: Big D design is where the only goal is to create appropriate solutions to any so-called problem provided by a client, where the drive toward resolution overwhelms exploration of other formal possibilities. This kind of work must always look like design, rather than, by contrast, looking like, well, design informed by things other than graphic design!

Louise: Let's follow through on the Goodwill example. He struck a chord.

Denise: Yes, I think he touched a major nerve.

Kali: My first reaction to his work was, "how familiar!" The thinking and form—it looked like CalArts work from the late eighties.

Louise: I think the work was incredibly nihilistic. It depressed me. The idea that even common sense or thoughtfulness could be abandoned and the work still be considered design.

Denise: For me Goodwill was one of the few designers attempting to break away from the dictates of Euro-determined design. Antistyle (and I agree, been-there-done-that), but also antimodern. And that's another step in the right direction as far as I'm concerned.

Louise: But his work gives up hope that design—not as a mere exercise in aesthetics, but as shaping of thought and thoughtful shaping—has significance. I can appreciate what you're saying, Denise. And yes, overaestheticized work is tiresome. But works intended as public communications done without intention to further that function! Sorry, but it's really a sign of "why bother, it's all crap and doesn't matter anyway" to me. Excuse me while I get a handkerchief, sniff, sniff.

Denise: Shaping significance is most closely tied today to shaping systems. And this is among the things Goodwill was attempting, whether he knew it or not. He is shaping systems that don't manifest as groovy computer form, that aren't modular and "high level" views, but systems that might move us past taste as a guiding principle, or personal expression, and into forms that reflect and interact with users, clients, designers, everybody.

Louise: So Denise, your answer is don't shape at all?!

Denise: No. But think of the way an imprinted address on a piece of direct mail interferes with tidy aesthetics. He's just corralling some of that. At least he wasn't quoting high-modern design as if it were so much vernacular.

Louise: But he was using vernacular; the vernacular of default!

Kali: Louise, you mean that "default" equals not originating or designing the form? And that he seems to be assuming, because he is being conceptual, that the form he creates will automatically be meaningful?

Louise: Yes. Actually, it's something I'd say was pervasive in much of the work we saw elsewhere. I call it the "style of the everyday." And it reflects what I believe is the continuing crisis of representation, that is, the problem that designers like Goodwill have with representing a world that is so full of complexity, information, and contradictions that no one feels up to the challenge of representing it. Instead we get nonrepresentation. Defaults. They leave everything "as is."

Kali: I have a different take on him. I perceive Goodwill as trying to distinguish himself by exploring issues such as designer as author, or designer as director of audience experience. The look and function of his work is decided in part by the user. But he should have been in contact with American designers, because these issues that he is struggling with were explored in the late eighties and nineties at schools like Cranbrook, CalArts, and Yale. He could have saved himself a lot of time if he had been exposed to these explorations.

Denise: Still, his method is at least one way to get design practice to reflect more depth, to represent actual living beings instead of martha-matons. This is the concern I continue to see surface over and over, in Europe, and the U.S. Goodwill seems to be trying to make things meaningful by disregarding or kicking at design Euro-standards. And I agree with this push. Though as Kali said, maybe it's what we saw going on in the U.S. a while ago.

Denise: Let's talk about what we might be carrying around as a sort of souvenir from this trip, something we refer to in our thoughts, a teeny muse.

Louise: I saw this textile design at Central St. Martins and RCA. The stuff was so compelling. It was conceptually based and so full of energy and visceral. By comparison, the graphic design work we saw looked limp.

Kali: I remember the dinner with Rick Vermeulen, and the chef who promised us a great meal and delivered! And Rick's work, which still resonates with me.

Denise: His is the one poster I put up upon returning. Very vital stuff, still, for me too.

Louise: There were those Leopold and Rudolf Blaschka glass sea creatures at the Design Museum in London. Their radiance outshined the "Graphics Now" show in the next room.

Louise: And Karel Marten's grandbaby announcement.

Denise: And the layers of history and decoration of the Amsterdam streets. The work you mention bore out passionate responses to making. Maybe as designers, we all just want to move beyond the replicable one-off, or that oh-so-clever graphic aloofness. These things we are reacting to have what in common?

Louise: Passion, yes. Caring. The sign that something matters!

Denise: I'm afraid I found so much joy in non-design things that it seems immaterial to our conversation. In Antwerp, the view out my window of the wrought iron pensione sign set against the massive carved stone tower of the cathedral. Or not understanding a politically charged argument over architecture, in Dutch, during a lecture at the back of a restaurant in Amsterdam with Henk Elenga occasionally translating in my ear. Or the intense red and green where that working-class strip mall was converted into a living lesson in art.

Louise: We're bad. No wonder so many cringe at calling themselves graphic designers. Even us champions of graphic design found so much more outside design to move us.

Kali: There's always room to grow. And what we're doing here in the states ain't so bad after all.

Denise: Don't you think we're in a unique position as Americans to play many sides at once?

Louise: We ARE in a unique position to ask what do we want to invent for this culture?

Denise: Right, we need to create rather than react.

Kali: This trip reminded me that when one is a full-time designer, there is little room for questioning, challenging, and shifting the profession. As teachers, we're in a privileged position to affect change with our students, and also maybe take risks in our own practice.

Louise: We have GOT to get over the Adbusters mentality in academia. Instead of critiquing everything and complaining, we have the opportunity to really address our society and culture. But we must have some sort of picture about our hopes and dreams for the culture and the society in which we live and then build something that will further that vision. But I want to emphasize the need to accept this culture as it is and insert ideas from and into that culture.

Denise: While I agree that the Adbusters approach isn't as productive as social service, for instance, it does inform about issues otherwise left unaddressed.

Kali: But it tends to ignore complexity. They are SO black and white. What about the person who has to feed their family and is in no position to protest? We can challenge and should challenge, yes, but please! Let's look at the bigger picture.

VISITATIONS REVISITED
Rudy VanderLans

The discussion piece "Visitations," which was published in "Rant" (*Emigre*, no. 64), generated a large number of critiques. Since the published piece was an edited version of an informal three-way conversation (a rant of sorts), certain ideas were perhaps not represented completely enough, so we felt it was fair to give the authors an opportunity to clarify and respond to some of the criticism. Following is a brief interview with Kali Nikitas and a short reply by Louise Sandhaus. —RVDL

Rudy: Quite a few people thought it was odd when you said: "And look at how few of the designers we visited were interested in what we were doing or what was happening in the U.S." You were being scolded for being pompous, aloof, self important . . . I'm guessing you were trying to get at something else. Care to clarify?

Kali: My intention was never to sound pompous or arrogant. It was merely an observation, and I was expressing a desire to have more dialogue about similarities or differences between countries in practice and education. Funny that it took the publication of our conversation in *Emigre #64* to get some heat into the discussion.

Rudy: All of you were described as not being "relevant" anymore, and hardly "current designers . . . more old-school academics," and that this is the reason why others in Europe are not interested in your work anymore. This comment intrigues me because it implies there are others out there who *are* relevant. At the risk of sending you even deeper into irrelevance, do you have any idea what and who is relevant in design today?

Kali: I am less interested in graphic design that is stylistically spectacular and limited in life span. I am more interested in how someone chooses to define their practice. In other words, what is "relevant" to me is someone's choices in practice and lifestyle and them trusting that the results of those choices will lead to great things.

Rudy: The entire issue #64 ("Rant"), including your "Visitations" piece, was critiqued by many for being obsessed with style. In *Adbusters*, Dmitri Siegel wrote: "Formal novelty is not of urgent interest to many young designers . . . Young designers are focused on creating a context in which they can do work that is satisfying and new" and "this novelty need not be based on formal qualities." Instead, he writes, "The next phase of innovation and debate will be toward renovating the context of its practice." Therefore, discussing its form is rather useless. In other words, there's a sense that we're not getting it. Are we not getting it?

Kali: All young designers that I know are obsessed with form. And not only that, they are the first to critique form. What does it mean when it's said that they are "creating a context in which they can do work that is satisfying and new"? Does that mean they want to have their own studios and do their own work *sans* clients? Or does it mean that they want to start working in cross-disciplinary ways that redefine graphic design altogether? In either case, and I will say it again, FORM MATTERS. Content is crucial. And content may drive form. But form is an integral part of the work, and to deny that is ridiculous and shortsighted. Even if it is possible to strip away personal style or character, the final form still conveys a message worth discussing. In some cases, that "stripping away" and denial of formal qualities is a knee jerk reaction to what has come before. It is a need for young designers to find a place in the design world that sets them apart. However, I would still talk about the work they come up with in terms of content, as well as form.

Rudy: Recently you and Louise visited Europe again. You mentioned you had a different experience. Did you revisit some of the studios you met on your first trip? What was different?

Kali: For this trip we were only in Holland. And, yes, we revisited some of the same studios and visited some others. Quite honestly, I was a bit gun-shy after some of the reaction to the "Rant" issue. It was very important for me to continue building relationships with these designers and not be seen as the American who barged in, gathered information, and ran back to the States bitching about what I did and did not see.

Personally, I was experiencing great disappointment in the profession at the time of my second trip. I came very close to quitting design and opening some flower shop anywhere in the world and living a life far away from graphic design. Surprisingly, the trip was really invigorating. I came home hopeful and happy. I can't put my finger on how or why. Maybe it had to do with coming to some conclusions about what I wanted from this profession and what I needed to do to find happiness again. Finding some of those answers made the trip worth its weight in gold.

REPLY BY LOUISE SANDHAUS

After getting a gander at the various responses to the "Visitations" rant appearing on blogs such as Design Observer and Speak Up, as well as in the publication *Adbusters*, this potentially cranky old gal of the possibly-has-been generation would like to offer a few reflections and clarifications, particularly about "style" and "context"—the heavy hitters of that conversation.

First, to clarify the purpose of my travels (physically and psychically) to Holland and London (places I've visited regularly since late 1994): I was trying to seek out ideas that might stir the pot during conversations at CalArts, and in my own practice, as we/I consider where graphic design might be going and where we might want to take it. Graphic design is a growing, living, changing discipline that is shaped by and responds to shifting social, technological, and economic contexts. I was out to garner some insights on those conditions and the responses to them through work being produced.

Part of what surfaced was that postmodernism, and by association work that might be seen as formally exuberant, seems to be the "current generation's" whipping boy. It seems to have been reduced to and relegated to history as a movement of "graphic free-for-all" and "personal expression and experimentation"—a representation that shrinks a significant cultural change to a vacuous visual style.

Postmodernism was the liberating social force after graphic design had lost its connection to context, and visual form had been reduced to reflecting universality, simplicity, conformity, and the illusion of global economic and social stability. Postmodernism was the impetus behind the upheaval of values that had become detached from the reality of the times. That we consider context in the first place— the very thing that allows for graphic design to evolve—is what this "movement," now reduced to a has-been style, allowed. The baby has been mistaken for the bathwater.

This misunderstanding might also be at the root of the complexities in discussing the value of visual form. If visual form has become equated with stylization and graphic novelty, no wonder it's receiving so much hate mail. As GRAPHIC designers, we create the means through which ideas are seen, experienced, and understood (for better or worse). I don't know what stuff should look like. I only know that to ignore visual form is to concede that what we do doesn't matter: that the visual is not important and is not capable of the kind of manifestation of intelligence attributed to words, not to mention the means of engagement that words have.

MAD DUTCH DISEASE: TEN PROPOSALS FOR A LECTURE ON DUTCH DESIGN

Michael Rock

Maybe we just got bored somewhere along the way. Maybe we just started to believe in our own irrelevance. Or maybe, after years of trying to get people to like what we do, we just gave up our attempts to win friends and influence people and retreated into our little private club where we know everyone and everyone knows us. But, whatever the reason, somewhere along the line we just stopped trying to really change anything and we settled for simply changing DESIGN itself.

The convoluted, challenging, intelligent, difficult, self-reflexive, coy, clever, often staggeringly beautiful work that results from this exhaustion, I call Dutch Design. I don't consider Dutch Design to be design generated in the Netherlands. I consider Dutch Design a kind of work, or an attitude about work, or even a brand of work that could theoretically occur anywhere at any time. Because of special conditions in the Netherlands, Dutch Design seems to flourish: primarily due to the fact that that there exists a culture that understands design, that so many study design, and so much money is injected into the system to support "design experiments." (In America the period during the high-tech bubble created a brief moment conducive to such work.) But any work that demonstrates the peculiar combination of irony, self-deprecation, and thinly veiled egoism can earn the title of Dutch Design.

There are several key themes—the rise of branding, the decline of nationalism and the public realm, and an emerging form of overt authorship—and some broad shifts—from public to private, from large scale to small, from optimism to irony—but

This is a shortened version of the Premsela Lecture, delivered on at the Verzetsmuseum in Amsterdam on March 11, 2004.

the form of this essay will be somewhat blurry. I have structured my essay as follows: I will present ten potential lectures on my own misreading of contemporary Dutch Design. Each chapter is a brief, a proposal, waiting to be developed by someone more adept and knowledgeable than I. So please take these as highly personal speculations from an enthusiastic outsider.

THE GREENHOUSE EFFECT

My first visit to Holland, as an American adult, was in 1984. I distinctly remember thinking that this is what my design professors were talking about. Good, modern design was everywhere. Signs had real typography. Bright colors—yellow, orange, and green—were employed by serious companies. Public buildings were "interesting." To plan and build a country using design as a key instrument is unfathomable for us. For whatever reason— maybe our country is just too big or our culture too eclectic—we have never believed in the notion of a "makeable society." In America, individualism and raw power always pummel consensus. "Action is typical of American style," wrote Daniel Bell, "thought and planning are not." (I realize the Dutch themselves may see this consensus culture as problematic, but in America it is cited, continuously, as an unattainable utopia.)

Our commitment to the private over public represents a vast difference between the ways we view the issue of "design." To understand that difference, one must realize that in America, design is always considered suspect: effete, luxurious, intellectual. America tends to be a deeply anti-intellectual, antiaesthetic place. So if our government builds something, it must look as awful and as cheap as possible, thus signifying (1) that no precious tax dollars were wasted on it; and (2) that no high flatulent "concepts" were passed off on an unwitting public. We have no tradition of aesthetic functionalism. We are suspicious of modernity. Modern smells expensive. Modern seems liberal, vaguely socialist. Modern is for white-wine swilling Northeastern and Hollywood Democrats.

When I scan a Dutch cityscape, or a poster kiosk or magazine rack, the array of "designed" infrastructure is staggering: stations, government buildings, museums, urban planning, conferences, institutes, festivals, etc. But, I wonder, what is the function of all these elaborate or exotic designs to the state that promotes them? I suppose when something is so obviously "designed" it suggests a social democratic commitment to culture, to the life of the nation. A challenging building or an unconventional book or a loco logo says: We're a good government! We invest in culture! We're daring and creative! We care about our people!

So now after twenty years of frequent visits, the Dutch landscape seems littered with fragments of contemporary design, indexical signs of an engaged, thoughtful, benevolent state and corporate governance. (To paraphrase an adage: Designers have crazy ideas everywhere; in Holland, they actually build them.) This fragmentation may be exacerbated by the current tendency to break up big projects into small commissions, encouraging young designers to make a name for themselves through some especially innovative design. Strange structures either crash-land in empty fields or get crammed together in conglomerations of urban renewal.

So much Design in one place creates an aggregation of exacerbated differ-ence. I wonder now, after a twenty-year ejaculation of making, if individual design doesn't need to signify anything anymore; it simply needs to look different from other designs. In that way design shifts from ideology to a kind of branding strategy and enters its fully linguistic state. The Dutch City becomes a Vegas version of a Dutch City with its myriad contemporary "attractions." It's Holland as an international design theme park.

POOR LITTLE RICH COUNTRY

So all that government incentive, corporate investment, and cheap design education paid off. Over the past two decades, Dutch Design has become simultaneously hot and cool. (Hot in that it's popular, cool in that it doesn't seem to try very hard or care too much.) What was once a local take on modernism has grown into a global brand.

But how did design become so central to the image of Holland? There is a famous group portrait that I like a lot: a cluster of earnest, hardworking young men—Ben Bos, Wim Crouwel, Benno Wissing, et al.—planning the overthrow of the Dutch aesthetic landscape. Their generation would take on all the major efforts of visual recon-struction: the airport, the telephone and postal systems, the rail and highway systems, etc. With that much money, time, effort, and talent thrown into the design of the nation, is it any wonder so much was done? Their name speaks volumes: Total Design. It could be a philosophy for the nation.

That first wave of Dutch corporate identity in the fifties and sixties may have been simply a knock-off of the work being developed in Germany and Switzerland at that time. Total Design loved Gerslter and Mueller-Brockman's hyper Swiss German rationalism. But an increasingly Dutch form of identity found its way into all sorts of designed objects: stamps, posters, trains, money, buildings, ships, highways, airports, etc. And in Holland, more than anywhere else—and much to our envy—corporate and government commissioners seemed to actually choose good design over bad.

The branding of Holland appeared to be overlaid with other, unassailable val-ues: efficiency, legibility, economy, beauty, etc. At least in the sixties these values were still discussed seriously; there appeared to exist an honest belief that the injection of design into the built environment would make it a better place. So like the Social Democratic politician demanding that the building be a "good" building, public infor-mation work demanded good design—which was usually interpreted to mean more or less Total Design modernism.

Somehow the heads of Dutch corporations and Dutch government agencies embraced the notion of not only the value of modern design but also promotion of Dutch talent through commissions. Certain things are possible in a state where the money looks the way it did in Holland back then. If the most staid organization of any state, the central bank, is sponsoring design like that, what is there left to rebel against?

In America we still feel it's our duty to try to inject good design into the fabric of a culture generally resistant to it. In Holland that cultural fabric is saturated, and it's a small country. But are all big projects done? Is Holland a country where *everything* is already designed?

CLASH OF THE TITANS

The answer of course is yes and no, and, at least in the late sixties, the thing to rebel against was Total Design's totalizing effect. In trying to understand the Dutch work I find interesting now, I keep going back to the oft-cited debate between Wim Crouwel and Jan van Toorn in November 1972. Crouwel seemed to argue for a seamless, rational rendering of information, the designer as information channel, the perfect expression of the "new objectivity." Van Toorn argued the position of the designer as editorial shaper, the one who adds content to content. Van Toorn saw (and sees) the designer's role as political commentator, even preaching "hindrance" rather than clarity.

But what we have learned in the meantime is that (1) neutrality is a myth or at least neutrality is a brand message in itself; and (2) hindrance and dissent as a method can also become a brand device. Despite their aesthetic, methodological, and political differences, both Crouwel and van Toorn are working at the "makeable society," one from the position of efficiency, modernization, and objectification; the other from the position of agitation, dialectic, and the enlightenment of the masses. Jan and Wim end up as two sides of the same Dutch coin. Both assume a patriarchal position, that is, as guardians of culture. (You rarely miss an underlying rhetoric of social value, no matter where you scratch the surface of Dutch Design.)

The ideology of a dominant culture consumes all discourse contained within it, including the discourse of resistance. So their difference now, in the age of what Max Kisman has dubbed the "style of styles," seems to be primarily formal. This disintegration of distinction does not in any way lessen the real ideological differences between the two men in 1972 but instead demonstrates the way in which the visual expressions of ideology have been absorbed into one master system that strips the meaning of all aesthetic gestures and reduces them to easily exchanged visual clichés.

DUMBAR FOR DUMMIES

For Americans, the ideological debates of the sixties and seventies were more or less invisible. We had our own conflicted relationship with Switzerland to work out. True Dutchification crept into our consciousness much later, and this "tagging" of official agencies was profoundly affected by one figure: Gert Dumbar. While we were following Jan van Toorn, Karel Martens, Anton Beeke, and later studios like Wild Plaka and Hard Werken, throughout the seventies, eighties, and nineties, it was this one designer—through his burgeoning studio stocked with legions of stagaires—who seemed to impress his subjectivity on every aspect of Dutch culture. For most of the rest of the world, Dutch graphic design—and remember I use that term as a category, not as a national description—in the eighties became synonymous with Dumbar Design.

For us, Dumbar seemed to impose a kind of irrational exuberance on the staid institutions of Dutch culture: the post office, the railway, the police, etc. Dumbar neatly synthesized the two competing strains of Dutchness: the systematic and the wonky. And he seemed to be able to sell his institutionalized wonkiness to even the most conservative commissioners. By 1995 Chris Vermaas, capturing the sensibility, warned that the continued application of Dumbarism to the organs of the state threatened to turn Holland into a LegoLand: "the Dutch policeman seems attached to his motorbike sitting on one big plastic peg and has a head that can spin around 360 degrees and come off in one piece."

Working from a palette of tried and true elements—brightness, off-kilteredness, geometric abstraction, angularity—Dumbarism became a kind of brand in itself that could be applied to anything, anywhere. Rather than an expression of a client's values, Dumbarism became a value in itself. To associate with Studio Dumbar meant adopting certain values suggested by Dumbar's own mythmaking apparatus, basically a systematic modernist approach to corporate identity peppered with a sprinkling of playful design elements. This approach allowed conservative, often privatizing clients to have it both ways: It promised efficiency and seeming individuality or freedom.

The effect of Dumbarism and the frenzy of identity designing over the eighties and nineties seemed to be that Holland became one continuous sea of logos. Everything was done. Everything was styled. The country took on a quality of a *Gesamtkunstwerk*: a total work of art and design. Every surface of the country was fondled. It recalls Loos' description—by way of Hal Foster—of the bourgeois gentleman subjected to the all-consuming design of his art nouveau environment:

> *The happy man suddenly felt deeply, deeply unhappy—He was precluded from all future living and striving, developing and desiring. His thought: this is what it means to learn to go about life with one's own corpse. Yes indeed, he is finished. He is complete.*

Are the young graphic designers living with the corpse of their parents' Dutch Design? Did Dumbar finish it off with terminal, nationwide overdesign? If not, what is left? Is there any room left for the Dutch Design imagination?

DUDE, WHERE'S MY COUNTRY?

At the moment of the ascendancy of Dumbarism and Dutch Design as international brands, the country itself was getting harder to find. Branding is a late cycle phenomenon, the next step once the thing itself is no longer enough. When the consumer needs added impetus to choose one more or less equivalent product over another, the package becomes almost as critical as the product. Does a thinning Holland need an ever-more-robust package? Is there a relationship between the rise of brand and the disappearance of nation?

Like everywhere else, Holland is under intense pressure. The contemporary nation is stretched: "The domination of information, media, and signs; the disaggregation of social structure into lifestyle; the general priority of consumption over production in everyday life and the constitution of identity and interests." What is Dutch anymore, anyway? Clearly what it means is changing. (The conservatives resort to the sly phrase "Dutch-values" to disguise an overt nationalist/racist appeal.) The demographics are brutal. The time-honored story of the battle between Catholic and Protestant is dissolving fast. What percentage of the country is Muslim? Who can speak Dutch? Who is even literate? While no one was looking, Holland became a porous concept.

The famous emblems of Dutchness dissolve through mergers and hostile takeover. The money first, then the post, then what? As production fades, Holland transforms into BeNeLux or MainPort: Europe's airport, seaport, and warehouse land (with its own special logo). It's the country as conduit. All that Delta Project territory to create land to store and move someone else's things headed somewhere else. There is a shift from commodity to experience. Everything—time, space, and service, as well as goods—becomes branded.

Some products so are inextricably linked to their nation they take on a quasi-public role. There is a subtle but profound shift that happens when major cultural figures privatize. Air France swallows KLM, although the deal is couched in a way that makes it seem like an equal marriage. PTT becomes a wholly owned subsidiary of TNT, based in Australia of all places. These great public institutions, flagships of the nation, become profit-driven corporations, subsidiaries of international conglomerates. What once was an expression of Dutch pride—PTT showcasing the best of Holland in the design of the stamps and phone cards, for instance, or KLM with their slow-motion swans and painfully matter-of-fact blue-suited flight attendants—either simply disappears or flips to clichés of Dutchness, turned back on the nation as marketing tools. The public institution represents the state; the private one attempts to represent the taste and lifestyle of its own market: McDonald's peddling McCroquets to the Dutch masses.

TWO BIG BOOKS

In the first five chapters I wanted to suggest an optimistic design culture ready and willing to engage the major challenges of rebuilding Holland, leading to a hyper-design state with increasingly less room for maneuvering. The next five look closely at contemporary reactions to that state and the concomitant rise in the desire for self-expression. It is at this point, I think, that design produced in the Netherlands starts to take on the qualities of full-blown Dutch Design.

To explore that shift from public to private a little further, I turn now to two big Dutch books: Wim Crouwel and Jolijn van de Wouw's PTT telephone book of 1977, and Irma Boom's commemorative book for the SHV corporation of 1999. I am curious specifically about the relationship between the designer and the work in two settings: one utterly public, the other obsessively private.

The telephone book may be the ultimate utilitarian object that is both open to, and includes, everybody. Its function is clearly stated and simply tested. The social contract between the designer and the public is clear and simple: I need to find a name; the number needs to be legible, etc. The designer has a responsibility, clearly, to clarity, legibility, efficient production, etc. You don't want personality or parody in the phone-book. So far, so good. This fits comfortably into the definition of Graphic Designer. Problem solver. A scientist of information.

But despite claims to the contrary, the phonebook is an expression of a kind of ideology: a belief that it was good for the public to read a certain way, a typographic aestheticism disguised as altruism. Under the cover of neutrality, the designer asserts his subjectivity; for instance, Crouwel uses the limited character set of phototypesetting to justify an all-lowercase alphabet: a long-time dream of modernist designers who saw different upper- and lowercase letterforms as an untenable illogic.

How, then, do we make sense of Irma Boom's role with SHV corporation (for whom Crouwel's Total Design had created the original house-style in 1965)? The Director of SHV commissioned Holland's most celebrated book designer to create a special volume commemorating the one-hundred-year anniversary of the company. Working in conjunction with an archivist for over five years, Boom shaped a narrative out of an undifferentiated lump of raw data. The meaning and narrative of the book is not a product of the words but almost exclusively the function of the sequence of the pages and the cropping of the images, the basic devices of design.

Boom's big book is fundamentally a different genre than Crouwel's big book, and the role defined for the designer is so antithetical as to almost demand a different title. The SHV book is a project for one man, representing all the power of his corporation, produced in a hyper-limited edition. (In typical Dutch pseudomodesty, the extravagant display of conspicuous consumption is hidden from view by limited distribution.) The book makes the signature of the designer part of its branding strategy. The book says: We are an enlightened company, we are rich, we are cultured, and we know the value of someone like Irma Boom. The corporation uses its association with her unassailable brilliance to advance its own image.

The difference between the two books, I think, is the difference between a hyper-Dutch and a hyper-American project. And it represents the move from the public to the private. But in both cases, the association with the designer has meaning. While Crouwel disappears in the phonebook, the PTT makes an overt commitment to modernity through a connection to Total Design. SHV licenses Boom's aura and Boom grafts her identity onto the content of the SHV book. (Crouwel opined in an interview that a recent Boom book on Otto Treumann was "in fact a book about her, not Otto Treumann.") A book that large and complex, with every page shaped by one person, becomes a kind of autobiography; and Boom is a constant, ghostly presence. It's not *just* a big book. It's an Irma Boom book. The designer, as author, supplies brand value or celebrity endorsement.

THE ORGANIZATION MEN (AND WOMEN)

The condition known as Dutch Design poses a special challenge. The Dutch designer— again a category, not a nationality—has a conflicted relationship with the idea of authorship (in the same way the Dutch seem to have issues with ambition and author- ity). There's the divided lust for expression on one side, and moral rectitude and modesty on the other, which seems to generate a range of singular behaviors.

To assuage, or at least to mask, the ambition and ego necessary to build the figure of the author, the Dutch designer positions him/herself, not as originator, but as one who marshals undeniable economic, legal, textual, demographic, and civic forces and follows them to their irrefutable conclusion. By this technique, the designer eschews celebrity, feigns anonymity, and assumes the role of systems manager.

This bifurcated relationship—dividing the desire to express and the drive for reason—is already present in Wim Crouwel's description of a rational design process. "The content determines the form, the typeface, the format, the cover, the binding. Every assignment can be divided into several factors, which are all interrelated. With each commission, as it were, you have to plot those factors along a horizontal and a vertical axis, stretch out a string and then see where it takes you." The image of the matrix is brutal; its findings, absolute. Notice the passivity, the submission to the data. You wait and see where the data takes you.

This matter-of-factism, this hyper-pragmatism, this surrender to the omnipo- tent effect of the diagram is present in all manner of Dutch work. Perhaps the strategy derives from a natural reaction to a country in which every centimeter is regulated by preordained rules. But the buildings of architects like MVDRV and their attendant doc- umentation and reliance on so-called Datascape, take that Dutch rationalism and stretch it to produce absurd, even parodic results. Research and analysis form a diagram, and diagram derives a building. The designers are represented as bystanders or objective sci- entists watching with grim satisfaction as their bizarre theories give rise to even more bizarre forms. See also Koolhaas's plan for New York's MoMA that simply uses the given zoning envelope as form generator—coupled with the title: "Architecture with- out Architects"; or also OMA's Seattle Public Library in which the Dewey Decimal organization of the library books drives a diagram that drives a building.

Critic Thomas Daniell put it nicely comparing the methods of the Japanese architect and the Dutch: paraphrasing: The Japanese architect begins with a poetic con- cept and refines it into plausibility, the Dutch architect begins with analysis and extrap- olates it into poetry. These Dutch buildings have a kind of brutal, self-evident ugliness to them. Of course they're ugly—current conditions, objectively measured, don't nec- essarily render beauty. Beauty would imply subjectivity. Facts are facts. You take the building the facts give you.

This authorial avoidance strategy seems to have spawned the enthusiasm for the generic, the recycled, the already done, the undersigned, and the preexisting that dominate contemporary design debates. Much of recent Dutch Design seems intent on erasing the sense that any designer imposed any subjectivity. Take Pascale Gatzen's reworking of photographed clothing. By copying an existing item, not from the original but from the ad, remaking it, and then rephotographing it and readvertising it, she calls the origination of the object into question. Is it her work? Klavers & Engelen make a simple change in orientation: a defamiliarization strategy. Or Hella Jorgenus's textile "Repeat" uses preexisting traditional textile designs reorganized by curious juxtaposition and unifying overlays. Or Experimental Jet Set's project that samples the work of a previous generation, its style stripped clean of any political associations. Or *Archis* magazine's use of found typographic style absolving the need for any subjectivity, that is, eliminating the designer's presumed responsibility to create distinct, unique identity. (More on that shortly.)

AUTHOR AS VALUE-ADDED

But if it is a Dutch Design trait to disappear into data or system, and at least feign a lack of real ambition or subjectivity, there is an emerging tendency in which the designer assumes a central role as character in his own work. This tests the way in which the treatment of given material—what Jan van Toorn might call the "critical perspective"—amounts to a kind of authorship.

Dumbar is one model of the designer as auteur, managing an army of underlings to impress his or her stamp on the broadest possible canvas. Dumbar—actually *not* Dumbar but Dumbar's studio—creates Dumbar signature work. Dumbar as the flamboyante stands for the work, gives it a public face, and provides a branded "personality." Irma Boom, working with SHV, seems to represent another model in which the designer uses the tools of design to construct meaning. But more recent work engages the subject in more complex and nuanced ways.

One well-publicized example of the fictionalized author can be discerned in Jop von Bennekom's self-motivated *Re* magazine. Von Bennekom links his magazine—which started as a school project at the Jan Van Eyck Academie—to "a typical Dutch approach. . . . A conceptual position of self-irony and self-questioning." Through this overt form, it becomes a magazine dedicated to his interests, proclivities, possessions, friends, life events, etc. Von Bennekom positions himself as both the originator and subject of the magazine. The magazine generates a fictional presence—that of the designer himself—that permeates every aspect of the project. Even as von Bennekom moves from sole proprietor to executive editor, or when the subject of a specific issue shifts to focus on a single individual, he serves as both author and subject in an intensely autobiographical project.

Archis represents another form of the emerging authorial voice as strategy. While the core of the magazine is still articles, reviews, critiques, and editorials, *Archis* seems to adopt another voice that appears spectrally among the articles, offering choices, garnering information, asking questions, and making jokes. But whose voice? The editor's? The designer's? A phantom that haunts its pages? Who is the "I" of *Archis*?

Since that voice has nothing ostensibly to do with the delivery of the content— that is, the articles and items that make up the body of the magazine—at first it would seem to be a van Toornian hindrance strategy. The designers editorialize through shaping the material. But the *Archis* authorial presence has none of van Toorn's desire for social reformation or political agitation. The *Archis* voice is that of the court jester; it's about richness, pleasure, irony, and humor—that is, value-added content and shading.

DRESSING DOWN

In typical Dutch fashion, no one dresses up to make an appearance. The Dutch author comes in unshaven and informal. His or her presence is almost always padded in irony and self-deprecation. There seems to be a close connection between the rise of the author and of subjectivity and the undesigning of design.

But what drove that shift to the undesigned design in the nineties and the attendant Dutch Design explosion internationally? While this may be in part a reaction to the slickness of the eighties and early nineties, I nominate one figure, Joop van den Ende, as the real source of inspiration. JVDE is of course the father of the worldwide global phenomenon known as *Big Brother* and bubble gum television.

Reality TV has exploded in the United States and around the world. Television producers love it because it's cheap, easy to make, easy to serialize, and, most importantly, easy to localize, hence the success of *Big Brother* around the globe. *Big Brother* satisfies a grim desire to inspect the dirty laundry of your neighbor. But in Holland, it seems to have a special resonance, perhaps because the whole country is a kind of artificial reality of closely packed neighbors, or perhaps due to the brutal efficiency of the concept. It seems to embody the "not one penny more" credo.

Recent work focuses on the banal: the areas untouched by Dumbarism and the sweeping overdesign gestures the years before. Van Lieshout's AVLville is a kind of artificial reality TV. The work seems to reference the standard, accidental items of an in-between space, but always with some ironic twist. Actually it's a romanticized banality. This work ignores the corporate, globalized reality of Phillips and PTT or Rabobank. The romanticized reality focuses on the generic apartment, the refugee camp, the abandoned embankment, and the vernacular language of the amateur do-it-yourself'er.

But the question is: Does banality have an agenda? Is anything advanced except the blasé, detached bemusement of the designer? Has Holland become so comfortable, so completely designed that the only thing left is ironic commentary on the act of designing itself? Does anyone think about a kind of makeable society or have we just given up? Is design simply a free-floating reaction, all verb without direct object?

We have all gotten used to accepting whatever comes along, whoever is in the house. One will get voted off each week but don't worry; the whole thing will start again next season. It's just a game.

WE ARE WHAT WE EAT

The production and consumption of style has accelerated so quickly, been broadcast so widely, that trends and countertrends develop simultaneously. Action and reaction are linked inextricably. This is due, at least in part, to the fact that there really is a culture of design here, a culture of experiment, discourse, and discovery.

I originally titled this talk "Mad Dutch Disease" an obvious allusion to Mad Cow Disease or more officially: Bovine Spongiform Encephalopathy. The scourge of Europe, Mad Cow is theorized to appear when cows eat feed that contains the remains of other cows. When our diet starts to be restricted to the point of devouring and regurgitating the trends of last week, we are in serious jeopardy of succumbing to a similar fate.

But as I mentioned at the beginning, I don't see Dutch Design as confined to the Netherlands. This is happening everywhere. It's just that, due to advantageous conditions, it seems more pronounced there. Our American flights of fancy are constantly quelled by the market. Because of that we use Holland as a kind of quarantined breeding ground, carefully observing what is sure to happen everywhere sooner or later.

Perhaps this is a better metaphor: The coyote builds his elaborate machine only to have it blow up in his face. I wonder if we have all worked ourselves into a trap of our own making. Or perhaps we have been building this elaborate contraption of a self-reflective design culture over the last twenty years only to realize that we may be its ultimate victims. When it comes time to hit the switch, who knows what the result will be?

WHY DESIGNERS CAN THINK
Ralph Caplan

In preparing a presentation for the AIGA on "angst in graphic design," I didn't have to look any further than the AIGA's own *Voice* for material. The complaints are various and standard. The clients you have, the clients you don't have, the annoying failure of the world at large (including your own mother) to understand what it is you do. In the summer of 2005 I spent two weeks at the Haystack Mountain School of Crafts, an idyllic blend of nature and architecture in Maine, where eighty people were blowing glass, throwing pots, weaving baskets, folding paper into pop-up books, hammering metal

Originally appeared on *Voice: AIGA Journal of Design* (December 13, 2005).

into jewelry, and turning wood into furniture or sculpture. In age they ranged from eighteen to ninety-three. In experience they ranged from beginner to professional, although the professionals tended to enroll in workshops in which they had no previous experience and therefore were themselves beginners. If there ever was an angst-free environment, that was it. At Haystack, as in Willie Nelson's Luckenbach, Texas, "ain't nobody feelin' no pain."

Euphoria, like angst, can be traced to multiple causes. Chief among them at Haystack was the fact that everyone there was doing exactly what he or she wanted to do. Moreover, *what they wanted to do was to make things*. I wonder how much of the dissatisfaction with professional design life is rooted in the disparity between what attracted you to the practice of design and what you now spend most of your days doing.

Over years of working with them, I have found designers in general—and graphic designers in particular—to be uncommonly intelligent, curious, and well-informed. I rarely talked about this, for it sounded patronizing and carried the arrogant implication that I was smart enough to assess the smartness of anyone else. But I did once mention it to my late friend Saul Bass, who responded suspiciously, "Are you trying to blow sunshine up my ass?"

I was not. My aim was not to flatter designers, but to clarify what to me was a mystery: the seeming incongruity between the intellectual prowess of designers and the limited educational requirements of the trade they followed. Unlike, say, doctors, lawyers, and teachers, designers did not have to go to college. Many did go; and almost all had some formal training. But art and design schools did not, for the most part, appear dedicated to fostering the life of the mind.

I was not alone in my skepticism. In a 1989 article called "Why Designers Can't Think," Michael Bierut wrote, "Almost all design schools today stress form over content, looks over brains, and seeing over thinking. . . ."

I agreed with Michael about the schools. But instead of holding them responsible for "why designers can't think," I had been struck by how brilliantly designers can and do think. Could the explanation lie in the design process itself, in the proclivities and gifts that lead people to become, or want to become, designers in the first place?

What do designers need to know, anyway? In the digital world, changes come too fast for that question to be answered specifically. We may get further by asking instead: What do designers feel an irresistible urge to do? Men and women, boys and girls, gravitate to design for any number of reasons; but common to all of them is the itch to make something—a picture, an artifact, a plan. That itch is satisfied by drawing, carving, shaping, molding—somehow using the hands to realize a concept in the mind.

If designers are more cerebral than expected, it may be because *designing* is more cerebral than expected. In an age when "digital" no longer refers to fingers, the work of the designer is no longer hands-on. That regrettable circumstance becomes truly deplorable with the realization that hands-on is never all that far from heads-on.

In saying that designers did not have to go to college, I was expressing a narrow and now dated view of college. I meant they did not have to go to the kind of college *I* went to. Times have changed and so have institutions of learning. Curricula at many design schools have become broader and more rigorous, while many liberal arts colleges have been, as the saying goes, dumbed down. "It's possible," Bierut complained, "to study graphic design for four years without any meaningful exposure to the fine arts, world literature, science, history, politics, or any of the other disciplines that unite us in a common culture." That is still true. But today that same meaningful exposure can be avoided for four years at colleges and universities across the country, no matter *what* the major field of study is. If design students could once graduate without encountering either William or Henry James, so can today's liberal arts students.

When I was talking recently with Milton Glaser about his drawings, he remarked, "Drawing is not about representation but about thinking. Trying to understand what you're looking at. . . . The brain sends a signal to the hand and the hand sends one back and there is an endless conversation between them."

The industrial designer Bruce Burdick said something similar in describing the notebooks of Leonardo da Vinci as "a private conversation between him and his hands."

In his book *The Hand*, neurologist Frank Wilson argues that the qualities needed for thinking are inseparable from the qualities needed for seeing, showing, and making. Glaser pursues the subject in his new book, *Drawing Is Thinking*—with a foreword by Dr. Wilson. Their demonstrations of, and insights into, the relationship between hand and mind may help us understand what makes designers so smart and what makes designers so anxious.

BIOGRAPHIES

PAOLA ANTONELLI is a writer and a curator in the Department of Architecture and Design at the Museum of Modern Art (MoMA).

DAVID BARRINGER (www.davidbarringer.com) writes fiction and design criticism for *I.D.*, *Eye*, and *AIGA Voice*, as well as for *Details*, *Mademoiselle*, and *Playboy*.

ROY R. BEHRENS is an art director for the *North American Review*, an author of several design books, and an editor at *Ballast Quarterly Review*.

MICHAEL BIERUT is the 2006 recipient of the Medal of the American Institute of Graphic Arts and a partner at Pentragram's New York office.

PETER BILAK teaches at the Royal Academy of Art in the Hague, and heads a type foundry, typotheque.com. He is also a co-editor at *DOT DOT DOT* magazine.

ANDREW BLAUVELT curates exhibitions on contemporary design and architecture as design director at the Walker Art Center in Minneapolis.

MAX BRUINSMA (maxbruinsma.nl) is an independent critic, curator, editor, and lecturer in the fields of graphic and media design, contemporary art, and culture.

RALPH CAPLAN is the author of *By Design* and *Cracking The Whip*. His column, "Noah's Archive," appears each month in *AIGA VOICE* (http://voice.aiga.org/).

FENELLA COLLINGRIDGE teaches architecture at the Royal College of Art, London, and is a design consultant with WDOwen Associates.

DENISE GONZALES CRISP is principal of SuperStove! and serves on the editorial board of *Design Criticism*. She is writing a textbook on typography.

NICK CURRIE, a.k.a. Momus, is an "electronic folk singer" with twenty albums to his credit. He appeared in the 2006 Whitney Biennial as an "unreliable tour guide."

MICHAEL DOOLEY is the creative director of MichaelDooley Design, contributing editor for *PRINT* magazine, and a writer for *AIGA/Voice* online.

WILLIAM DRENTTEL works in partnership with Jessica Helfand at Winterhouse Studio. Drenttel is president emeritus of the American Institute of Graphic Arts.

JOHANNA DRUCKER is the Robertson Professor of Media Studies at the University of Virginia and an internationally-known book artist.

ROB GIAMPIETRO is a professor at Parsons School of Design and a principal at Giampietro+Smith, a design firm based in New York City.

JESSICA HELFAND is senior critic in graphic design at Yale School of Art and the author of several books on graphic design and cultural criticism.

STEVEN HELLER is the co-chair of the School of Visual Arts MFA Designer as Author program and co-founder of the MFA in Design Criticism.

KARRIE JACOBS was the founding editor-in-chief of *Dwell Magazine*. She writes for *Metropolis* and is a contributing editor at *Travel + Leisure*.

JEFFERY KEEDY, a professor in the graphic design program at CalArts, has had designs and essays published in *Eye, I.D., Émigré*, and *Adbusters*.

EMILY KING is the design editor of *Frieze* magazine, and her latest book, *Robert Brownjohn: Sex and Typography*, was published by Laurence King in 2005.

MAUD LAVIN is a professor and graduate director of visual and critical studies at the School of the Art Institute of Chicago.

ELLEN LUPTON is director of the graphic design MFA program at Maryland Institute College of Art and has authored, edited, and co-authored over a dozen books.

VICTOR MARGOLIN is emeritus professor of design history at the University of Illinois, Chicago and is writing his newest book on the world history of design.

RANDY NAKAMURA is a graphic designer and writer based in Los Angeles. He has an MFA from CalArts.

KALI NIKITAS is the chair of the Department of Visual Arts at Northeastern University and a partner of Graphic Design for Love (+$).

WILLIAM OWEN is a strategy consultant and writer. He is director of WDOwen Associates, a service design consulting company.

AUTHOR PHIL PATTON writes about automobile design for the *New York Times*. He is also a contributing editor for *I.D.* and *Departures* magazines.

ALAN ROBERTSON is senior lecturer in communication design on the Bachelor of Design at Unitec New Zealand. He occasionally writes for *TypoGraphic*.

MICHAEL ROCK is a professor of design at the Yale School of Art and a partner in the design studio 2x4 in New York City.

CHRISTINE ROSEN is a fellow at the Ethics & Public Policy Center in Washington, D.C. and senior editor of *The New Atlantis: A Journal of Technology & Society*.

LOUISE SANDHAUS is director of the graphic design program at CalArts and has her own studio, LSD. Her writing has appeared in *Step*, *PRINT*, *Eye*, and *Émigré*.

ADRIAN SHAUGHNESSY is creative director of This is Real Art. His latest book is *How to be a Graphic Designer Without Losing Your Soul*.

TEAL TRIGGS is professor of graphic design at the London College of Communication. She has published extensively on feminism, graphic design, and typography.

ALICE TWEMLOW contributes to *Eye*, *I.D.*, and *PRINT*, and authored *What is Graphic Design For?* She has taught at RISD, Parsons, and University of the Arts.

VÉRONIQUE VIENNE is the co-editor of *The Education of an Art Director*. She is also the author of the bestselling book, *The Art of Doing Nothing*.

INDEX

Books from Allworth Press

Allworth Press is an imprint of Allworth Communications, Inc. Selected titles are listed below.

Looking Closer 3: Classic Writings on Graphic Design
edited by Michael Bierut, Jessica Helfand, Steven Heller, and Rick Poynor
(paperback, 6¾ × 9⅞, 304 pages, $18.95)

Looking Closer 2: Critical Writings on Graphic Design
edited by Michael Bierut, William Drenttel, Steven Heller, and DK Holland
(paperback, 6¾ × 9⅞, 288 pages, $18.95)

Looking Closer: Critical Writings on Graphic Design
edited by Michael Bierut, William Drenttel, Steven Heller, and DK Holland
(paperback, 6¾ × 10, 256 pages, $18.95)

AIGA Professional Practices in Graphic Design: The American Institute of Graphic Arts
edited by Tad Crawford (paperback, 6¾ × 9⅞, 320 pages, $24.95)

Graphic Design Humor: The Art of Graphic Wit
by Steve Heller (paperback, 6¾ × 9⅞, 288 pages, $21.95)

Design Issues: How Graphic Design Informs Society
edited by DK Holland (paperback, 6¾ × 9⅞, 288 pages, $21.95)

Graphic Design and Reading: Explorations of an Uneasy Relationship
edited by Gunnar Swanson (paperback, 6¾ × 9⅞, 256 pages, $19.95)

The Graphic Design Reader
by Steven Heller (paperback with flaps, 5½ × 8½, 320 pages, $19.95)

The Education of an E-Designer
edited by Steven Heller (paperback, 6¾ × 9⅞, 352 pages, $21.95)

The Education of a Graphic Designer
edited by Steven Heller (paperback, 6¾ × 9⅞, 288 pages, $18.95)

The Education of an Illustrator
edited by Steven Heller and Marshall Arisman (paperback, 6¾ × 9⅞, 288 pages, $19.95)

Business and Legal Forms for Graphic Designers, Revised Edition
by Tad Crawford and Eva Doman Bruck (paperback, 8½ × 11, 240 pages, includes CD-ROM, $24.95)
Careers By Design: A Business Guide for Graphic Designers, Third Edition *by Roz Goldfarb* (paperback, 6 × 9, 232 pages, $19.95)

Please write to request our free catalog. To order by credit card, call 1-800-491-2808 or send a check or money order to Allworth Press, 10 East 23rd Street, Suite 510, New York, NY 10010. Include $5 for shipping and handling for the first book ordered and $1 for each additional book. Ten dollars plus $1 for each additional book if ordering from Canada. New York State residents must add sales tax.

To see our complete catalog on the World Wide Web, or to order online, you can find us at ***www.allworth.com***.